ORIGO

STEPPING STONES 2.0

COMPREHENSIVE MATHEMATICS

AUTHORS

James Burnett
Calvin Irons
Peter Stowasser
Allan Turton

PROGRAM CONSULTANTS

Diana Lambdin
Frank Lester, Jr.
Kit Norris

CONTRIBUTING WRITERS

Debi DePaul
Beth Lewis

STUDENT BOOK A

ORIGO
EDUCATION

ORIGO STEPPING STONES 2.0 STUDENT JOURNAL

ORIGO Stepping Stones 2.0 is a world-class comprehensive program, developed by a team of experts to provide a balanced approach to teach and learn mathematics. The Student Journal consists of two parts — Book A and Book B. Book A comprises Modules 1 to 6, and Book B Modules 7 to 12. Each book has Lesson and Practice pages, a complete Contents, Student Glossary, and Teacher Index.

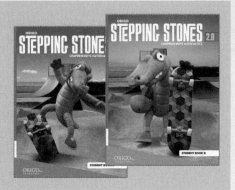

LESSON PAGES

There are two pages for each of the 12 lessons in every module. This sample shows the key components.

9.8 Length: Converting metric units

Step In This number line represents one meter.

0

Write a number at the right-hand end to mark the line in centimeters.

Write another number at the right-hand end to mark the line in millimeters.

Where would you draw a mark to show the length that is 50 cm long?
Use your ruler to determine the halfway mark and label the point.

What are all the different ways you could describe and write that length?

You could describe the length in millimeters, and as a fraction of a meter, which could be written as a decimal fraction or common fraction.

Think about the relationship between each metric unit. Then write the missing length.

| | meter | is equivalent to | 150 centimeters | is equivalent to | 1,500 millimeters |

What do you know about kilometers? How many meters are equivalent to one kilometer?

Step Up I. Measure each strip. Write the length in millimeters, then as a decimal fraction of a meter.

a. _____ mm _____ m

b. _____ mm _____ m

c. _____ mm _____ m

◆ 340 *ORIGO Stepping Stones* · Grade 5 · 9.8

---

2. Write equivalent lengths.

a. 3.2 m $3\frac{2}{10}$ m   _____ cm   _____ mm

b. _____ m   _____ m   425 cm   _____ mm

c. _____ m   _____ m   _____ cm   6,540 mm

d. _____ m $\frac{67}{1000}$ m   _____ cm   _____ mm

3. Write each length as a decimal fraction, then as a mixed number.

a. 3,650 m   _____ km   _____ km

b. 2,780 m   _____ km   _____ km

c. 4,190 m   _____ km   _____ km

d. 1,325 m   _____ km   _____ km

Step Ahead Choose the number that makes the most sense to complete the sentence.

a. 0.4 $\frac{1}{4}$ 0.04   The book is _____ m thick.

b. $1\frac{5}{10}$ 1.5   150   Cody can stand and leap _____ cm.

ORIGO Stepping Stones · Grade 5 · 9.8   341 ◆

---

1 Module number and Lesson number.

2 The lesson title tells the content of the lesson. It has two parts: the stem (or big idea), and the leaf (which gives more details).

3 The Step In is designed to generate classroom discourse. Open questions are used to make students think about many methods or answers.

4 For Grade 5, Book A shows a blue diamond beside each page number and index references are in blue. Book B shows a green diamond and index references are in green.

5 Step Up provides appropriate written work for the student.

6 The Step Ahead puts a twist on each lesson to develop higher order thinking skills.

PRACTICE PAGES

Lessons 2, 4, 6, 8, 10, and 12 each provide two pages for maintaining concepts and skills. These samples show the key components.

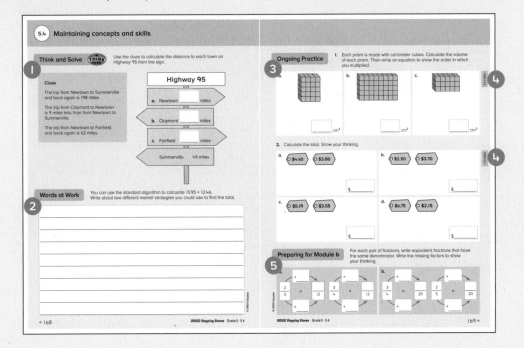

1. The *ORIGO Think Tanks* are a popular way for students to practice problem solving. There are three Think Tank problems in each module.

2. The development of written language is essential. These activities aim to help students develop their academic vocabulary, and provide opportunities for students to write their thinking.

3. Ongoing Practice revisits content previously learned. Question 1 always revisits content from a previous module, and Question 2 revisits content from the current module.

4. This tab shows the originating lesson.

5. Each right-hand page provides content that prepares students for the next module.

6. Regular written practice of mental strategies is essential. There are three computation practice pages that focus on specific strategies in each module.

CONTENTS

BOOK A

MODULE 1

1.1	Number: Reviewing six-digit numbers	6
1.2	Number: Reading and writing seven-digit numbers	8
1.3	Number: Locating seven-digit numbers on a number line	12
1.4	Number: Comparing and ordering seven-digit numbers	14
1.5	Number: Reading and writing eight- and nine-digit numbers	18
1.6	Number: Working with millions expressed as fractions	20
1.7	Number: Rounding numbers with up to nine digits	24
1.8	Algebra: Investigating order with one operation	26
1.9	Algebra: Investigating order with two operations	30
1.10	Algebra: Working with expressions (without parentheses)	32
1.11	Algebra: Working with expressions (with parentheses)	36
1.12	Algebra: Working with expressions (with and without parentheses)	38

MODULE 2

2.1	Multiplication: Reviewing the standard algorithm	44
2.2	Multiplication: Using the standard algorithm with three- and four-digit factors	46
2.3	Multiplication: Using the standard algorithm with two two-digit factors	50
2.4	Multiplication: Using the standard algorithm with two- and three-digit factors	52
2.5	Multiplication: Extending the standard algorithm	56
2.6	Multiplication: Solving word problems	58
2.7	Volume: Developing the concept	62
2.8	Volume: Analyzing unit cubes and measuring volume	64
2.9	Volume: Developing a formula	68
2.10	Volume: Finding the dimensions of prisms with a given volume	70
2.11	Volume: Composing and decomposing prisms	74
2.12	Volume: Solving real-world problems	76

MODULE 3

3.1	Decimal fractions: Reviewing tenths and hundredths (area model)	82
3.2	Decimal fractions: Reviewing tenths and hundredths (number line)	84
3.3	Decimal fractions: Introducing thousandths	88
3.4	Decimal fractions: Reading and writing thousandths (without zeros and teens)	90
3.5	Decimal fractions: Reading and writing thousandths (with zeros and teens)	94
3.6	Decimal fractions: Recording in expanded form	96
3.7	Decimal fractions: Locating thousandths on a number line	100
3.8	Decimal fractions: Comparing and ordering thousandths	102
3.9	Decimal fractions: Comparing and ordering with unequal places	106
3.10	Decimal fractions: Rounding thousandths	108
3.11	Decimal fractions: Rounding with unequal decimal places	112
3.12	Decimal fractions: Interpreting results on a line plot	114

MODULE 4

4.1	Common fractions: Reviewing equivalent fractions (related denominators)	120
4.2	Common fractions: Reviewing equivalent fractions (related and unrelated denominators)	122
4.3	Common fractions: Reviewing the relationship with mixed numbers	126
4.4	Common fractions: Converting improper fractions to mixed numbers	128
4.5	Common fractions: Converting mixed numbers to improper fractions	132
4.6	Common fractions: Solving word problems	134
4.7	Length: Converting between inches and feet	138
4.8	Length: Converting customary units	140
4.9	Capacity: Converting customary units	144
4.10	Mass: Converting customary units	146
4.11	Mass/capacity: Solving word problems (customary units)	150
4.12	Mass: Solving real-world problems on a line plot	152

MODULE 5

5.1	Decimal fractions: Reviewing addition strategies (without composing)	158
5.2	Decimal fractions: Adding (with composing)	160
5.3	Decimal fractions: Using the standard algorithm to add (with composing)	164
5.4	Decimal fractions: Using the standard algorithm to add more than two addends	166
5.5	Decimal fractions: Subtracting tenths and hundredths	170
5.6	Decimal fractions: Using the standard algorithm to subtract	172
5.7	Decimal fractions: Subtracting tenths (decomposing ones)	176
5.8	Decimal fractions: Subtracting hundredths (decomposing tenths)	178
5.9	Decimal fractions: Subtracting (decomposing multiple places)	182
5.10	2D shapes: Identifying parallelograms	184
5.11	2D shapes: Exploring categories of quadrilaterals	188
5.12	2D shapes: Identifying categories of triangles	190

MODULE 6

6.1	Common fractions: Making comparisons and estimates	196
6.2	Common fractions: Reviewing addition strategies (same denominators)	198
6.3	Common fractions: Adding (related denominators)	202
6.4	Common fractions: Adding (unrelated denominators)	204
6.5	Common fractions: Adding mixed numbers (related denominators)	208
6.6	Common fractions: Adding mixed numbers (unrelated denominators)	210
6.7	Common fractions: Adding mixed numbers with unrelated denominators (composing whole numbers)	214
6.8	Division: Reviewing strategies	216
6.9	Division: Analyzing partitioning strategies	220
6.10	Division: Three- and four-digit dividends and one-digit divisors (with remainders)	222
6.11	Division: Three- and four-digit dividends with divisors that are two-digit multiples of five or ten	226
6.12	Division: Three- and four-digit dividends and any two-digit divisor	228

STUDENT GLOSSARY AND TEACHER INDEX — 234

ORIGO Stepping Stones • Grade 5

CONTENTS

BOOK B

MODULE 7

7.1	Common fractions: Exploring strategies to subtract (same denominators)	244
7.2	Common fractions: Subtracting (related denominators)	246
7.3	Common fractions: Subtracting (unrelated denominators)	250
7.4	Common fractions: Subtracting mixed numbers (related denominators)	252
7.5	Common fractions: Subtracting mixed numbers (unrelated denominators)	256
7.6	Common fractions: Subtracting mixed numbers with unrelated denominators (decomposing whole numbers)	258
7.7	Common fractions: Reinforcing subtraction strategies (related and unrelated denominators)	262
7.8	Common fractions: Solving word problems involving mixed numbers	264
7.9	Number: Building a picture of one billion and beyond	268
7.10	Number: Working with exponents	270
7.11	Number: Exploring place-value patterns	274
7.12	Number: Representing whole numbers using exponents	276

MODULE 8

8.1	Common fractions: Reviewing multiplication by whole numbers	282
8.2	Common fractions: Relating unit fractions to division	284
8.3	Common fractions: Finding a fraction of a whole number (unit fractions)	288
8.4	Common fractions: Finding a fraction of a whole number pictorially (non-unit fractions)	290
8.5	Common fractions: Finding a fraction of a whole number symbolically (non-unit fractions)	294
8.6	Common fractions: Solving word problems involving multiplying with whole numbers	296
8.7	Common fractions: Multiplying two common fractions pictorially	300
8.8	Common fractions: Multiplying two common fractions symbolically	302
8.9	Common fractions: Multiplying whole numbers and mixed numbers	306
8.10	Common fractions: Multiplying common fractions and mixed numbers	308
8.11	Common fractions: Exploring multiplication by fractions less than, equal to, or greater than one	312
8.12	Common fractions: Solving word problems	314

MODULE 9

9.1	Common fractions: Relating fractions to division	320
9.2	Common fractions: Dividing a whole number by a unit fraction pictorially	322
9.3	Common fractions: Dividing a whole number by a unit fraction using multiplication	326
9.4	Common fractions: Solving word problems involving multiplication or division with a unit fraction	328
9.5	Common fractions: Dividing a unit fraction by a whole number pictorially	332
9.6	Common fractions: Dividing a unit fraction by a whole number using multiplication	334
9.7	Common fractions: Solving word problems involving unit fractions	338
9.8	Length: Converting metric units	340
9.9	Mass: Converting metric units	344
9.10	Capacity: Converting metric units	346
9.11	Length/mass/capacity: Solving word problems (metric units)	350
9.12	Mass/data: Interpreting a line plot to solve problems	352

MODULE 10

10.1	Decimal fractions: Multiplying by a whole number	358
10.2	Decimal fractions: Reinforcing strategies for multiplying by a whole number	360
10.3	Decimal fractions: Multiplying tenths by tenths	364
10.4	Decimal fractions: Multiplying with whole numbers using partial products	366
10.5	Decimal fractions: Multiplying two decimal fractions using partial products	370
10.6	Decimal fractions: Dividing whole numbers by decimal fractions	372
10.7	Decimal fractions: Dividing decimal fractions by whole numbers	376
10.8	Decimal fractions: Dividing decimal fractions by decimal fractions	378
10.9	Decimal fractions: Reinforcing the think-multiplication strategy to divide	382
10.10	Decimal fractions: Adjusting the divisor	384
10.11	Decimal fractions: Adjusting the dividend and divisor	388
10.12	Decimal fractions: Solving multiplication and division word problems	390

MODULE 11

11.1	Algebra: Reviewing number patterns	396
11.2	Algebra: Examining relationships between two numerical patterns	398
11.3	Algebra: Introducing the coordinate plane	402
11.4	Algebra: Relating tables to ordered pairs	404
11.5	Algebra: Representing patterns on coordinate grids	408
11.6	Algebra: Interpreting coordinate grids	410
11.7	Multiplication: Using the double-and-halve strategy to multiply dollars and cents	414
11.8	Multiplication: Using a nearby number to multiply dollars and cents	416
11.9	Multiplication: Reinforcing strategies to multiply dollars and cents	420
11.10	Perimeter: Solving word problems	422
11.11	Area: Solving word problems	426
11.12	Volume: Solving word problems	428

MODULE 12

12.1	Division: Recording steps (three- and four-digit dividends)	434
12.2	Division: Developing the standard algorithm	436
12.3	Division: Introducing the standard algorithm	440
12.4	Division: Working with the standard algorithm	442
12.5	Division: Working with the standard algorithm (with remainders)	446
12.6	Division: Investigating methods to divide by a two-digit multiple of ten	448
12.7	Division: Working with four-digit dividends and two-digit divisors	452
12.8	Division: Solving word problems (one- and two-digit divisors)	454
12.9	Division: Making estimates to solve problems	458
12.10	Division: Partitioning dollar-and-cent amounts	460
12.11	Division: Extending partitioning strategies to divide dollar-and-cent amounts	464
12.12	Division: Calculating unit costs to determine best buys (dollars and cents)	466

STUDENT GLOSSARY AND TEACHER INDEX	472

Step In

What number is represented on this abacus?

Draw one more bead on the ten thousands rod.

Write the new number.

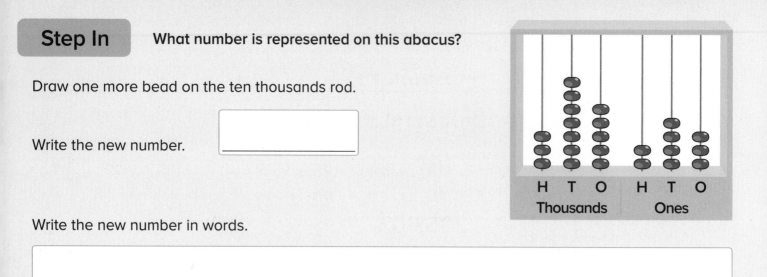

H T O H T O
Thousands   Ones

Write the new number in words.

Look at this abacus.
Draw a red bead on one of the rods to the left of the blue bead.

How can you describe the relationship between the red and blue beads?

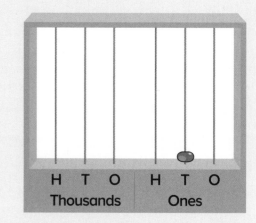

H T O H T O
Thousands   Ones

Step Up

1. Draw beads on each abacus to represent the number.

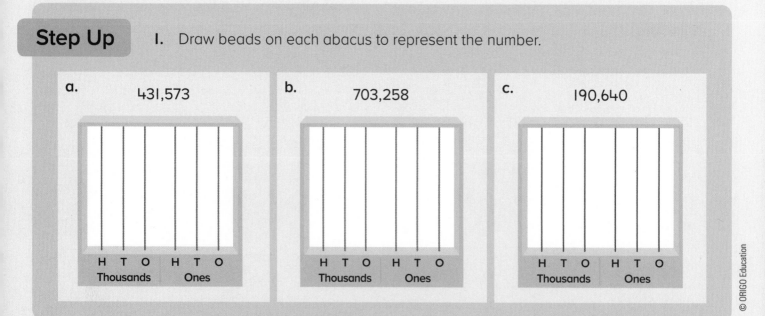

a. 431,573

H T O H T O
Thousands Ones

b. 703,258

H T O H T O
Thousands Ones

c. 190,640

H T O H T O
Thousands Ones

2. Complete the missing parts.

a.
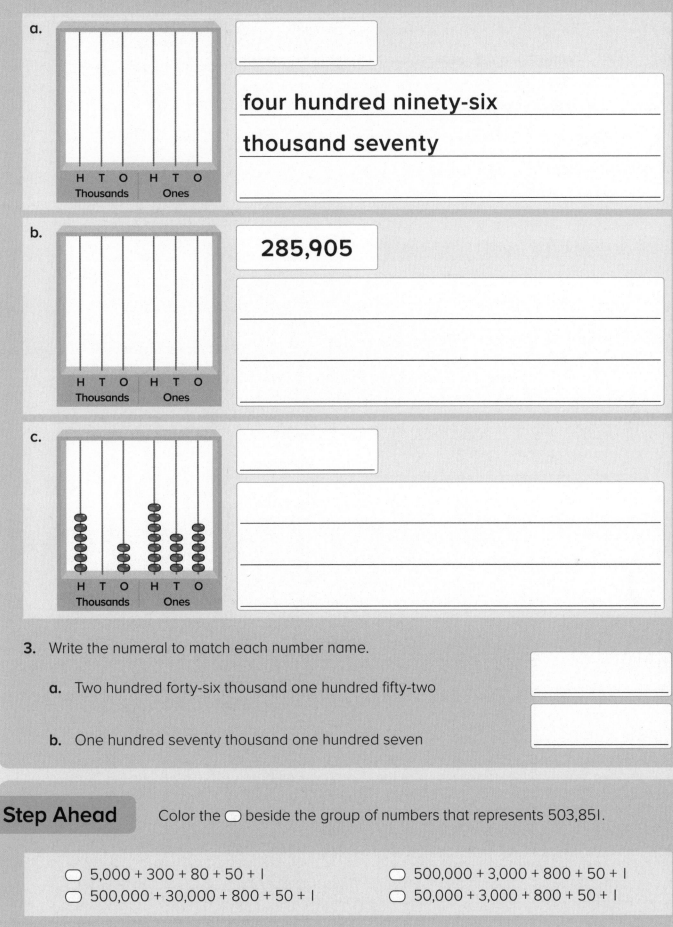

H T O | H T O
Thousands | Ones

four hundred ninety-six
thousand seventy

b.

H T O | H T O
Thousands | Ones

285,905

c.

H T O | H T O
Thousands | Ones

3. Write the numeral to match each number name.

a. Two hundred forty-six thousand one hundred fifty-two

b. One hundred seventy thousand one hundred seven

Step Ahead   Color the ○ beside the group of numbers that represents 503,851.

○ 5,000 + 300 + 80 + 50 + 1
○ 500,000 + 30,000 + 800 + 50 + 1

○ 500,000 + 3,000 + 800 + 50 + 1
○ 50,000 + 3,000 + 800 + 50 + 1

Step In What numbers greater than 900,000 do you know?

What do you remember about the number one million?

How could you show one million with base-10 blocks?
How many thousands blocks would you need?

How would you say the number on this expander?

What place-value names do you say?

Read this number and write it on the expander.

five million four hundred twenty thousand two hundred eighteen

How did you know where to write each digit?
How did you know where to write the zero?

Zeros are written when there is no value in a place.

Step Up I. Read the number name. Then write the matching number on each expander.

a. one million seven hundred fifteen thousand twenty-nine

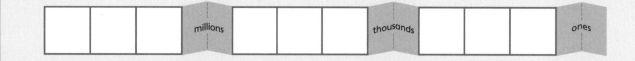

b. four million three hundred eighty thousand two hundred one

2. Read the number on the expander. Then write the matching number in words.

a.

| | | 7 | millions | 0 | 5 | 6 | thousands | 9 | 3 | 0 | ones |

b.

| | | 5 | millions | 1 | 0 | 8 | thousands | 0 | 0 | 5 | ones |

3. Read the number name. Then write the matching numeral.

a. two million eight hundred three thousand

b. five million eight hundred thirty-three thousand
four hundred two

c. one million eighteen thousand three hundred
forty-two

d. nine million eighty-three thousand
four hundred twenty

Step Ahead

Read the number on the expander.
Then write in words the number that is **10 thousand greater.**

| | | 5 | millions | 2 | 0 | 8 | thousands | 6 | 1 | 5 | ones |

Computation Practice

★ Complete the equations. Then write each letter above its matching product at the bottom of the page. Some letters appear more than once.

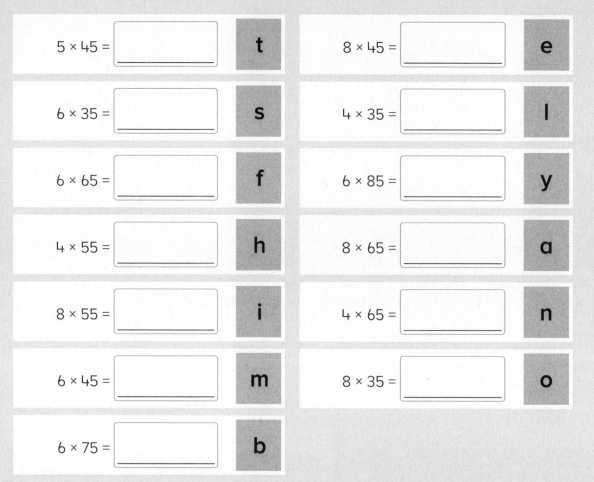

5 × 45 = _____ **t**

6 × 35 = _____ **s**

6 × 65 = _____ **f**

4 × 55 = _____ **h**

8 × 55 = _____ **i**

6 × 45 = _____ **m**

6 × 75 = _____ **b**

8 × 45 = _____ **e**

4 × 35 = _____ **l**

6 × 85 = _____ **y**

8 × 65 = _____ **a**

4 × 65 = _____ **n**

8 × 35 = _____ **o**

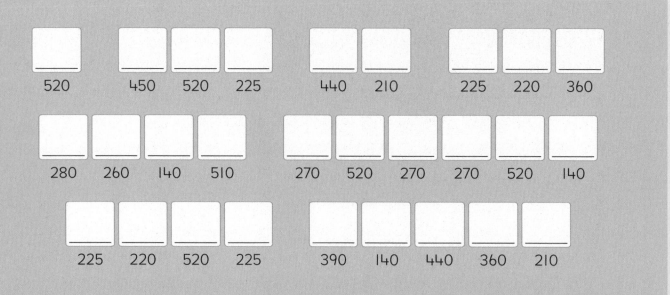

520   450   520   225   440   210   225   220   360

280   260   140   510   270   520   270   270   520   140

225   220   520   225   390   140   440   360   210

Ongoing Practice

I. Use this number line to help you write the totals below.

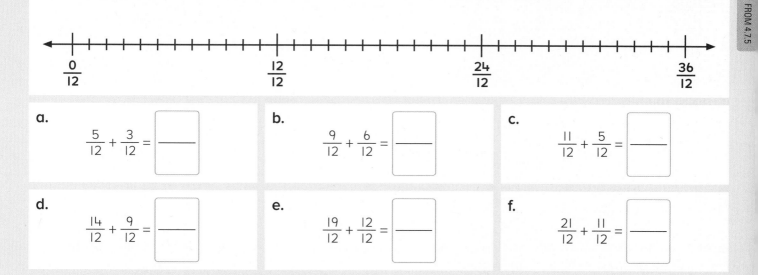

$$\frac{0}{12} \qquad \frac{12}{12} \qquad \frac{24}{12} \qquad \frac{36}{12}$$

a. $\frac{5}{12} + \frac{3}{12} = $ ____

b. $\frac{9}{12} + \frac{6}{12} = $ ____

c. $\frac{11}{12} + \frac{5}{12} = $ ____

d. $\frac{14}{12} + \frac{9}{12} = $ ____

e. $\frac{19}{12} + \frac{12}{12} = $ ____

f. $\frac{21}{12} + \frac{11}{12} = $ ____

2. Write the matching number on each expander.

a. eight million ninety-eight thousand seven hundred two

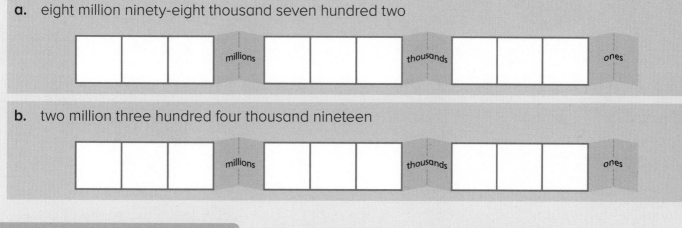

millions   thousands   ones

b. two million three hundred four thousand nineteen

millions   thousands   ones

Preparing for Module 2

Estimate each product. Then use the standard multiplication algorithm to calculate the exact product.

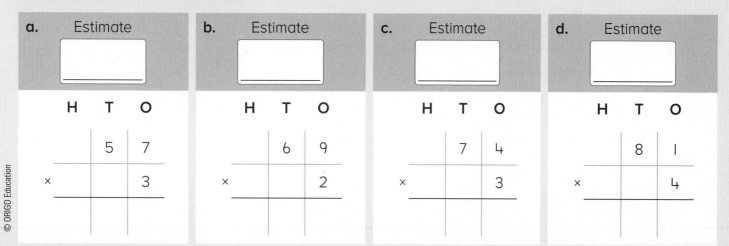

a. Estimate

H	T	O
	5	7
×		3

b. Estimate

H	T	O
	6	9
×		2

c. Estimate

H	T	O
	7	4
×		3

d. Estimate

H	T	O
	8	1
×		4

Step In

This poster was used to show the total funds raised to help build a new wing at a hospital.

What amount was raised?

What does each mark on the poster represent?

What amount is each month showing?
How do you know?

How can you figure out the increase in the amount raised from one arrow to the next on the poster?

Where do you think September might be located?
How did you decide?

How could you use the marks to help you locate each of these amounts?

$1,290,000	$1,920,000	$920,000
$810,000	$180,000	$1,180,000

Help Build the Hospital Wing

December — $2,000,000

October

August

$1,000,000

May

March

$1,290,000 is just a little less than the third mark above $1,000,000.

Step Up

1. Draw a line from each number to its position on the number line.

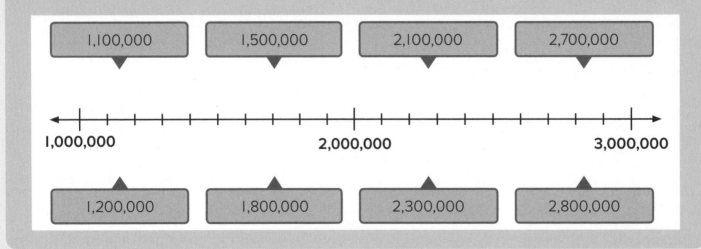

1,100,000   1,500,000   2,100,000   2,700,000

1,000,000   2,000,000   3,000,000

1,200,000   1,800,000   2,300,000   2,800,000

2. Write the number shown by each arrow.

a.

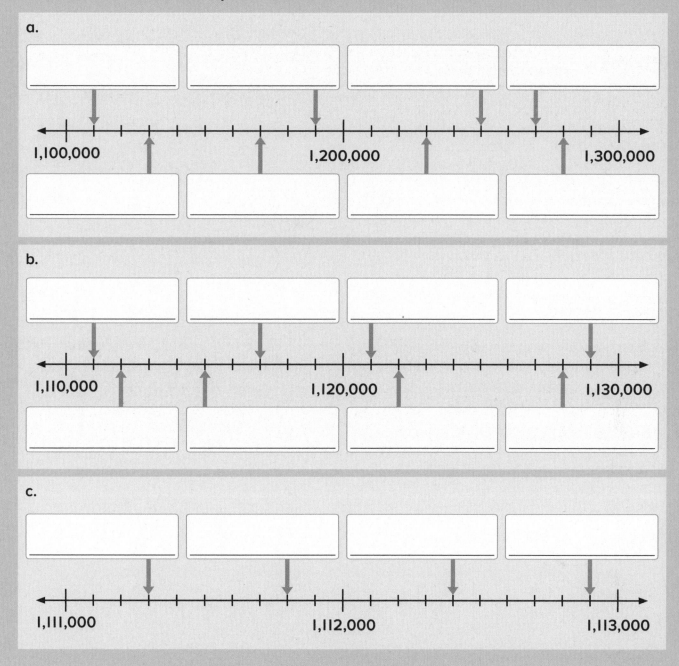

1,100,000   1,200,000   1,300,000

b.

1,110,000   1,120,000   1,130,000

c.

1,111,000   1,112,000   1,113,000

Step Ahead   Mark and label the number line to show the donations that were received each year.

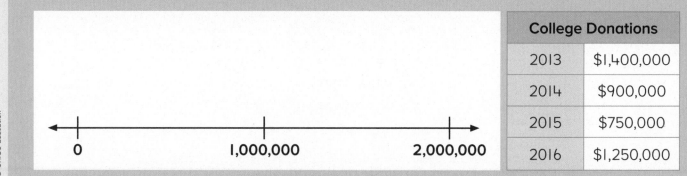

0   1,000,000   2,000,000

College Donations	
2013	$1,400,000
2014	$900,000
2015	$750,000
2016	$1,250,000

Step In

Look at these digit cards. Imagine you use each digit once to form a number.

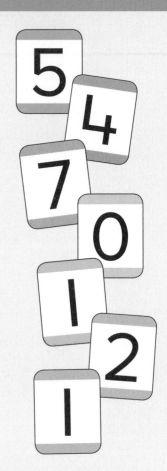

Is this number possible? How do you know? **7,013,542**

What number(s) could you form to match these descriptions?

- The greatest number that ends in zero
- The least number that ends in zero
- Numbers between 1,000,000 and 1,100,000
- Numbers between 4,500,000 and 4,700,000
- The number that is as close to 5,000,000 as possible
- The least and greatest numbers

What strategy did you use to figure out the numbers?

Did your strategy work for every description?

Step Up

1. Look at these digit cards.

8 1 4 9 5 6 3

Use each digit once to make these.

	greatest	least
a. the **greatest** and **least** numbers		
b. the greatest **even** number		
c. the least **even** number		

d. any three numbers that are between 4,500,000 and 5,000,000

2. Roll a number cube seven times. Write the numbers you roll on these cards.

Use each digit once to make these.

greatest	least

a. the **greatest** and **least** numbers

b. the greatest **odd** number

c. the greatest **even** number

d. a number that is as close to 3,000,000 as possible

e. a number that is as close to 1,000,000 as possible

f. the three **least** numbers

g. the three **greatest** numbers

3. These are the top seven scores from a popular online game:

Fiona 3,685,125   Allan 2,487,102   Hugo 2,690,300   Cathy 2,599,305

Carmen 2,358,521   Mateo 2,609,301   Cary 2,490,999

Write the scores for the players who came 4th, 5th, and 6th.

4th: _____   5th: _____   6th: _____

Step Ahead

The number 123 can be written backward as 321.
The difference between the two numbers is 198.

Write a seven-digit number forward and backward
so the difference is less than 10,000.
Show your thinking on page 42.

My number: _____

My difference: _____

Think and Solve THINK TANK

Wendell can move shapes between scales to make the number of kilograms on each scale the same.

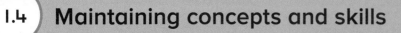

A   B   C   D

⬤ weighs 3 kg   ⬤ weighs 9 kg   ⬛ weighs 6 kg

a. Which shapes can Wendell move?

b. How many kilograms will be on each scale after the moves? _____ kg

Words at Work

Research the populations of four different states. Write the numbers in order from least to greatest. Then write how you know that your order is correct.

Ongoing Practice

1. Add these mixed numbers. Show your thinking.

a.

$4\frac{4}{6} + 2\frac{1}{6} =$ ☐

b.

$3\frac{2}{5} + 1\frac{1}{5} =$ ☐

c.

$3\frac{2}{8} + 4\frac{5}{8} =$ ☐

2. Write the number shown by each arrow.

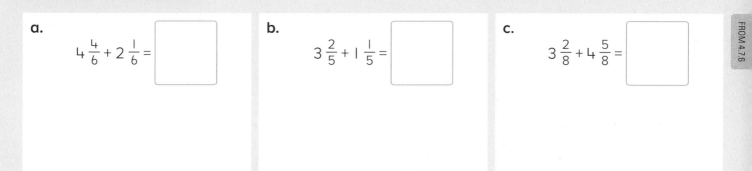

a. _____

b. _____

c. _____

4,108,000   4,109,000   4,110,000

d. _____

e. _____

f. _____

Preparing for Module 2

Calculate each partial product. Then write the total of the four products.

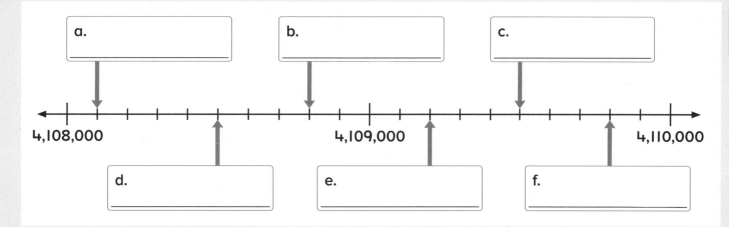

30

8

20   6

38 × 26

30 × 20 = _____

30 × 6 = _____

8 × 20 = _____

8 × 6 = _____

Total _____

Step In

Where have you seen eight- or nine-digit numbers recorded?

What place values are said when you say a nine-digit number?

Complete the number name below to show how you read the number on this expander.

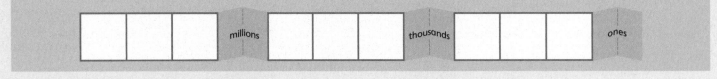

| 1 | 3 | 5 | millions | 2 | 7 | 4 | thousands | 3 | 1 | 2 | ones |

_____ hundred _____ million _____ hundred _____ thousand _____ hundred _____

Read this number.   two hundred forty-six million seven hundred five thousand ninety

Write it on the expander. Then write the matching numeral below.

| | | | millions | | | | thousands | | | | ones |

How did you decide where to write the commas?

How do they help you read the numeral?

Step Up

1. Read the number name. Then write the matching number on the expander.

a. seventy-three million five hundred thirty thousand six hundred three

| | | | millions | | | | thousands | | | | ones |

b. four hundred eighty million five thousand three hundred fifty-eight

| | | | millions | | | | thousands | | | | ones |

c. seven hundred three million three thousand forty

| | | | millions | | | | thousands | | | | ones |

2. Write the numeral and number name to match the number on the expander.

a.

| | 3 | 5 | millions | 5 | 9 | 2 | thousands | 8 | 0 | 5 | ones |

b.

| 3 | 0 | 9 | millions | 0 | 4 | 7 | thousands | 5 | 0 | 0 | ones |

3. Write the matching numeral or number name.

a. 70,293,430 _____

b. one hundred eight million four thousand two hundred seventy-five _____

c. 418,720,912 _____

Step Ahead   Read this number name. Then write the number that is **10 million less**.

fourteen million three thousand twenty-three

Step In Mark and label the location of one million on this number line.

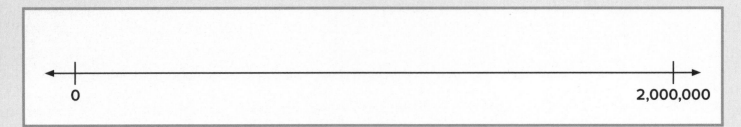

0   2,000,000

Draw more marks to partition the distance between each million into fourths of a million.

What number does each mark represent? How do you know?

What fraction of one million does the third mark represent? How do you know?

Write the whole numbers below the number line. Then write the fractions above the number line.

Record fractions equal to or greater than one whole as a mixed number, for example, 1, $1\frac{1}{4}$, $1\frac{2}{4}$.

What quarter million is closest to 1,483,000?
How did you figure it out?
How would you write it as a decimal fraction?

Step Up 1. Draw a line to show the position of each number on the number line. Be as accurate as possible.

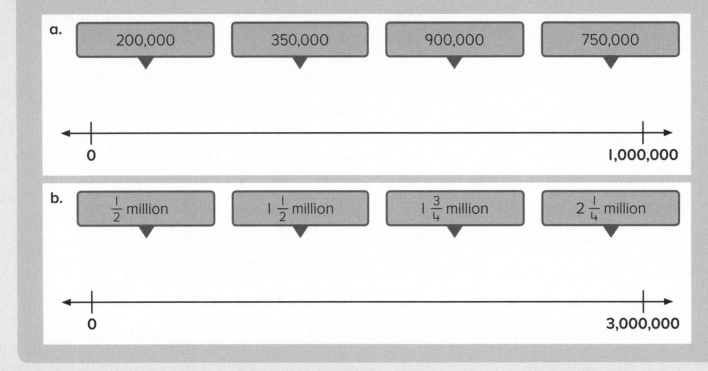

a.

| 200,000 | 350,000 | 900,000 | 750,000 |

0   1,000,000

b.

| $\frac{1}{2}$ million | $1\frac{1}{2}$ million | $1\frac{3}{4}$ million | $2\frac{1}{4}$ million |

0   3,000,000

2. Write each amount as a whole number.

a. $\frac{1}{4}$ million _____

b. $4\frac{1}{2}$ million _____

c. $2\frac{3}{4}$ million _____

d. $3\frac{1}{4}$ million _____

3. Look at this list of state populations*. Which state has a population closest to each of these?

POPULATION	
Alaska	738,432
Colorado	5,456,574
Connecticut	3,590,886
Indiana	6,619,680
Nevada	2,890,845
New Jersey	8,958,013
New Mexico	2,085,109
North Carolina	10,042,802
Tennessee	6,600,299
Wisconsin	5,771,337

*2015 US Census Bureau estimate

a. $5\frac{3}{4}$ million _____

b. 2 million _____

c. $3\frac{1}{2}$ million _____

d. $6\frac{1}{2}$ million _____

e. $2\frac{3}{4}$ million _____

f. $5\frac{1}{4}$ million _____

4. Look at this list of country populations**. Which country has the population closest to each of these?

POPULATION	
Malaysia	30,513,848
Cameroon	23,739,218
Canada	35,099,836
Taiwan	23,415,126
Poland	38,562,189

**2015 CIA World Factbook online

a. 38.5 million _____

b. 24 million _____

c. 36.25 million _____

d. 23.5 million _____

Step Ahead   Imagine you round a number to the nearest $\frac{1}{4}$ million and get 3.75 million.

Write three possible starting numbers. Try to use as many different digits as possible in each.

_____   _____   _____

© ORIGO Education

Computation Practice

★ Complete the equations. Write each letter above its matching total at the bottom of the page. Some letters appear more than once.

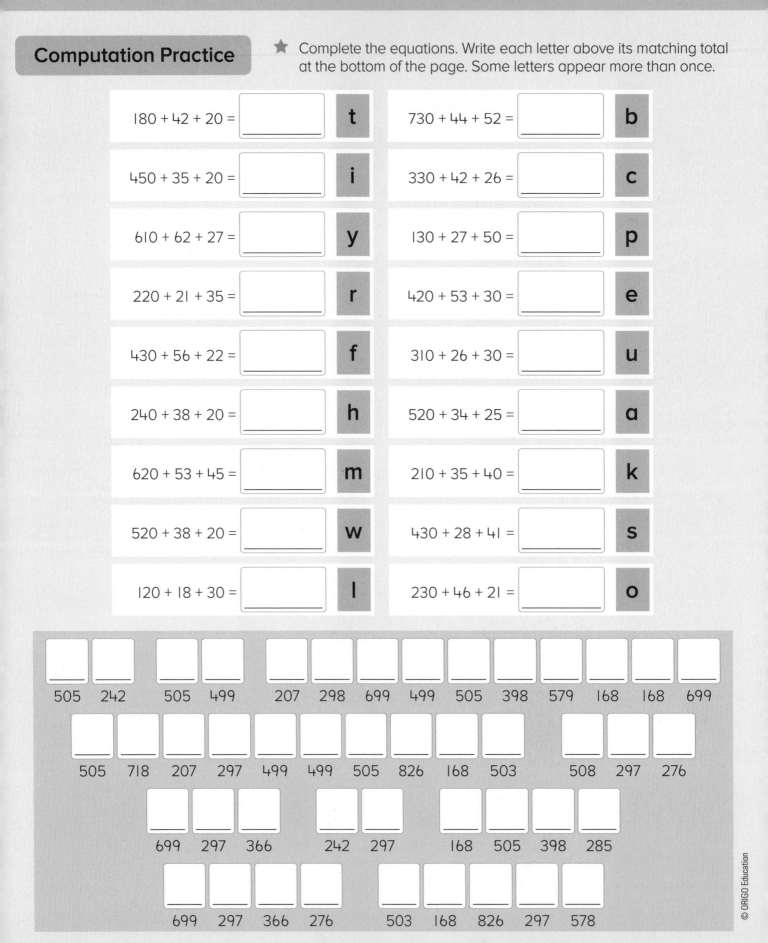

180 + 42 + 20 = ____ **t**

450 + 35 + 20 = ____ **i**

610 + 62 + 27 = ____ **y**

220 + 21 + 35 = ____ **r**

430 + 56 + 22 = ____ **f**

240 + 38 + 20 = ____ **h**

620 + 53 + 45 = ____ **m**

520 + 38 + 20 = ____ **w**

120 + 18 + 30 = ____ **l**

730 + 44 + 52 = ____ **b**

330 + 42 + 26 = ____ **c**

130 + 27 + 50 = ____ **p**

420 + 53 + 30 = ____ **e**

310 + 26 + 30 = ____ **u**

520 + 34 + 25 = ____ **a**

210 + 35 + 40 = ____ **k**

430 + 28 + 41 = ____ **s**

230 + 46 + 21 = ____ **o**

505	242		505	499		207	298	699	499	505	398	579	168	168	699

505	718	207	297	499	499	505	826	168	503		508	297	276

699	297	366		242	297		168	505	398	285

699	297	366	276		503	168	826	297	578

Ongoing Practice

1. Calculate the difference. Draw jumps on the number line to show your thinking.

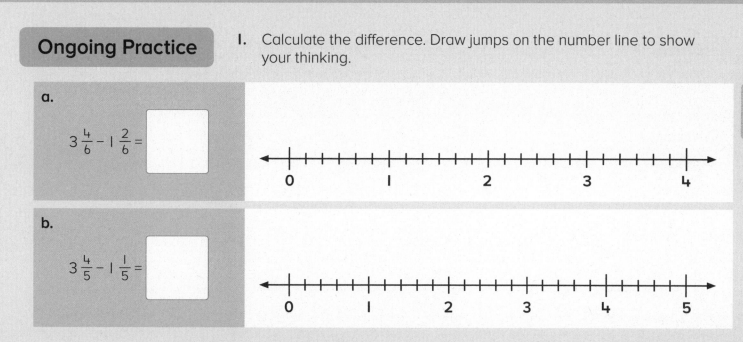

a.

$3\frac{4}{6} - 1\frac{2}{6} =$ ☐

b.

$3\frac{4}{5} - 1\frac{1}{5} =$ ☐

FROM 4.7.9

2. Write the matching number or number name.

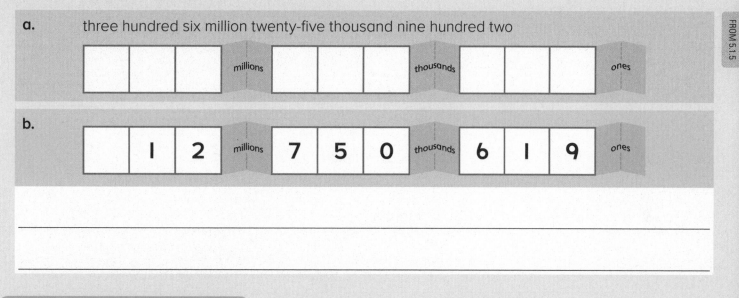

a. three hundred six million twenty-five thousand nine hundred two

| | | | millions | | | | thousands | | | | ones |

b.

| | 1 | 2 | millions | 7 | 5 | 0 | thousands | 6 | 1 | 9 | ones |

FROM 5.1.5

_____

_____

Preparing for Module 2

Solve each problem. Show your thinking.

a. Each pallet holds 255 large books and 420 small books. There are 7 pallets. How many books are packed in total?

_____ books

b. A dairy farm produces 2,490 gallons of milk each day. How much milk will be produced in 9 days?

_____ gallons

Step In

This table shows the number of motor vehicles that were produced by different countries or regions around the world*.

Country/Region	2012	2013	2014	2015
China	19,271,808	22,116,825	23,731,600	24,503,326
European Union	16,275,525	16,246,974	17,127,469	18,477,481
United States	10,335,765	11,066,432	11,660,702	12,100,095
Japan	9,943,077	9,630,181	9,774,665	9,278,238

*OICA Production Statistics 2012–2015

How many motor vehicles were produced by the United States in each year shown?

Which country or region produced closest to 20,000,000 motor vehicles in 2014? How can you figure it out? What digit did you look at to help you decide?

Draw an arrow on this number line to show the approximate location of the number of motor vehicles produced in Japan in 2014.

9,000,000   10,000,000

How would you round this number to the nearest million?

How would you round this number to the nearest hundred thousand?

How does the number line support your thinking?

Step Up

1. Use the table above to complete these.

a. Round the number of motor vehicles produced in each of these places to the nearest **million**.

China (2015) _____

United States (2013) _____

b. Round the number of motor vehicles produced in each of these places to the nearest **hundred thousand**.

European Union (2012) _____

Japan (2014) _____

This table shows the number of registered vehicles in different countries*.

Country	Registered Vehicles
Brazil	81,600,729
China	250,138,212
Indonesia	104,211,132
Australia	17,180,596
United States	265,043,362

*WHO Global status report on road safety 2015

2. Write the countries that have more than 100,000,000 registered vehicles.

3. Round the number of registered vehicles to the nearest **ten**, **hundred**, and **thousand**.

Country	Nearest Ten	Nearest Hundred	Nearest Thousand
China			
Indonesia			
United States			

4. Round the number of registered vehicles to the nearest **ten thousand** and the nearest **hundred thousand**.

Country	Nearest Ten Thousand	Nearest Hundred Thousand
Brazil		
Australia		
United States		

Step Ahead

How would you round this number to the nearest **thousand**? Explain your thinking. Then write the new number.

52,460,308

Step In

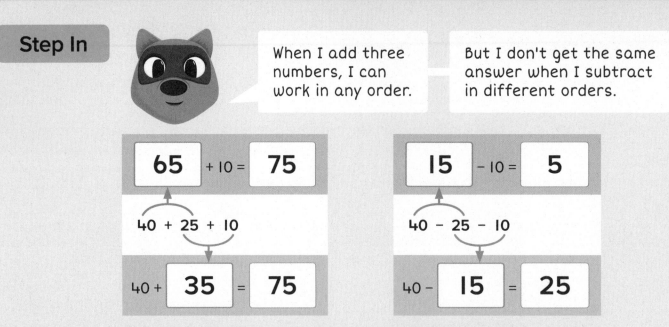

When I add three numbers, I can work in any order.

But I don't get the same answer when I subtract in different orders.

| 65 | + 10 = | 75 |
| 40 + 25 + 10 |
| 40 + | 35 | = 75 |

| 15 | – 10 = | 5 |
| 40 – 25 – 10 |
| 40 – | 15 | = 25 |

What do you think would happen if you multiply or divide in different orders?

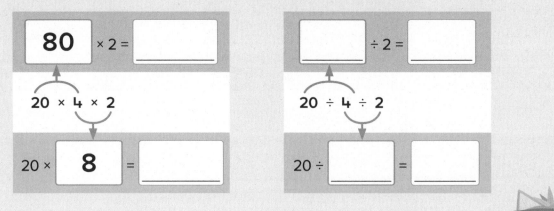

| 80 | × 2 = |
| 20 × 4 × 2 |
| 20 × | 8 | = |

| | ÷ 2 = |
| 20 ÷ 4 ÷ 2 |
| 20 ÷ | | = |

What do you notice? Which operations can you work with in different orders?

Step Up   1.   Add to calculate the missing numbers. Write the totals.

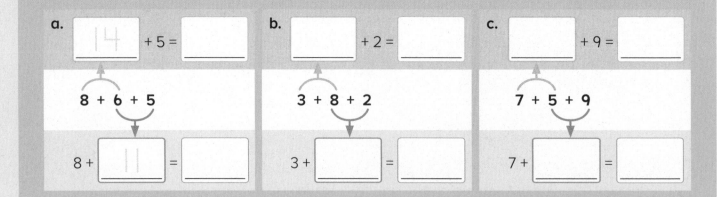

a.
| 14 | + 5 = |
| 8 + 6 + 5 |
| 8 + | 11 | = |

b.
| | + 2 = |
| 3 + 8 + 2 |
| 3 + | | = |

c.
| | + 9 = |
| 7 + 5 + 9 |
| 7 + | | = |

2. Write the missing numbers. Then write the answers.

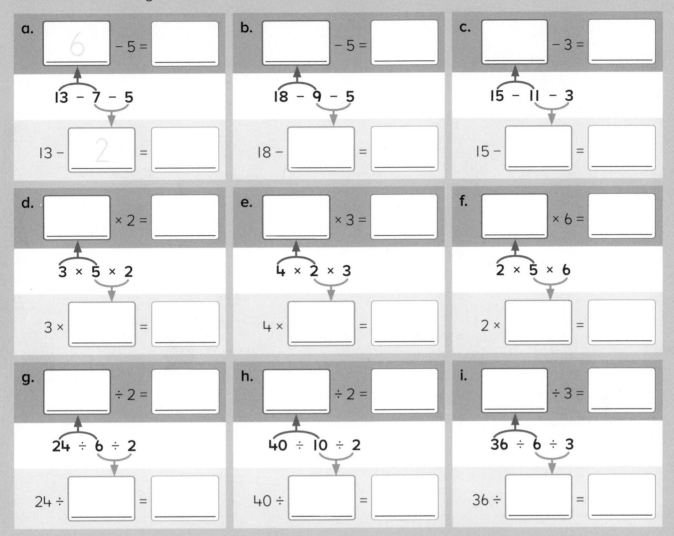

a. ⬜6⬜ – 5 = ⬜

13 – 7 – 5

13 – ⬜2⬜ = ⬜

b. ⬜ – 5 = ⬜

18 – 9 – 5

18 – ⬜ = ⬜

c. ⬜ – 3 = ⬜

15 – 11 – 3

15 – ⬜ = ⬜

d. ⬜ × 2 = ⬜

3 × 5 × 2

3 × ⬜ = ⬜

e. ⬜ × 3 = ⬜

4 × 2 × 3

4 × ⬜ = ⬜

f. ⬜ × 6 = ⬜

2 × 5 × 6

2 × ⬜ = ⬜

g. ⬜ ÷ 2 = ⬜

24 ÷ 6 ÷ 2

24 ÷ ⬜ = ⬜

h. ⬜ ÷ 2 = ⬜

40 ÷ 10 ÷ 2

40 ÷ ⬜ = ⬜

i. ⬜ ÷ 3 = ⬜

36 ÷ 6 ÷ 3

36 ÷ ⬜ = ⬜

3. Look at your answers in Questions 1 and 2. Write what you notice.

_____

_____

Step Ahead   Write numbers to make true equations. Use a calculator to help.

_____ + _____ + _____ = 64

_____ × _____ × _____ = 64

_____ – _____ – _____ = 64

_____ ÷ _____ ÷ _____ = 64

Think and Solve 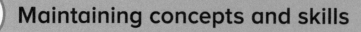 At Dave's Diner, 2 sandwiches and 2 drinks cost $12.
You can buy 5 drinks for the cost of one sandwich.

a. What does one sandwich cost? $_____

b. What does one drink cost? $_____

Dave's Diner

2 sandwiches
and 2 drinks
for $12

Words at Work Write about the operations you know you can work with in different orders.
Be sure to use examples.

Ongoing Practice

1. Split the total into two numbers that are easier to divide. Divide the two parts then complete the equation.

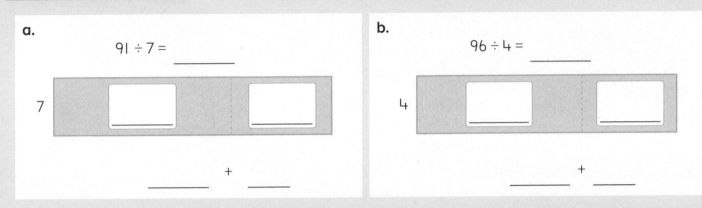

a.

$91 \div 7 =$ _____

7

_____ + _____

b.

$96 \div 4 =$ _____

4

_____ + _____

2. Round each number to the nearest **thousand**, **ten thousand**, and **hundred thousand**.

	Nearest 1,000	Nearest 10,000	Nearest 100,000
79,072,113			
407,892,918			
190,089,745			
218,107,112			
381,609,498			
60,299,001			

Preparing for Module 2

Write an equation to show the order in which you would multiply these three numbers.

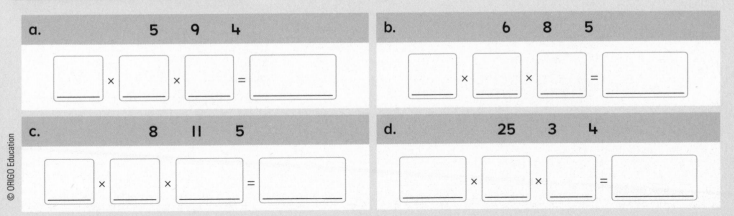

a.   5   9   4

[ ] × [ ] × [ ] = [ ]

b.   6   8   5

[ ] × [ ] × [ ] = [ ]

c.   8   11   5

[ ] × [ ] × [ ] = [ ]

d.   25   3   4

[ ] × [ ] × [ ] = [ ]

Step In

How could you figure out the number of cubes in this prism?

This prism is 4 layers high. Each layer has 6 rows and 3 cubes in each row. So I would multiply 4 × 6 × 3.

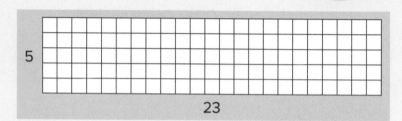

What would you write to show your thinking?

Which part is easier to multiply? Why?

How many cubes are in the prism?

You don't need parentheses for multiplication, but they do tell which two factors to multiply first.

Here is another example where parentheses are used to help.

How would you calculate the total number of squares in this array?

5

23

The rows can be split into parts to make it easier to figure out. How have these rows been partitioned?

5

20   + 3

Look at these equations. What do you notice?

$$5 × 23 = 5 × (20 + 3)$$

$$5 × (20 + 3) = (5 × 20) + (5 × 3)$$

Step Up

1. Write an equation with parentheses to show how to calculate the total number of cubes in each prism. Make sure you write the total.

a.

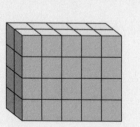

_____

b.

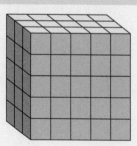

_____

2. For each equation, write the product. Then circle the part that shows how you multiplied.

a.

$(7 \times 4) \times 5 =$ _____ $= 7 \times (4 \times 5)$

b.

$(2 \times 8) \times 6 =$ _____ $= 2 \times (8 \times 6)$

c.

$(3 \times 4) \times 5 =$ _____ $= 3 \times (4 \times 5)$

d.

$(9 \times 2) \times 5 =$ _____ $= 9 \times (2 \times 5)$

3. Color each rectangle to show how you could split it into two parts to calculate the area. Complete each equation.

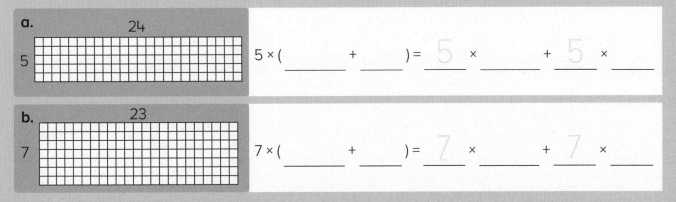

a.

24

5

$5 \times ($ _____ $+$ _____ $) =$ 5 $\times$ _____ $+$ 5 $\times$ _____

b.

23

7

$7 \times ($ _____ $+$ _____ $) =$ 7 $\times$ _____ $+$ 7 $\times$ _____

4. Luke and Giselle calculated two products in different ways.
Complete the equations to show their thinking. Then write the products.

a. 4 × 28

Luke $4 \times (20 + 8) = 4 \times$ _____ $+ 4 \times$ _____

Giselle $4 \times (25 + 3) = 4 \times$ _____ $+ 4 \times$ _____

$4 \times 28 =$ _____

b. 3 × 36

Luke $3 \times (30 + 6) = 3 \times$ _____ $+ 3 \times$ _____

Giselle $3 \times (33 + 3) = 3 \times$ _____ $+ 3 \times$ _____

$3 \times 36 =$ _____

Step Ahead

8 × 49

$8 \times (40 + 9) = 8 \times$ _____ $+$ _____ $\times$ _____ $=$ _____

a. Complete both equations.

$8 \times (50 - 1) = 8 \times$ _____ $-$ _____ $\times$ _____ $=$ _____

b. What do you notice about the two equations? Which operations are used?

_____

_____

_____

Step In Look at these problems. What steps would you use to calculate each answer?

Logan bought a new shirt for $39, shorts for $19, and shoes for $75. What was the total cost?	Kay bought 3 boxes of muffins. In each box, there were 4 flavors with 6 muffins of each flavor. How many muffins did she buy?

What expression could you write to solve each problem?

Why are parentheses not needed?

> An **expression** is a combination of numbers and operations that do not show a relationship, for example, 5 × 8 or 40 + 3.

Look at these word problems. What steps would you use to calculate each answer?
Write one expression for each to show how you would calculate the answer.

Richard bought a cap for $18 and 4 pairs of socks for $9 a pair. What was the total cost?	One box of muffins is $12. Deana used a $50 bill to pay for 3 boxes of muffins. How much change should she get back?

Why are parentheses not needed for these expressions?

> Remember, without parentheses, multiplication and division are always done before addition or subtraction.

Step Up 1. Write an equation to represent each problem.
Use a letter for the unknown amount.

a. Marcos has already saved $85. He plans to save $6 each week for the next 5 weeks. How much will he have saved after 5 weeks?	**b.** Hailey needs 6 strips of ribbon. Each strip is 5 ft long. The ribbon costs $2 a foot. What is the total cost of the ribbon she needs?

2. Write an equation to represent each problem. Use a letter for the unknown amount.

a. A road rally began at 8 a.m. The first car finished the race in $2\frac{1}{2}$ hours. The last car crossed the finish line $\frac{3}{4}$ of an hour later. What time did the last car finish the race?

FINISH

_____

b. Katherine gave $15 to each of her five children. Andre also gave the children $60 to share equally. How much money was each child given?

_____

c. Small bottles of water are 55 cents each. Large bottles are 95 cents each. How much more do 6 small bottles cost than 3 large bottles?

_____

d. Small stickers are in rows of 3 and large stickers are in rows of 2. How many stickers are in 6 rows of small stickers and 4 rows of large stickers?

_____

3. Circle the part that you would calculate first in each of these expressions.

a. $75 + 5 \times 12$

b. $75 \times 5 - 12$

c. $75 - 5 \times 12$

d. $75 \div 5 - 12$

e. $75 \div 5 - 12$

f. $75 \times 5 + 12$

g. $75 + 5 - 12$

h. $75 \div 5 + 12$

Step Ahead   Write a word problem that matches this expression.

$$75 \times 5 + 12$$

_____

_____

_____

_____

_____

Computation Practice

★ Write the differences in the grid below.

Across	Down
a. 792 – 550	**a.** 574 – 350
c. 283 – 110	**b.** 395 – 140
e. 883 – 360	**c.** 372 – 240
f. 785 – 340	**d.** 768 – 450
h. 468 – 230	**g.** 962 – 530
j. 873 – 450	**i.** 486 – 130
l. 585 – 320	**j.** 681 – 250
n. 393 – 150	**k.** 562 – 240
o. 292 – 120	**l.** 547 – 310
p. 976 – 220	**m.** 866 – 330

Ongoing Practice

I. Split the total into three numbers that are easier to divide. Divide the parts then complete the equation.

a.

$$485 \div 5 = \underline{\hspace{2cm}}$$

5

_____ + _____ + _____

b.

$$684 \div 6 = \underline{\hspace{2cm}}$$

6

_____ + _____

2. Write the missing numbers.

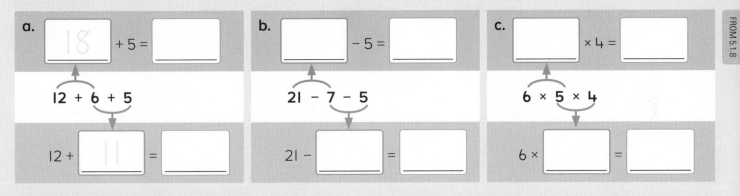

a.

18 + 5 = _____

12 + 6 + 5

12 + 11 = _____

b.

_____ − 5 = _____

21 − 7 − 5

21 − _____ = _____

c.

_____ × 4 = _____

6 × 5 × 4

6 × _____ = _____

Preparing for Module 2

Each small square represents I yard by I yard. Write the dimensions of the whole rectangle. Then write how you will use the dimensions to calculate the area.

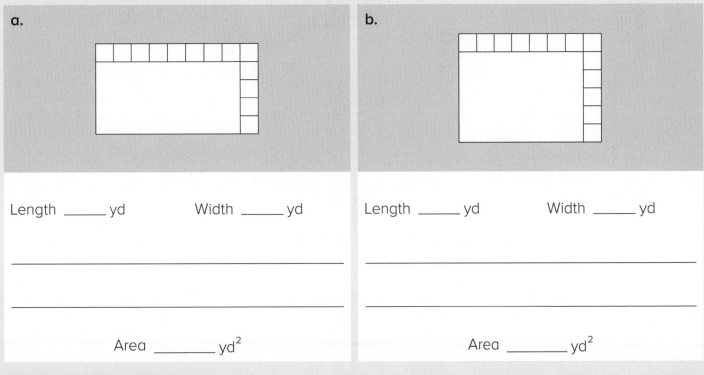

a.

Length _____ yd   Width _____ yd

_____

_____

Area _____ yd²

b.

Length _____ yd   Width _____ yd

_____

_____

Area _____ yd²

Step In

Look at these word problems.

A school used 4 buses for a trip to a football game. Each bus carried 25 students and 10 teachers. How many passengers were on all 4 buses?

Sara had $50. She bought a $35 game. At the checkout, $5 was taken off the price of the game. How much did she have left after she paid for the game?

Write an expression you could use to solve each problem. Why are parentheses needed in each expression?

If you changed these expressions to equations, what steps could you use to calculate each answer?

Could you rewrite the expressions without parentheses and still get the correct answer? How?

Look at these word problems.

Six students bought food for $28 and drinks for $11. They shared the cost equally. How much did each student pay?

Cooper earns $85 each week and spends $68 each week. He saves what is left over. How much will he save in 12 weeks?

Write an expression that uses parentheses to show how you could calculate each answer.

If you changed these expressions to equations, what steps could you use to calculate each answer?

Step Up

1. Color the ⬭ beside the expression that matches the steps you would use to calculate the answer to the problem.

a. Each book costs $8 plus 50 cents for tax. How much will you pay for 6 books?

- ◯ 6 × (8 + 0.50)
- ◯ 8 + 0.50 × 6
- ◯ 6 × 8 + 0.50
- ◯ (6 × 8) + 0.50

b. A web page displays 12 photos of cats and 23 photos of dogs in one single array. If there are 5 rows of photos, how many columns of photos are there?

- ◯ (12 + 23) ÷ 5
- ◯ 12 + (23 ÷ 5)
- ◯ 12 + (23 ÷ 5)
- ◯ 12 ÷ 5 + 23

c. Julia had $35 and bought an $18 game. Then her grandmother gave her $5. How much does she have now?

- ◯ 35 − (18 + 5)
- ◯ 35 − (18 − 5)
- ◯ (35 − 18) + 5
- ◯ 35 + (5 − 18)

d. The perimeter of a rectangle is 22 feet. The two long sides total 14 feet. What is the width of the rectangle?

- ◯ 22 − 14 ÷ 2
- ◯ 22 − (14 ÷ 2)
- ◯ (22 − 14) ÷ 2
- ◯ (22 ÷ 2) − 14

2. Write an equation to represent each problem. Use a letter for the unknown amount.

a. Large bottles of water that normally cost $2.50 have been reduced by 60 cents. What is the total cost of 5 large bottles of water?

_____

b. A marching band has 38 people in red uniforms, and 38 people in white uniforms. They are all arranged in rows of 4. How many rows are there?

_____

c. James runs 4 miles every morning and 7 miles every evening. How far does he run in 5 days?

_____

d. Alisa bought 3 shirts for $29 each and then spent $15 on lunch. She has $31 left. How much money did she have before?

_____

e. 35 pictures are arranged in 8 equal rows with an extra row of 3 pictures. How many pictures are in each of the first 8 rows?

_____

f. A rectangular room has an area of 384 sq ft with floor tiles covering one part of it and carpet covering the other. The tiled part is 8 ft long. The carpeted part is 24 ft long. What is the width of the room?

_____

3. In each equation, draw parentheses if they are needed to make it true.

a. $5 \times 0 + 20 = 100$ **b.** $26 + 47 + 5 = 78$ **c.** $24 \div 4 \times 2 = 3$

d. $38 - 21 + 38 = 55$ **e.** $12 - 8 \times 4 = 16$ **f.** $2 \times 32 \div 4 = 16$

g. $3 + 7 \times 4 \div 2 = 20$ **h.** $100 = 31 + 9 \times 2 + 20$ **i.** $55 \div 5 - 6 + 1 = 4$

Step Ahead   Write a word problem to match this expression. $8 \times (4 + 5)$

_____

_____

_____

Step In

Ricardo bought three trading cards that cost **$6** each. He paid with a **$20** bill. How much change should he receive?

What expression would you write to calculate the change?

Jessica wrote this equation.

$$20 - 3 \times 6 = \boxed{}$$

What part of the equation should you do first? How do you know?

Why are parentheses not needed in Jessica's equation?

Could you use them anyway?

You don't have to use parentheses, but they can make it clearer.

Step Up

1. Read the problem. Then color the ⬭ beside the thinking you would use to calculate the answer.

a.

Noah had $40.
He bought 4 tickets that cost $7 each.

How much money does he have left?

○ $40 - 4 \times 7$
○ $(40 - 4) \times 7$
○ $4 \times 7 - 40$

b.

9 red apples and 3 green apples were shared equally among 6 children.

How many apples were in each share?

○ $9 + 3 \div 6$
○ $(9 + 3) \div 6$
○ $(9 + 3) - 6$

c.

Ethan has $100 to buy some clothes. A jacket costs $63 which is 9 times as much as the cost of a T-shirt.

How much change will Ethan get if he buys the T-shirt?

○ $63 \div 9 - 100$
○ $(100 - 93) \div 9$
○ $100 - 63 \div 9$

2. Write an expression to show how you would solve each problem. Then write the solution.

Problem	Expression	Solution
a. Mary buys a sandwich for $7 and a drink for $4. She pays with a $20 bill. How much change will she get?		
b. On Saturday, Ryan watches 1.5 hours of TV in the morning and the same amount at night. On Sunday, he watches twice as much TV. How much TV does he watch on Sunday?		
c. 25 boys and 17 girls are split into 6 equal teams. How many people are on each team?		
d. A pair of skates costs $4 to rent. Valentina rents 3 pairs. She pays with cash and gets $3 in change. How much money did she give to the cashier?		

3. Write **true** or **false** beside each statement.

a. $(247 + 85) \times 16$ is 16 times greater than **247 + 85**. _____

b. $1{,}738 \times 46 - 35$ is 46 times greater than **1,738 − 35**. _____

Step Ahead   **a.** Write a word problem that uses more than one operation.

_____

_____

_____

_____

b. Exchange problems with another student and write the answer to their problem here.

_____

Think and Solve THINK TANK

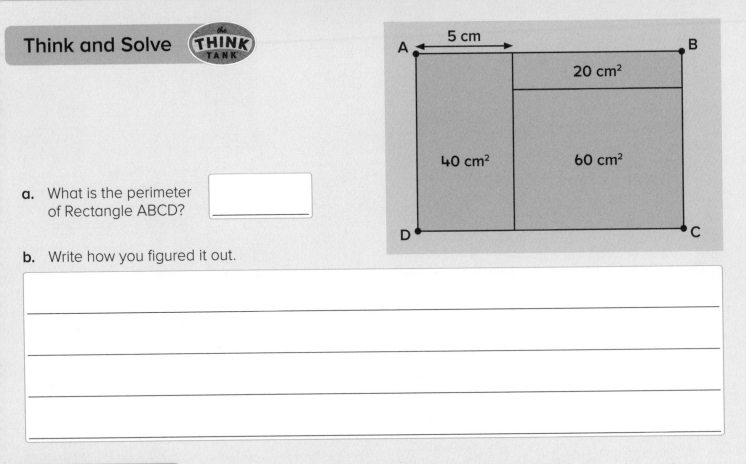

a. What is the perimeter of Rectangle ABCD?

b. Write how you figured it out.

Words at Work

Write in words how you would solve this problem. Then write an equation to match your thinking.

A farmer bought some laying hens. He split them into five equal groups.
Each group had double the number of red hens as white hens.
Each group had half the number of red hens as speckled hens.
There were 20 speckled hens in each group. How many hens did the farmer buy?

Ongoing Practice

I. Write equations to calculate each quotient.

$$24 \div 6 = 4$$
Dividend   Divisor   Quotient

a.
$256 \div 4 = \boxed{}$

$240 \div 4 = \underline{}$

$16 \div 4 = \underline{}$

b.
$384 \div 6 = \boxed{}$

$360 \div 6 = \underline{}$

$\underline{} \div 6 = \underline{}$

c.
$378 \div 7 = \boxed{}$

$\underline{} \div 7 = \underline{}$

$\underline{} \div 7 = \underline{}$

d.
$392 \div 8 = \boxed{}$

$\underline{} \div 8 = \underline{}$

$\underline{} \div 8 = \underline{}$

e.
$477 \div 9 = \boxed{}$

$\underline{} \div 9 = \underline{}$

$\underline{} \div 9 = \underline{}$

f.
$495 \div 5 = \boxed{}$

$\underline{} \div 5 = \underline{}$

$\underline{} \div 5 = \underline{}$

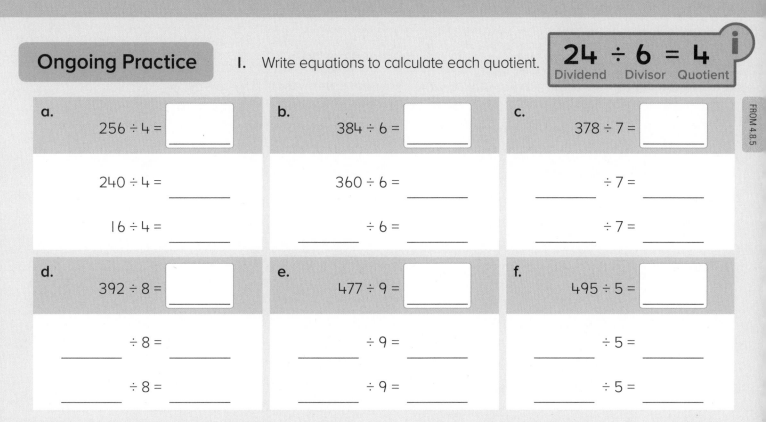

2. Write an equation to represent each problem. Use a letter for the unknown amount.

a. Abey has $20. How much change will she receive if she buys 6 books at $2.50 each?

b. How much money will Max need to buy 3 T-shirts at $12 each and a pair of shorts for $24?

c. Janice has $15. She earns $28 more, then buys two songs for $1.99 each. How much money does she have left?

d. Victor runs 4 miles a day for 5 days then runs 10 miles a day on the weekend. How far does he run in one week?

Preparing for Module 2

Calculate the area of the orange shape. Show your thinking.

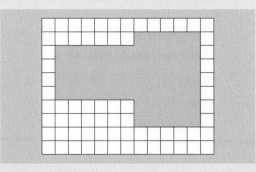

Area $\underline{}$ sq units

Step In

A room at the Seasons Hotel costs $132 for one night.
About how much is the total cost for three nights?

How would you calculate the exact cost?

Layla multiplied the parts to figure out the total cost.

What steps did she follow?

What is the total cost? How do you know?

Write the total cost in the empty boxes.

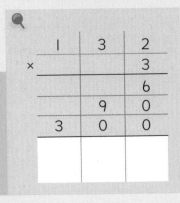

	1	3	2
×			3
			6
		9	0
	3	0	0

Cody used the standard algorithm for multiplication to calculate the total cost.
He followed these steps.

Step 1	Step 2	Step 3

Step 1

H	T	O
1	3	2
×		3
		6

Step 2

H	T	O
1	3	2
×		3
	9	6

Step 3

H	T	O
1	3	2
×		3
3	9	6

What numbers did he multiply in each step?

Compare the two methods above. How are they the same? How are they different?

How could you use Cody's method to calculate 2,312 × 3?

Step Up

1. Estimate each product. Then use the standard multiplication algorithm to calculate the exact answer.

a. Estimate

H	T	O
3	1	2
×		3

b. Estimate

H	T	O
4	2	4
×		2

c. Estimate

H	T	O
2	1	2
×		4

d. Estimate

H	T	O
1	3	1
×		3

2. Estimate each product. Then use the standard multiplication algorithm to calculate the exact answer.

a. Estimate
_____

H	T	O
1	0	3
×		3

b. Estimate
_____

H	T	O
3	4	1
×		2

c. Estimate
_____

H	T	O
1	2	3
×		3

d. Estimate
_____

H	T	O
2	1	0
×		4

e. Estimate
_____

Th	H	T	O
1	3	1	2
×			3

f. Estimate
_____

Th	H	T	O
2	4	4	1
×			2

g. Estimate
_____

Th	H	T	O
1	0	1	2
×			4

h. Estimate
_____

Th	H	T	O
3	1	2	3
×			3

i. Estimate
_____

3	0	3	1
×			3

j. Estimate
_____

1	1	0	2
×			4

k. Estimate
_____

2	4	3	0
×			2

l. Estimate
_____

3	2	0	2
×			3

Step Ahead

Look at each card below. Draw a ✔ on the card that shows partial products that match this standard multiplication algorithm.

3 × 3 = 9	3 × 3 = 9
1 × 3 = 3	10 × 3 = 30
3 × 3 = 9	300 × 3 = 900
2 × 3 = 6	2,000 × 3 = 6,000

3 × 3 = 9
10 × 3 = 30
30 × 3 = 90
200 × 3 = 600

2	3	1	3
×			3
6	9	3	9

Step In

About how much is the total cost of three of these screens?

○ $172

How would you calculate the exact cost?

Nancy figured it out like this. What steps did she follow?

```
    172
  ×   3
  ------
      6
    210
    300
  ------
  $516
```

What other methods could you use?

Charlie used the standard multiplication algorithm.

Step 1	Step 2	Step 3

H	T	O
1	7	2
×		3
		6

H	T	O
²1	7	2
×		3
	1	6

H	T	O
²1	7	2
×		3
5	1	6

What numbers did he multiply in each step?

What does the 2 in the hundreds place represent?

How did he use this digit?

Compare the two methods above.
How are they the same? How are they different?

How could you use Charlie's method to calculate 3,261 × 4?

Step Up

I. Write your estimate. Then use the standard multiplication algorithm to calculate the exact product.

a. Estimate

	4	2	6
×			3

b. Estimate

	3	7	5
×			5

c. Estimate

	6	4	2
×			4

d. Estimate

	5	2	8
×			7

e. Estimate

	5	8	0
×			4

f. Estimate

	7	5	3
×			6

g. Estimate

	3	0	9
×			8

h. Estimate

	9	1	9
×			3

i. Estimate

	3	4	2	5
×				3

j. Estimate

	5	7	9	1
×				6

k. Estimate

	4	0	3	9
×				4

Step Ahead

Write the correct product. Then describe the mistake in words.

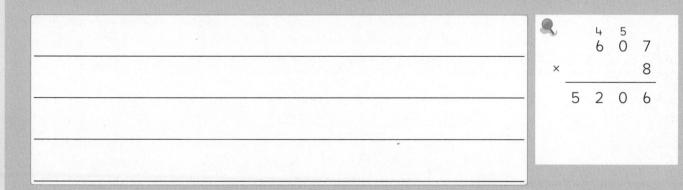

		4	5	
	6	0	7	
×				8
	5	2	0	6

Computation Practice

Time Taken:

⭐ Complete these facts as fast as you can. Use the classroom clock to time yourself.

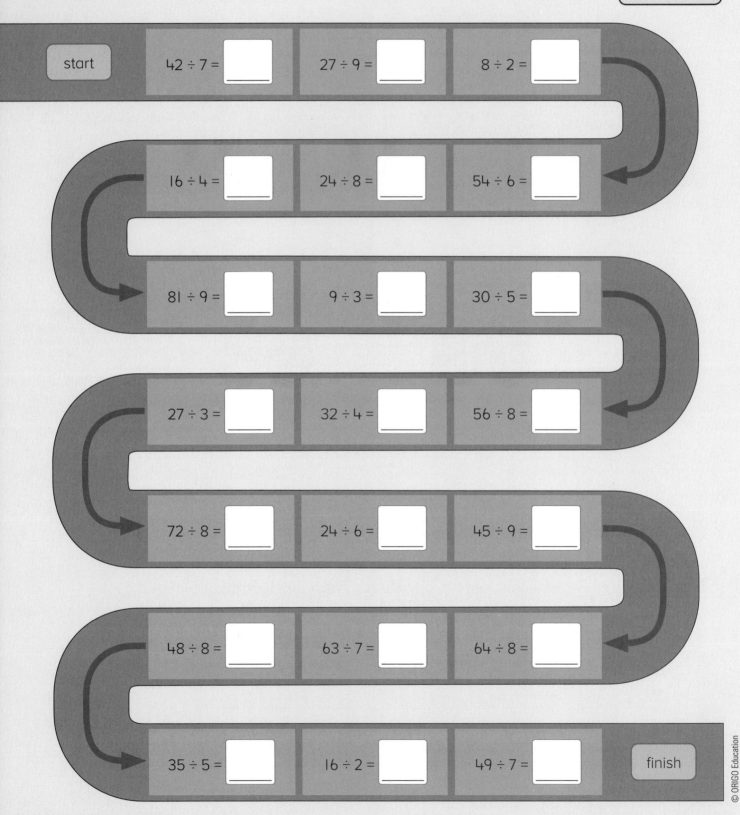

start

42 ÷ 7 =

27 ÷ 9 =

8 ÷ 2 =

16 ÷ 4 =

24 ÷ 8 =

54 ÷ 6 =

81 ÷ 9 =

9 ÷ 3 =

30 ÷ 5 =

27 ÷ 3 =

32 ÷ 4 =

56 ÷ 8 =

72 ÷ 8 =

24 ÷ 6 =

45 ÷ 9 =

48 ÷ 8 =

63 ÷ 7 =

64 ÷ 8 =

35 ÷ 5 =

16 ÷ 2 =

49 ÷ 7 =

finish

1. Write the missing lengths in meters and centimeters. Then draw lines to show where the other lengths are located on the measuring tape.

FROM 4.5.6

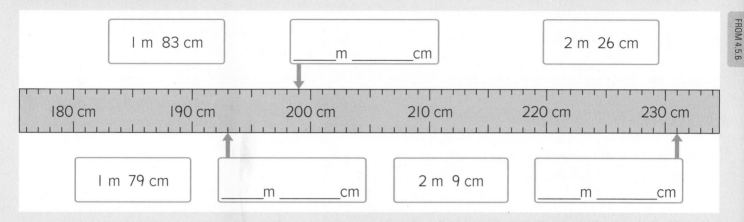

2. Estimate each product. Then use the standard multiplication algorithm to calculate the exact answer.

FROM 5.2.2

a.
Estimate _____

	1	8	2
×			4

b.
Estimate _____

	3	2	4
×			2

c.
Estimate _____

	1	4	1
×			5

d.
Estimate _____

	2	3	6
×			3

e.
Estimate _____

	4	8	2	5
×				2

f.
Estimate _____

	5	8	0	3
×				5

g.
Estimate _____

	3	2	6	1
×				7

Preparing for Module 3

Draw a line to show the location of each decimal fraction. Be as accurate as possible.

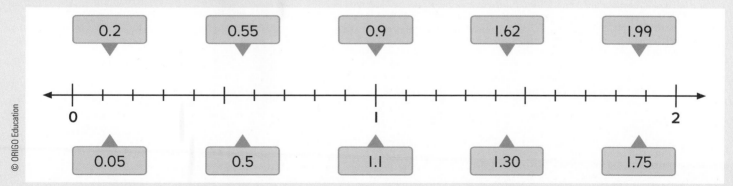

Step In

A school hall has a rectangular floor. Its dimensions are 24 yd × 32 yd.

How would you estimate the area of the floor?

How would you calculate the exact area?

John drew this diagram. How will it help him figure out the area of the floor?

Write the partial product inside each part of the diagram.

What is the area? How do you know?

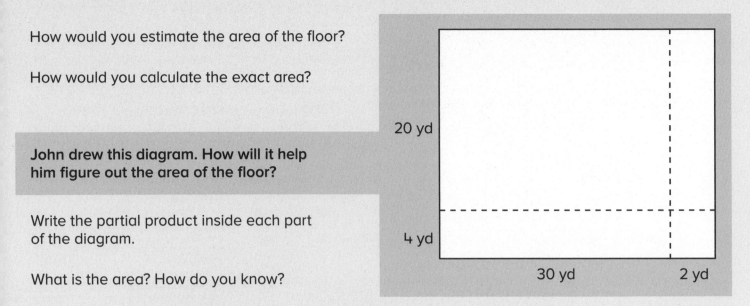

20 yd

4 yd

30 yd   2 yd

Teresa used the standard multiplication algorithm to calculate the exact area.

Step 1	Step 2	Step 3	Step 4	Step 5
H T O	H T O	H T O	H T O	H T O
2 4	2 4	2 4	2 4	2 4
× 3 2	× 3 2	× 3 2	× 3 2	× 3 2
8	4 8	4 8	4 8	4 8
		2 0	7 2 0	7 2 0
				7 6 8

Does it matter which factor is written in the top row? How do you know?
What numbers did she multiply in each step?

Compare the partial-products method and the standard algorithm. How are they similar?

Look carefully at the numbers being multiplied in each step of the algorithm.
Where are the matching partial products in John's diagram?

What is another way you could calculate the area?

I would break the rectangle into two parts. That is 24 × 3 tens plus 24 × 2 ones.

© ORIGO Education

I. A builder made some quick calculations. Make an estimate, then check each calculation and mark it with a ✔ or a ✘. If it is not correct, write the correct calculation to the side.

a.
```
    39
×   41
    39
  156
  195
```

b.
```
    29
×   31
    29
  870
  899
```

c.
```
    26
×   35
  130
  780
  910
```

d.
```
    70
×   61
    70
 3600
 3670
```

e.
```
    53
×   27
  371
 1060
 1431
```

f.
```
    39
×   62
    78
  234
  302
```

Riku thinks following the standard algorithm with these two examples will give different products. Is she correct? Explain your thinking.

```
    14          6
×    6      ×  14
```

Multiplication: Using the standard algorithm with two- and three-digit factors

Step In

A ferry seats 136 people.
It makes 24 trips each day.

Does the ferry carry more or fewer than 2,500 people each day?

How could you calculate the exact number?

Thomas drew this diagram to calculate the exact number.
How will it help him?
Write the partial products inside each part of the diagram.

	20	4
100		
30		
6		

Leila used the standard algorithm to calculate the exact number.

How did she calculate the number in the first row?
What numbers should she write in the second row?

		1	1 2	
		1	3	6
	×		2	4
	5	4	4	

It can get confusing if too many regrouping digits are recorded. Sometimes it is easier to cross them out after using them.

Cross out the regrouping digits that have been recorded.

Then multiply the numbers in the second row. What is the total?

Step Up

1. Write the partial product inside each part of the diagram below. Then add these to calculate the area.

$32 \times 145 =$ [ ]

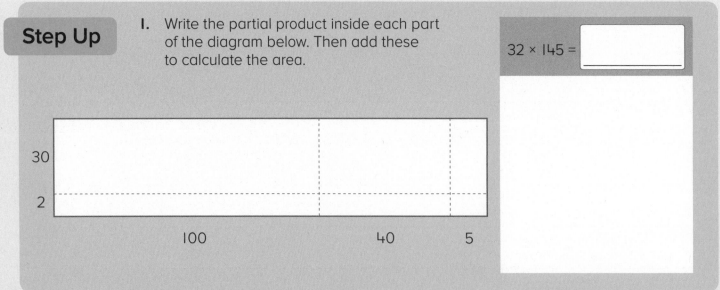

	100	40	5
30			
2			

2. Use the standard multiplication algorithm to calculate the exact product.
Then estimate the product to check that your answer makes sense.

a.

```
    1  4  2
×      2  1
_____
```

b.

```
    6  7  5
×      4  2
_____
```

c.

```
    2  1  4
×      4  2
_____
```

d.

```
    1  7  3
×      3  2
_____
```

e.

```
    3  2  9
×      5  4
_____
```

f.

```
    2  0  8
×      7  3
_____
```

Step Ahead

Look at this calculation.
Describe the mistake in words.

		1	4	6
×			5	4
		5	8	4
	7	3	0	
1	3	1	4	

Think and Solve

THINK TANK

Write **+**, **−**, **×** or **÷** in each ◯ to make a true equation.

$$(60 \bigcirc 6) \bigcirc 9 \bigcirc 2 \bigcirc 3 = 12$$

Rewrite the order of operations you used in the above equation.
Then write five different numbers to make it true.

$$(\boxed{} \bigcirc \boxed{}) \bigcirc \boxed{} \bigcirc \boxed{} \bigcirc \boxed{} = 12$$

Words at Work

Write how you would estimate the product of 347 and 42.

Ongoing Practice

1. Complete each of these.

a. 16 meters

(is equivalent to)

_____ cm

b. 8 meters

(is equivalent to)

_____ mm

c. 220 millimeters

(is equivalent to)

_____ cm

d. 12 $\frac{1}{2}$ centimeters

(is equivalent to)

_____ mm

e. 22 $\frac{1}{2}$ centimeters

(is equivalent to)

_____ mm

f. 6 $\frac{1}{2}$ centimeters

(is equivalent to)

_____ mm

2. Complete these.

a.
$$\begin{array}{r} 6\ 3 \\ \times\ \ 2\ 7 \\ \hline \end{array}$$

b.
$$\begin{array}{r} 4\ 2 \\ \times\ \ 3\ 6 \\ \hline \end{array}$$

c.
$$\begin{array}{r} 2\ 9 \\ \times\ \ 5\ 8 \\ \hline \end{array}$$

d.
$$\begin{array}{r} 8\ 2 \\ \times\ \ 6\ 4 \\ \hline \end{array}$$

Preparing for Module 3

Complete the missing parts. Each large square is one whole.

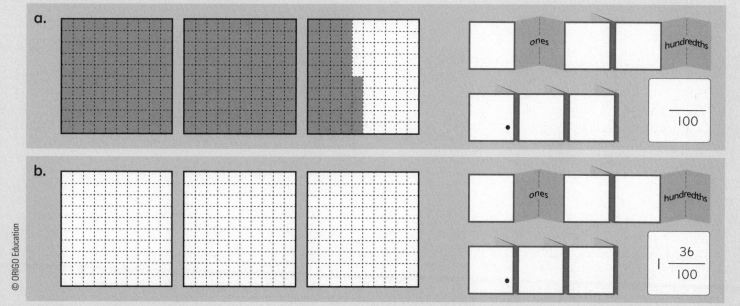

a.

ones ... hundredths

$\frac{}{100}$

b.

ones ... hundredths

$1\frac{36}{100}$

Step In

The local park is rectangular and measures 134 yd by 232 yd.

How could you calculate the area of the park?

Mia drew this diagram of a rectangle split into parts to make it easier to multiply.

Write the partial product inside each part of her diagram.

Add the partial products in your head and write the area of the park below.

Area is _____ yd²

	200	30	2
100			
30			
4			

Alejandro used the standard multiplication algorithm to calculate the area. What steps did he follow?

Look carefully at the third and fifth rows of the algorithm. What do you notice?

Why is the product in the fifth row 100 times greater than the product in the third row?

```
        1  1
        1  3  4
   ×    2  3  2
   _____
  1     2  6  8
  1  4  0  2  0
  2  6  8  0  0
   _____
  3  1  0  8  8
```

Step Up

1. Write the partial product inside each part of the diagram below. Then add these to calculate the area.

153 × 328 = _____

	300	20	8
100			
50			
3			

2. Use the standard multiplication algorithm to calculate the exact product.
Then estimate the product to check that your answer makes sense.

a.
```
    1  3  4  2
  ×        1  2
  _____
```

b.
```
       5  8  7
  ×    4  2  0
  _____
```

c.
```
       1  6  1
  ×    2  5  1
  _____
```

d.
```
    1  0  4  2
  ×     3  2  1
  _____
```

e.
```
       4  2  7
  ×    2  0  5
  _____
```

f.
```
    3  5  2  6
  ×     2  3  5
  _____
```

Step Ahead   Color the ⬭ beside the estimate you think is closest to the exact product.

a. 127 × 53
- ◯ 600
- ◯ 6,000
- ◯ 60,000
- ◯ 600,000

b. 7,325 × 49
- ◯ 35,000
- ◯ 13,500
- ◯ 350,000
- ◯ 280,000

c. 308 × 426
- ◯ 12,000
- ◯ 120,000
- ◯ 1,200
- ◯ 13,000

d. 6,906 × 720
- ◯ 42,000
- ◯ 4,200,000
- ◯ 420,000
- ◯ 460,000

Step In

This table shows the payments players received for each game, and the number of games they played.

Player	Payment	Games Played
A	$4,350	4
B	$1,025	5
C	$895	11
D	$12,352	32
E	$20,499	18

Which player earned the greatest total amount of money?

How could you estimate the total amount that Player A received?

Player A earned almost $4,500 for each game. Double 4,500 is 9,000, then double that is 18,000.

The player earned about $4,500 but I will use 5,000 to help me. 4 × 5,000 is 20,000, then subtract 4 × 500. 20,000 take 2,000 is 18,000.

How would you estimate the total amount that Player E received?

Step Up

1. Look at the table above. Use the standard algorithm to calculate the total amount paid to each of these players.

a. Player B	b. Player C	c. Player D

2. Estimate then use the standard algorithm to solve each problem.

a. The distance from Ruby's house to the stadium is 2,617 feet. The distance from Damon's house to the stadium is 15 times farther. How far is it from Damon's house to the stadium?

b. Each half of a basketball court is 47 feet long. The width of the court is 50 feet. What is the area of the court?

c. Membership for a club costs $245 a season. There are 4,043 members. How much money is paid to the club for memberships?

d. There are 28 seats in each row. There are 42 rows in each section. What is the total number of seats in 3 sections?

Step Ahead

Look at the table at the top of page 58. There are 82 regular games in one season. Estimate the amount that each player below would earn if they played every game. Write your estimates, then use a calculator to check them.

Player A	Player B	Player C	Player D
$_____	$_____	$_____	$_____

Computation Practice   The more there is of me, the less you see. What am I?

★ Complete the equations. Find each product in the grid below and cross out the letter above.
Then write the remaining letters at the bottom of the page.

$5 \times 8 \times 4 = $ ___

$2 \times 7 \times 5 = $ ___

$4 \times 5 \times 2 = $ ___

$5 \times 8 \times 7 = $ ___

$7 \times 6 \times 5 = $ ___

$5 \times 6 \times 2 = $ ___

$6 \times 5 \times 0 = $ ___

$9 \times 5 \times 4 = $ ___

$5 \times 9 \times 6 = $ ___

$4 \times 6 \times 5 = $ ___

$2 \times 5 \times 9 = $ ___

$5 \times 5 \times 7 = $ ___

$9 \times 1 \times 5 = $ ___

$8 \times 5 \times 9 = $ ___

$4 \times 7 \times 5 = $ ___

$5 \times 6 \times 5 = $ ___

E	N	D	A	N	G	E	R
160	180	190	50	210	360	270	240
K	N	O	T	S	N	E	T
100	0	45	150	70	20	60	175
P	E	S	T	S	U	D	S
120	200	40	140	170	280	90	75

Write the letters in order from the ❋ to the bottom-right corner.

Ongoing Practice

1. Complete each of these.

a. 1 ft 10 in

is equivalent to

_____ inches

b. 2 ft 3 in

is equivalent to

_____ inches

c. 3 ft 4 in

is equivalent to

_____ inches

d. 4 ft 2 in

is equivalent to

_____ inches

e. 3 ft 9 in

is equivalent to

_____ inches

f. 5 ft 1 in

is equivalent to

_____ inches

2. Estimate the product, then use the standard algorithm to calculate the problem.

a. A school bought 24 new computers for $1,238 each. Ten of the computers are for teachers. What is the total cost of the computers for students?

b. A roller coaster carries 32 people. It makes 186 trips each day. What is the greatest number of people who could ride the roller coaster in one day?

Preparing for Module 3

Write the matching number on the expander or in words.

a. three and sixty hundredths

ones   hundredths

b. 7.09

_____

c. four and sixteen hundredths

ones   hundredths

Step In

Place base-10 ones blocks on this base picture so it is six layers high.

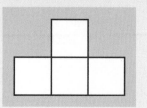

How can you calculate the number of blocks that are used?

Complete this table to help you. What do you notice?

Number of cubes in base	Number of layers	Total number of cubes
4	1	4
4	2	8
4	3	
4		
4		
4		

The total number of cubes tells you the volume of the object.

How can you calculate the total number of cubes for any number of layers?

Volume is the amount of space an object occupies.

What do you need to know?

Andrew builds another stack of cubes. His stack has seven layers, with five cubes in each layer. What is the volume of his stack of cubes?

Step Up

1. Place base-10 ones blocks on this base picture. Build the number of layers to match the data in the table. Then complete the table.

Number of cubes in base	Number of layers	Total number of cubes
6	1	6
6	2	12
6	3	
6	4	

2. Complete these tables. You can use ones blocks to help.

a.

Number of cubes in base	Number of layers	Total number of cubes
5	1	
	2	
	3	
	4	

b.

Number of cubes in base	Number of layers	Total number of cubes
6	1	
	3	
	5	
	7	

c.

Number of cubes in base	Number of layers	Total number of cubes
7	2	
	4	
	6	
	8	

Step Ahead

1. Use 32 ones blocks to make an object that is the same on each layer. Draw the base of your object.

2. Write the missing numbers.

a. Number of blocks in base _____

b. Number of layers _____

Step In

Laura plans to store these boxes in the garage.

How can she compare the amount of space that each box will occupy?

To measure the space, she decides to fill each box with objects that are the same shape. How will this help?

Look at these objects.

Which object would you use to measure the volume of each of the boxes above?

How did you decide?

Laura chose to use centimeter cubes to find the volume of the jewelery box.

Does she need to fill the whole box with cubes?

What is an easier way to calculate the volume?

> Just find the number of cubes in one layer.
> Then find the number of layers.

Step Up

1. Use base-10 ones blocks to cover the area of this rectangle. Then complete the table.

Dimensions of the base of the prism (cm)	Number of layers	Total number of centimeter cubes
×	1	
×	2	
×	3	
×	4	

2. Use base-10 ones blocks to cover the area of this rectangle. Then complete the table.

Dimensions of the base of the prism (cm)	Number of layers	Total number of centimeter cubes
×	1	
×	2	
×	3	
×	5	

3. Complete each table to show the total number of centimeter cubes in each prism.

Dimensions of the base (cm)	Number of layers	Total number of centimeter cubes
4 × 5	1	
4 × 5	2	
4 × 5	3	
4 × 5	5	
4 × 5	8	

Dimensions of the base (cm)	Number of layers	Total number of centimeter cubes
8 × 3	1	
8 × 3	2	
8 × 3	4	
8 × 3	5	
8 × 3	10	

4. Write a rule to calculate the total number of cubes in a prism when you know the dimensions of the base and the number of layers. Use your answers to Question 3 to help.

Step Ahead

Carlos pours cubes into this container to calculate the volume. He counts 78 cubes. Do you think his calculation is accurate? Explain your thinking.

Think and Solve (THINK TANK)

There are △, ▮, and ▱ in the set of blocks.

For every 2 △, there are 3 ▮.

For every 6 ▮, there are 7 ▱.

a. What is the least number of blocks that could be in the set?

_____ blocks

b. How many of each block would there be?

_____ cones

_____ cylinders

_____ cubes

Words at Work

Write a word problem that involves multiplying a three-digit number by a two-digit number. Then write how you find the solution.

Ongoing Practice

1. Complete each of these to find an equivalent fraction.

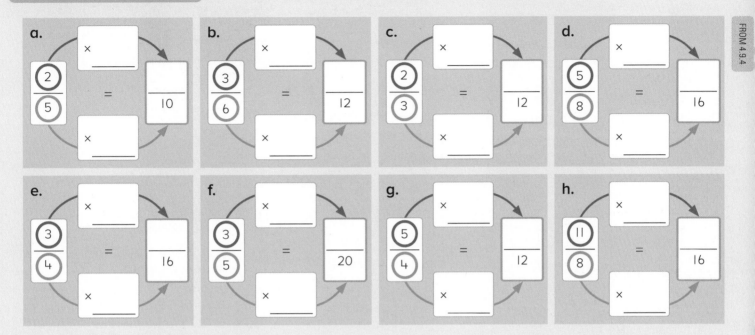

a. $\dfrac{2}{5} = \dfrac{}{10}$

b. $\dfrac{3}{6} = \dfrac{}{12}$

c. $\dfrac{2}{3} = \dfrac{}{12}$

d. $\dfrac{5}{8} = \dfrac{}{16}$

e. $\dfrac{3}{4} = \dfrac{}{16}$

f. $\dfrac{3}{5} = \dfrac{}{20}$

g. $\dfrac{5}{4} = \dfrac{}{12}$

h. $\dfrac{11}{8} = \dfrac{}{16}$

2. Place base-10 ones blocks on the base picture. Build the number of layers to match the data in the table. Then complete the table.

Number of cubes in base	Number of layers	Total number of cubes
8	1	8
8	2	
8	3	
8	6	
8	10	

Preparing for Module 3

Write each decimal fraction in expanded form.

a. 7.45

b. 9.07

c. 1.73

2.9 Volume: Developing a formula

Step In

How can you figure out the volume of this prism without counting each individual cube?

I know there are 8 cubes in the base. There are 4 layers. 8 + 8 + 8 + 8 = 32.

Oscar multiplied the height of the prism by the number of cubes in the base.

Base	Height
8 cubes	4 layers

8 × 4 = 32 cubes
Volume is 32 cubes.

Peta multiplied the dimensions.

Length	Width	Height
4 cubes	2 cubes	4 cubes

4 × 2 × 4 = 32 cubes
Volume is 32 cubes.

How are their methods similar?

What rule could you write to match each method?

Look at Peta's method.
Does it matter in what order she multiplies the dimensions?
How do you know?

Volume is usually measured in cubic units. The abbreviation for cubic centimeter is cm^3.

Step Up

1. Imagine you built this prism with base-10 ones cubes.

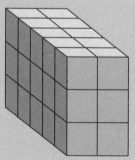

a. Complete this table.

Length (cubes)	Width (cubes)	Height (cubes)	Total number of cubes

b. Write the volume of the prism. _____ cm^3

2. Here are the dimensions of another prism.

Length 8 cm   Width 3 cm   Height 5 cm

Write how you can calculate the volume without counting cubes.

_____

3. Use your rule from Question 2 to calculate the volume of these prisms.

	Length (cm)	Width (cm)	Height (cm)	Volume (cm³)
a.	5	4	3	
b.	9	6	4	
c.	7	5	5	
d.	7	6	3	

4. Calculate the volume of each prism.
Then write an equation to show the order you used to multiply the dimensions.

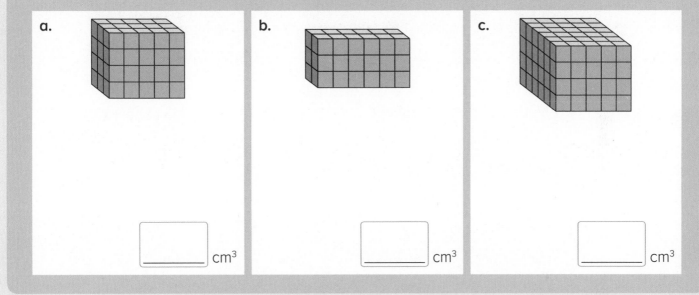

a.

_____ cm³

b.

_____ cm³

c.

_____ cm³

Step Ahead   This square-based pyramid has been built with base-10 ones blocks.

Calculate the volume of the pyramid. Show your thinking.

_____ cm³

Step In

The volume of a box is 60 in³. Write some possible dimensions for the box.

☐ × ☐ × ☐ = 60 in³   ☐ × ☐ × ☐ = 60 in³   ☐ × ☐ × ☐ = 60 in³

How did you figure out the dimensions?

What do you notice about each of the dimensions?

> Each dimension is a factor of 60.
> 60 has a lot of factors.

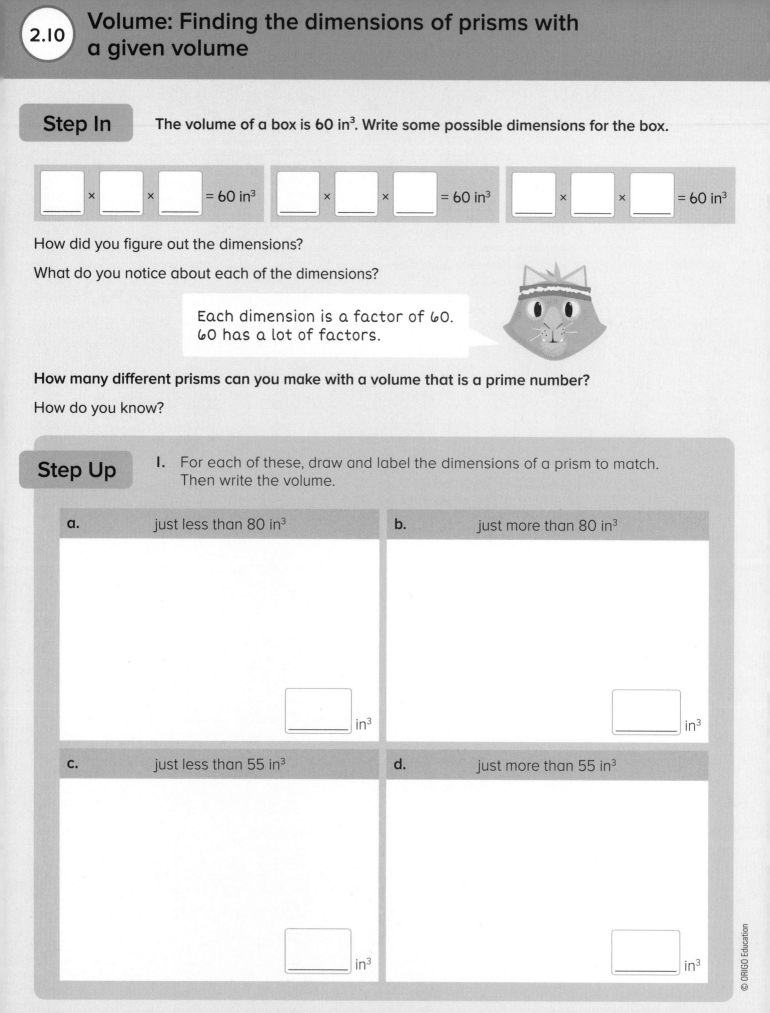

How many different prisms can you make with a volume that is a prime number?

How do you know?

Step Up

1. For each of these, draw and label the dimensions of a prism to match. Then write the volume.

a. just less than 80 in³

_____ in³

b. just more than 80 in³

_____ in³

c. just less than 55 in³

_____ in³

d. just more than 55 in³

_____ in³

2. Complete each table to show the dimensions of four different prisms that have the same volume.

a.

Volume is 36 in³		
Length	Width	Height

b.

Volume is 64 in³		
Length	Width	Height

c.

Volume is 100 in³		
Length	Width	Height

d.

Volume is 72 in³		
Length	Width	Height

3. Write the dimensions of another prism that has the same volume as 4 cm × 8 cm × 10 cm.

Length _____ cm   Width _____ cm   Height _____ cm

Step Ahead

Prism A is made with inch cubes. It is 4 cubes long, 5 cubes wide, and 2 cubes high. Prism B is made with centimeter cubes. It is 10 cubes long, 2 cubes wide, and 2 cubes high.

Which prism has the **greater volume**? Explain your thinking.

Computation Practice

What is another name for the female red kangaroo?

★ Complete the equations. Then write each letter above its matching factor below.

$4 \times \boxed{} = 36$ **l**

$2 \times \boxed{} = 48$ **l**

$2 \times \boxed{} = 150$ **h**

$5 \times \boxed{} = 35$ **e**

$2 \times \boxed{} = 90$ **e**

$4 \times \boxed{} = 88$ **e**

$2 \times \boxed{} = 70$ **y**

$5 \times \boxed{} = 150$ **t**

$4 \times \boxed{} = 60$ **b**

$2 \times \boxed{} = 24$ **f**

$4 \times \boxed{} = 200$ **r**

$4 \times \boxed{} = 100$ **u**

$\boxed{}$	$\boxed{}$	$\boxed{}$
30	75	22

$\boxed{}$	$\boxed{}$	$\boxed{}$	$\boxed{}$		$\boxed{}$	$\boxed{}$	$\boxed{}$	$\boxed{}$	$\boxed{}$
15	9	25	7		12	24	35	45	50

Write the missing factors as fast as you can.

$5 \times \boxed{} = 100$

$2 \times \boxed{} = 180$

$4 \times \boxed{} = 120$

$2 \times \boxed{} = 110$

$5 \times \boxed{} = 55$

$2 \times \boxed{} = 44$

$4 \times \boxed{} = 48$

$5 \times \boxed{} = 45$

$4 \times \boxed{} = 84$

Ongoing Practice

1. For each pair of fractions, complete the diagram to show equivalent fractions that have a common denominator. Then complete the sentence.

a.

$\dfrac{2}{3}$ and $\dfrac{3}{4}$

A common multiple is _____

so a common denominator is _____.

×4

$\dfrac{2}{3} = \dfrac{}{}$

×4

×3

$\dfrac{3}{4} = \dfrac{}{}$

×3

b.

$\dfrac{1}{3}$ and $\dfrac{4}{5}$

A common multiple is _____

so a common denominator is _____.

× ___

$\dfrac{}{} = \dfrac{}{}$

× ___

× ___

$\dfrac{}{} = \dfrac{}{}$

× ___

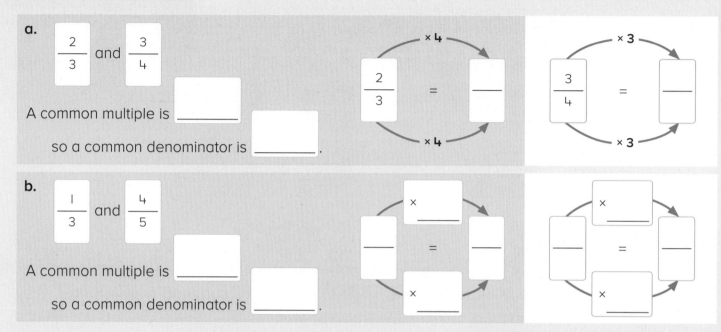

2. Complete the table to show the total number of centimeter cubes in each prism.

Dimensions of the base (cm)	Number of layers	Total number of centimeter cubes	Dimensions of the base (cm)	Number of layers	Total number of centimeter cubes
6 × 4	1		7 × 5	2	
6 × 4	2		7 × 5	4	
6 × 4	5		7 × 5	6	
6 × 4	10		7 × 5	10	

Preparing for Module 3

The distance between each whole number is one whole. Draw a line to join each number to its approximate location on the number line. Be as accurate as possible.

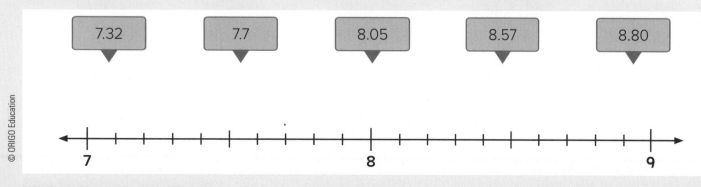

7.32   7.7   8.05   8.57   8.80

7   8   9

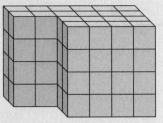

Step In

The base of this prism has six sides.
It is called a hexagonal-based prism.

How could you calculate the volume of this prism?

Sheree split the prism into two rectangular-based prisms.

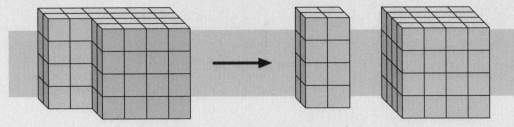

How will breaking the prism into parts help her calculate the volume?

What equation would you write to match?

Dixon used a different strategy. He added more blocks to change the hexagonal-based prism into a rectangular-based prism.

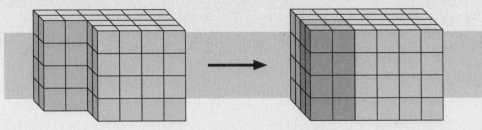

How could Dixon's strategy help him calculate the volume of the prism?

What equation would you write to match?

Step Up

I. Each of these small cubes is 1 cm³. Calculate the volume of the prism. Write an equation to show your thinking.

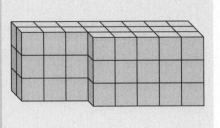

_____ cm³

2. These prisms are made with centimeter cubes. Calculate the volume of each prism.
Show your thinking.

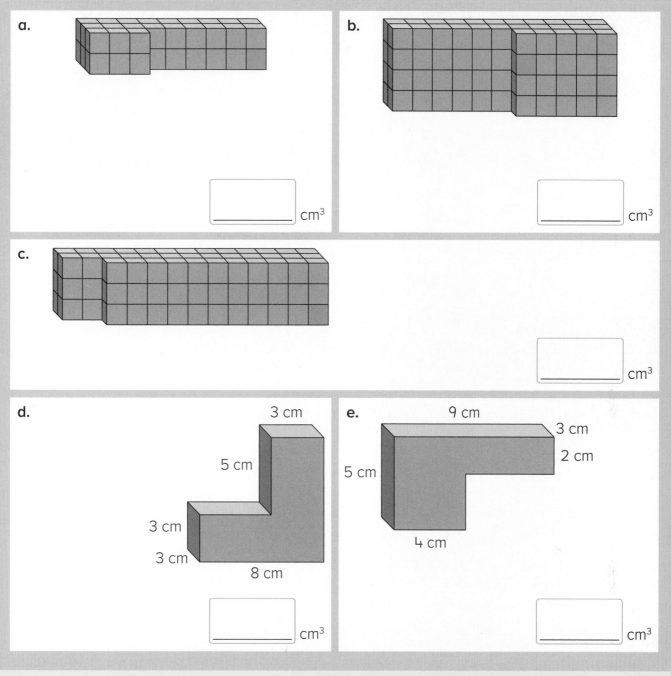

a.

_____ cm³

b.

_____ cm³

c.

_____ cm³

d.

3 cm

5 cm

3 cm

3 cm

8 cm

_____ cm³

e.

9 cm

3 cm

2 cm

5 cm

4 cm

_____ cm³

Step Ahead

Some centimeter cubes have been removed from the middle of this prism.
Calculate the volume of the new object. Show your thinking.

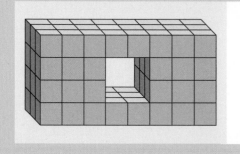

_____ cm³

Step In

Nicole is moving some household items into storage.
She decides to pack the items into boxes.
Boxes are sold in these three sizes.

What is the volume of each box?
How do you know?

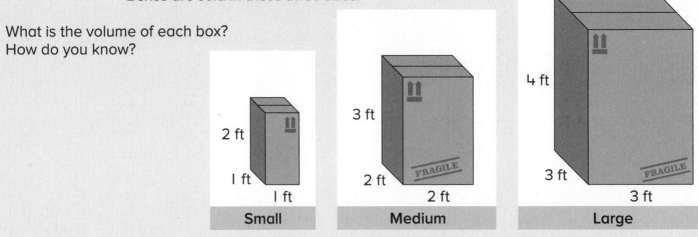

| Small | Medium | Large |

Write the volume above each box.

Gavin rents some storage space with the dimensions 10 ft × 10 ft × 8 ft.
What is the volume of the storage space?

He buys and fills five large boxes and five medium boxes.
How much space do the boxes occupy in storage?

How much storage space does he have left?

Think about the dimensions of the boxes and the dimensions of the storage space.

What size box would you use to fill the storage space? Why?

The height of the storage space is 8 feet, so there
would be some space left if I used the medium boxes.

Step Up

1. Use the box sizes above. Calculate the total volume that each group of boxes
would occupy. Show your thinking.

a. 2 large boxes and 3 medium boxes

b. 3 large boxes, 2 medium boxes,
and 6 small boxes

_____ ft³

_____ ft³

2. Use the box sizes shown on page 76 to solve these problems. Show your thinking.

a. Stella buys and fills 4 boxes of each size. What is the total volume of the boxes?

_____ ft³

b. Andre has 5 medium boxes in the attic and 2 large boxes in the basement. Which group of boxes has the greater volume?

_____

c. Daniela has a storage space measuring 9 ft × 9 ft × 9 ft. What is the greatest number of medium boxes she can pack into this space?

_____ medium boxes

Step Ahead

Look at Question 2c above. After Daniela packs the boxes into storage, how much space will be left? Show your thinking.

_____ ft³

Think and Solve THINK TANK

Same shapes cost the same amount.

a. 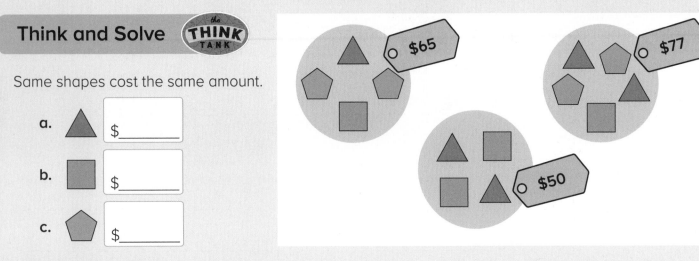 $ _____

b. $ _____

c. $ _____

Words at Work

Read the clues. Choose matching words from the list and write them in the grid. Some words are not used.

Clues Across

2. ___ the dimensions of a prism in any order to calculate the volume.

5. To calculate the volume of a rectangular-based prism, multiply the length by the ___ by the height.

6. Volume is the amount of ___ something occupies.

Clues Down

1. Volume is measured in ___ units.

3. Each dimension of a ___ is a factor of the volume.

4. To measure volume with cubes there should be no ___ or overlaps between the cubes.

height
length
width
prism
multiply
divide
volume
gaps
holes
space
cubes
cubic
object
room

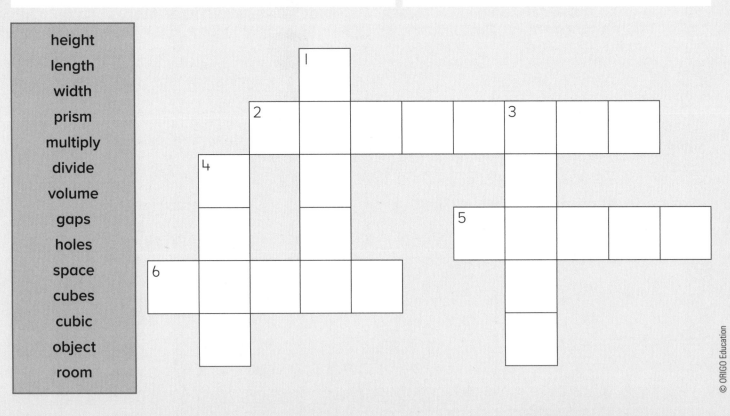

Ongoing Practice

1. Compare the fractions in each pair to a benchmark such as $\frac{1}{2}$ or 1. Then write **<** or **>** to make a true statement. Write your thinking.

a. $\frac{2}{7}$ ◯ $\frac{4}{9}$

b. $\frac{5}{6}$ ◯ $\frac{7}{8}$

c. $\frac{3}{4}$ ◯ $\frac{7}{9}$

d. $\frac{2}{3}$ ◯ $\frac{5}{7}$

FROM 4.9.8

2. Complete each table to show the dimensions of three different prisms that have the same volume.

a.

Volume = 48 in³		
Length	Width	Height

b.

Volume = 60 in³		
Length	Width	Height

FROM 5.2.10

Preparing for Module 3

Write **<**, **>**, or **=** to make each statement true. Use what you know about equivalence to help you.

a. $\frac{3}{10}$ ◯ $\frac{7}{100}$

b. $\frac{12}{10}$ ◯ $\frac{125}{100}$

c. $\frac{280}{100}$ ◯ $\frac{28}{10}$

d. $\frac{145}{100}$ ◯ $\frac{100}{10}$

e. $2\frac{4}{10}$ ◯ $2\frac{55}{100}$

f. $1\frac{80}{100}$ ◯ $1\frac{8}{10}$

g. $3\frac{7}{10}$ ◯ $1\frac{7}{100}$

h. $4\frac{9}{100}$ ◯ $4\frac{8}{10}$

Step In

This large square represents one whole.
Color parts to match the number
on the expander below.

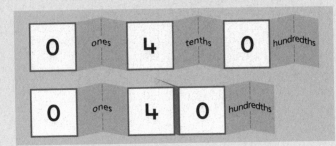

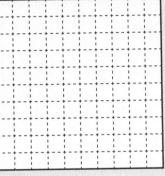

What decimal fraction would you write to match the expander?

What other decimal fractions are possible?

What common fraction would you write?

Each large square represents one whole.

How would you color them to show the
number on this expander?

Write the mixed number to match.
Then write the decimal fraction.

_____
100

_____ . _____

Step Up

1. Each large square is one whole. Color parts to show the decimal fraction.
   Then write the matching common fraction.

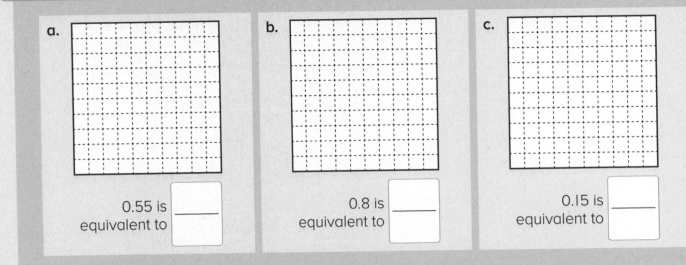

a.

0.55 is _____
equivalent to _____

b.

0.8 is _____
equivalent to _____

c.

0.15 is _____
equivalent to _____

2. Complete the missing parts. Each large square is one whole.

a.

ones			hundredths

. | | | $\frac{}{100}$

b.

2 ones	1	5 hundredths

. | | | $\frac{}{100}$

c.

ones		hundredths

1 . 9 0 | $\frac{}{100}$

d.

ones		hundredths

. | | | $\frac{}{100}$

Step Ahead   Each large square is one whole. Color parts to show a fraction that matches each description.

a. greater than 0.6
but less than $\frac{4}{5}$

b. less than $\frac{3}{4}$
but greater than 0.5

c. more than 0.8
but less than 1

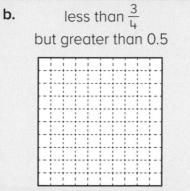
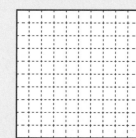

© ORIGO Education

Step In

Each large square represents one whole. What decimal fraction would you write to show the amount that is shaded?

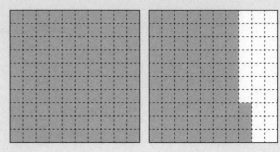

What mixed number would you write?

On this number line, the distance between each whole number is one whole.

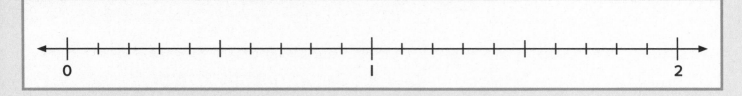

Where would 1.73 be on this number line?

What section of this number line represents decimal fractions that are greater than 1.2 but less than 1.5? What are some numbers you could show in that section?

Show the position of 1.8 and 1.80 on the number line.
What do you notice about each number's position? Why does this happen?

Step Up

1. On this number line, the distance between each whole number is one whole. Draw a line to show the position of each decimal fraction. Be as accurate as possible.

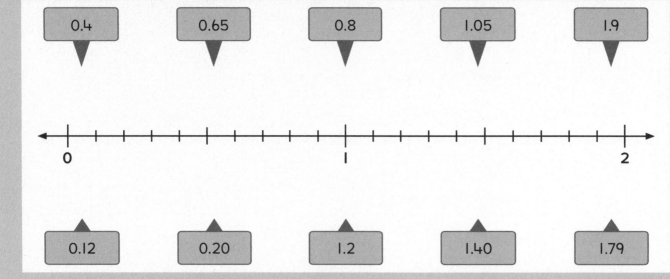

2. On each number line, the distance between each whole number is one whole.
Complete the missing parts.

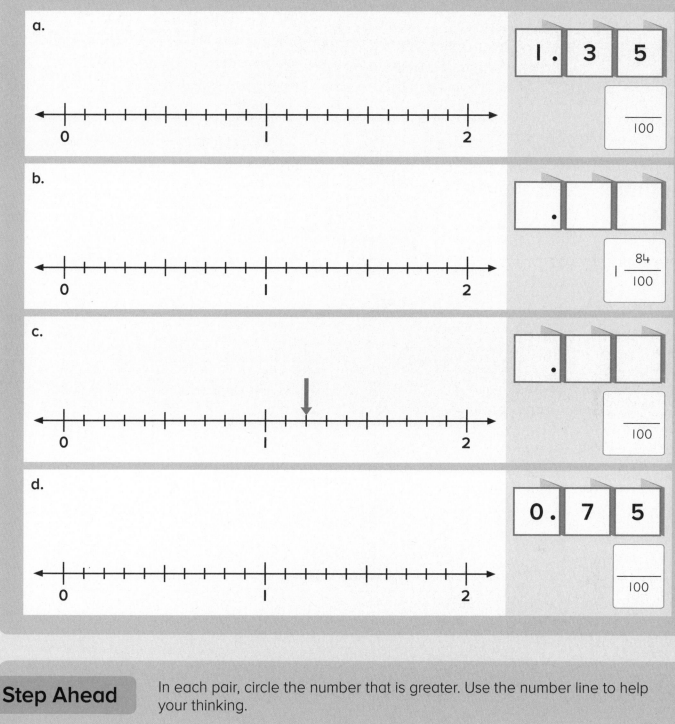

a.

```
←——|——|——|——|——|——|——|——|——|——|——|——|——|——|——|——→
    0                     1                     2
```

| 1 . | 3 | 5 |

$$\frac{}{100}$$

b.

```
←——|——|——|——|——|——|——|——|——|——|——|——|——|——|——|——→
    0                     1                     2
```

| | . | | |

$$1\frac{84}{100}$$

c.

```
←——|——|——|——|——|——|——|——|——↓——|——|——|——|——|——|——→
    0                     1                     2
```

| | . | | |

$$\frac{}{100}$$

d.

| 0 . | 7 | 5 |

```
←——|——|——|——|——|——|——|——|——|——|——|——|——|——|——|——→
    0                     1                     2
```

$$\frac{}{100}$$

Step Ahead   In each pair, circle the number that is greater. Use the number line to help your thinking.

```
←——|——|——|——|——|——|——|——|——|——|——|——|——|——|——|——→
    0                     1                     2
```

a.

$1\frac{27}{100}$ 1.5

b.

$1\frac{3}{10}$ 0.95

c.

1.68 $1\frac{4}{5}$

Computation Practice

Why can any hamburger run a mile in less than four minutes?

★ Complete the equations. Then write each letter above its matching total at the bottom of the page.

$3.25 + $4.40 = $_____ **u**

$5.15 + $2.80 = $_____ **a**

$1.35 + $2.30 = $_____ **c**

$3.40 + $3.15 = $_____ **t**

$3.25 + $5.50 = $_____ **a**

$4.24 + $1.40 = $_____ **e**

$2.35 + $3.15 = $_____ **o**

$2.41 + $6.35 = $_____ **s**

$1.22 + $3.35 = $_____ **f**

$6.74 + $1.14 = $_____ **o**

$5.43 + $1.36 = $_____ **i**

$1.34 + $7.12 = $_____ **i**

$2.55 + $2.14 = $_____ **e**

$2.64 + $4.05 = $_____ **d**

$6.51 + $3.27 = $_____ **s**

$5.32 + $4.33 = $_____ **s**

$3.14 + $2.51 = $_____ **b**

$3.30 + $5.25 = $_____ **t**

$2.71 + $2.28 = $_____ **f**

$5.65	$5.64	$3.65	$8.75	$7.65	$8.76	$4.69		$6.79	$6.55

$8.46	$9.78		$4.99	$7.95	$9.65	$8.55		$4.57	$5.50	$7.88	$6.69

© ORIGO Education

Ongoing Practice

I. Estimate the total cost. Show your thinking.

a.

○ $349   ○ $291

Estimate $_____

b.

○ $204   ○ $278

Estimate $_____

2. Each large square is one whole. Shade parts to show the decimal fraction.
Then write the matching common fraction.

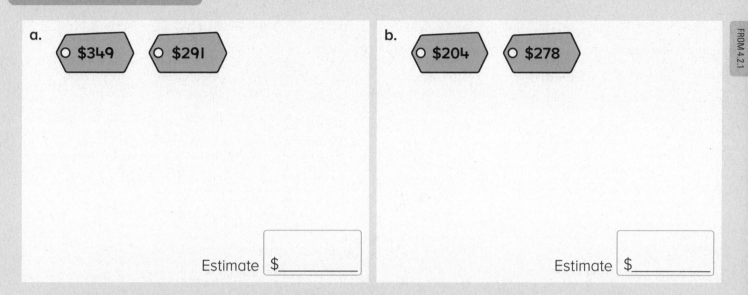

a.

0.35 is equivalent to ___/100

b.

0.05 is equivalent to ___

c.

0.5 is equivalent to ___

Preparing for Module 4

In each shape, color parts to show the first fraction. Then draw more lines to show an equivalent fraction and complete the diagram.

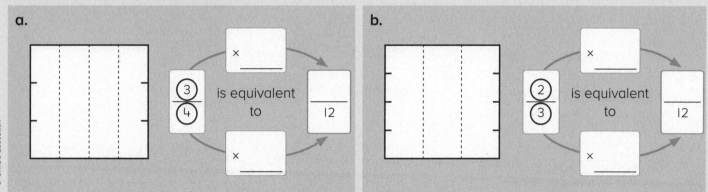

a.

$\frac{3}{4}$ is equivalent to

× ___

× ___

___/12

b.

$\frac{2}{3}$ is equivalent to

× ___

× ___

___/12

Step In   What do you call one of the ten equal parts that form one whole?

Complete the **first row** of this table.

Fraction Word	Ones	tenths	hundredths	thousandths	Decimal Fraction	Common Fraction
	0	I	0	0	0.1	

What do you call one of the ten equal parts that form one-tenth? What fraction of the whole is it?

Complete the **second row** of the table.

The large square below is one whole. How has it been divided?

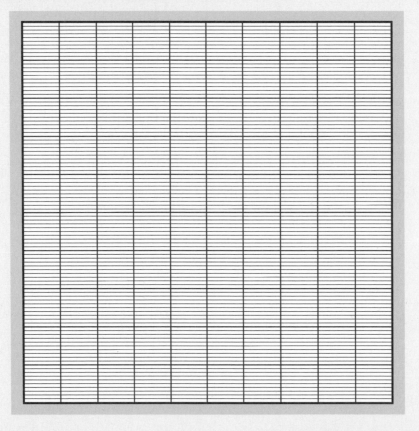

What do you call one of the ten equal parts that form one-hundredth? What fraction of the whole is it?

Complete the **third row** of the table.

Color parts of the large square to match the decimal fraction on the expander.

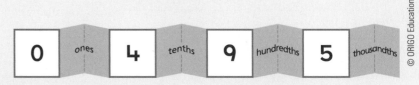

© ORIGO Education

Step Up

Each large square is one whole. Shade parts of the whole to match the decimal fraction on the expander.

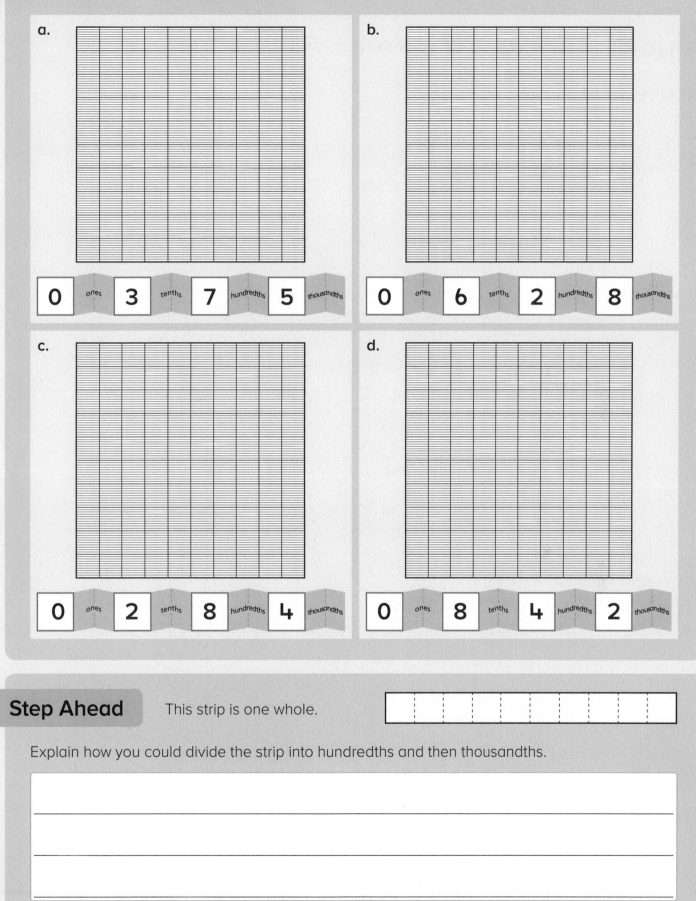

a.

| 0 | ones | 3 | tenths | 7 | hundredths | 5 | thousandths |

b.

| 0 | ones | 6 | tenths | 2 | hundredths | 8 | thousandths |

c.

| 0 | ones | 2 | tenths | 8 | hundredths | 4 | thousandths |

d.

| 0 | ones | 8 | tenths | 4 | hundredths | 2 | thousandths |

Step Ahead

This strip is one whole.

Explain how you could divide the strip into hundredths and then thousandths.

_____

_____

_____

Step In

Each large square is one whole.

What fraction has been shaded?
How do you know?

Write the decimal fraction and mixed number that matches the shaded amount. Then write the number that matches the shaded amount on the expander.

ones   tenths

Draw more lines on the square above to divide the tenths into hundredths.

How many hundredths are shaded? How would you read this number?

Write the decimal fraction and mixed number that matches the shaded amount. Then write the number that matches the shaded amount on the expander.

ones   hundredths

Imagine you drew more lines to divide the hundredths into thousandths.

How many thousandths would be shaded? How could you read this number?

Write a decimal fraction and mixed number to show the fraction that would be shaded. Then write the number that matches the shaded amount on the expander.

ones   thousandths

Look at this place-value chart.

The decimal point tells the position of the ones place. The ones place is the center of our place-value system.

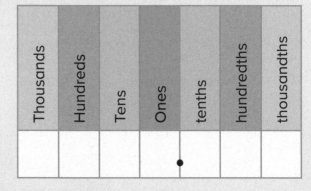

Thousands	Hundreds	Tens	Ones	tenths	hundredths	thousandths
			·			

What do you notice about the places on either side of the ones place?

Write **one and four hundred thousandths** on the chart.

© ORIGO Education

I. Write the matching number on the expander. Then write the numeral to match.

a. four and six hundred thousandths

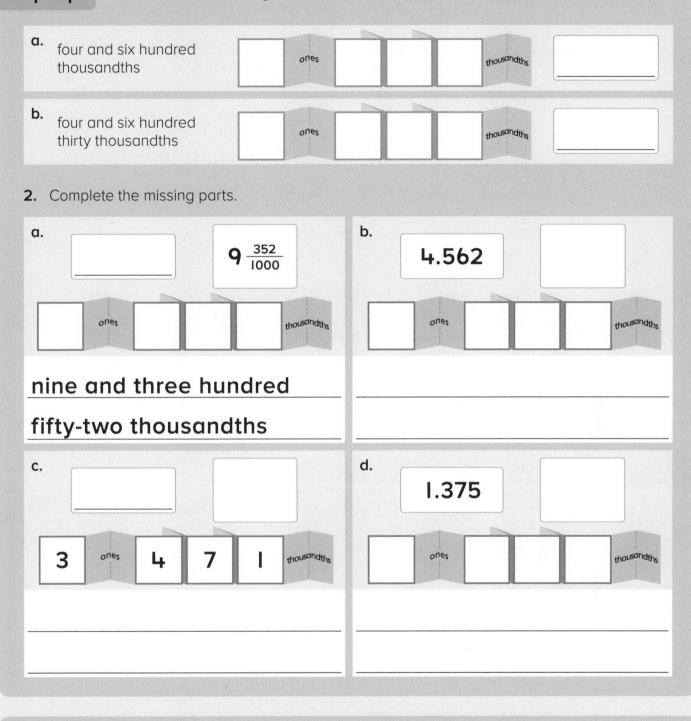

ones | thousandths

b. four and six hundred thirty thousandths

ones | thousandths

2. Complete the missing parts.

a.

$9\frac{352}{1000}$

ones | thousandths

nine and three hundred fifty-two thousandths

b.

4.562

ones | thousandths

c.

3 ones 4 7 1 thousandths

d.

1.375

ones | thousandths

Use the digits **2**, **4**, **5**, and **9** to write four different decimal fractions that are all greater than 2 but less than 3.

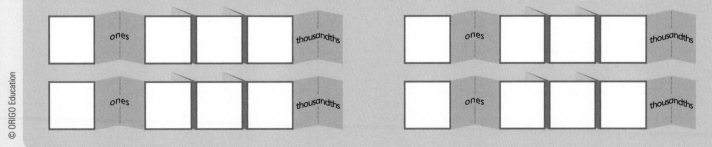

ones | thousandths

ones | thousandths

ones | thousandths

ones | thousandths

Think and Solve THINK TANK This ⭐ means **multiply the two factors and subtract 2.**

4 ⭐ 5 = 18

Look at these and figure out what 😊 is doing.

5 😊 11 = 8   9 😊 15 = 12   8 😊 0 = 4   100 😊 50 = 75

Complete these.

a.

10 😊 20 = ☐

b.

24 😊 12 = ☐

c.

4 😊 ☐ = 5

d. What is 😊 doing?

Words at Work Write three different ways to show the decimal fraction 2.785.

© ORIGO Education

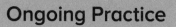

Ongoing Practice

I. Use the standard addition algorithm to calculate the total.

a.

```
    5   I   9   8
    I   4   0   2
+   3   2   I   5
_____
```

b.

```
    3   I   5   4   2
    I   6   5   0   9
+       I   7   4   2
_____
```

c.

```
    2   7   9   9   I
    I   0   0   5   7
+   I   I   2   I   2
_____
```

FROM 4.2.5

2. Each large square is one whole. Shade parts of the whole to match the number on the expander.

FROM 5.3.3

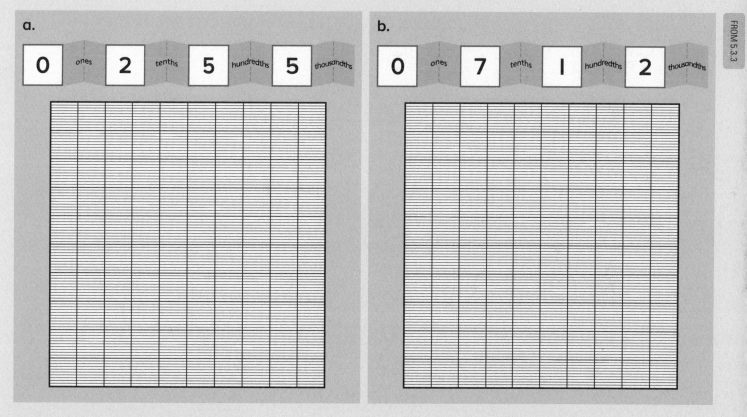

a.

| 0 ones | 2 tenths | 5 hundredths | 5 thousandths |

b.

| 0 ones | 7 tenths | I hundredths | 2 thousandths |

Preparing for Module 4

Write each fraction as a whole number.

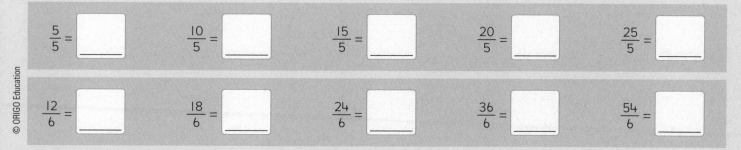

$\frac{5}{5} =$ ___ $\frac{10}{5} =$ ___ $\frac{15}{5} =$ ___ $\frac{20}{5} =$ ___ $\frac{25}{5} =$ ___

$\frac{12}{6} =$ ___ $\frac{18}{6} =$ ___ $\frac{24}{6} =$ ___ $\frac{36}{6} =$ ___ $\frac{54}{6} =$ ___

Step In

This large square is one whole.

Color parts of the square to match the decimal fraction on this expander.

| 0 | ones | 7 | tenths | 0 | hundredths | 5 | thousandths |

How did you know what number of parts to color? How would you read the number?

Seven hundred five thousandths.

What common fraction could you write to match 0.705?

Color more parts to show 0.730. What common fractions could you write to match 0.730?

Step Up

I. Write the matching number. Then write the numeral to match.

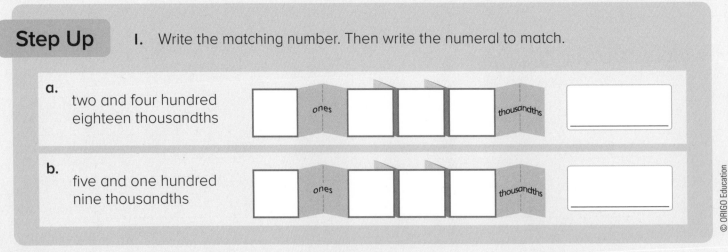

a. two and four hundred eighteen thousandths

| | ones | | | | thousandths | |

b. five and one hundred nine thousandths

| | ones | | | | thousandths | |

2. Complete the missing parts.

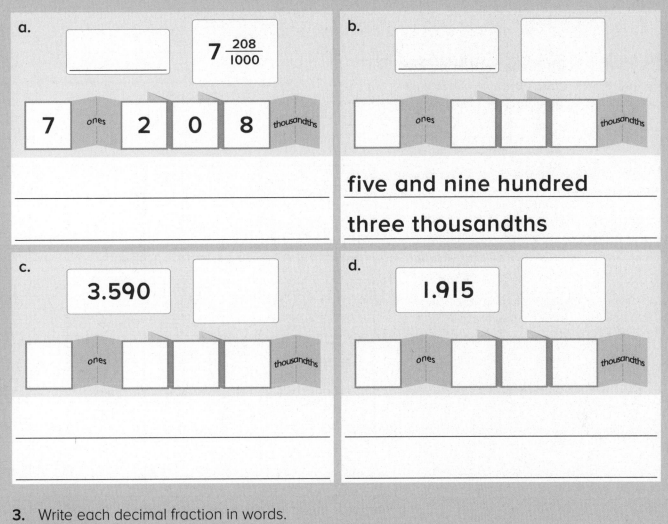

a.

[   ] $7\frac{208}{1000}$

| 7 | ones | 2 | 0 | 8 | thousandths |

_____

b.

[   ] [   ]

| | ones | | | | thousandths |

five and nine hundred three thousandths

c.

3.590 [   ]

| | ones | | | | thousandths |

_____

d.

1.915 [   ]

| | ones | | | | thousandths |

_____

3. Write each decimal fraction in words.

a.	8.052	_____
b.	3.709	_____
c.	5.011	_____

Step Ahead

Sumi says 1.370 is greater than 1.37. William says they are the same. Who do you think is correct? Explain your thinking.

_____

Step In

How do you say the decimal fraction on this closed expander?

3.	8	0	5

What mixed number could you write to match?

How would you describe the value of each digit?

Trina wrote the decimal fraction in expanded form.
She wrote the expanded form in two different ways.

Method A $(3 \times 1) + (8 \times 0.1) + (5 \times 0.001)$

Method B $(3 \times 1) + (8 \times \frac{1}{10}) + (5 \times \frac{1}{1000})$

Does each method give you the same sum? How do you know?
Why are the hundredths not expanded?

David knew another way to write the decimal fractions in expanded form.
He wrote the decimal fraction like this.

Method C $(8 \times 0.1) + (3 \times 1) + (5 \times 0.001)$

Does his method give the same sum?

Does it matter what order the place values are expanded?

How could you use David's method with common fractions?

Step Up

1. Write the missing numbers.

a.
9.164

$(\boxed{} \times 1) + (\boxed{} \times 0.1) + (\boxed{} \times 0.01) + (\boxed{} \times 0.001)$

b.
5.207

$(\boxed{} \times 1) + (\boxed{} \times 0.1) + (\boxed{} \times 0.001)$

c.
8.046

$(\boxed{} \times 1) + (\boxed{} \times 0.01) + (\boxed{} \times 0.001)$

d.
2.179

$(\boxed{} \times 1) + (\boxed{} \times 0.1) + (\boxed{} \times 0.01) + (\boxed{} \times 0.001)$

2. Write each decimal fraction in expanded form using one of the methods from page 96.

a.

6.256

b.

1.907

c.

5.005

d.

1.840

3. Write the decimal fraction that has been expanded.

a. $(5 \times 1) + (2 \times 0.1) + (3 \times 0.001)$

b. $(1 \times 0.01) + (9 \times 0.001) + (6 \times 1)$

c. $(9 \times \frac{1}{10}) + (7 \times \frac{1}{100}) + (8 \times \frac{1}{1000})$

d. $(7 \times 1) + (4 \times \frac{1}{1000}) + (9 \times \frac{1}{10})$

Step Ahead For each of these, color the ◯ beside the statement that is true.

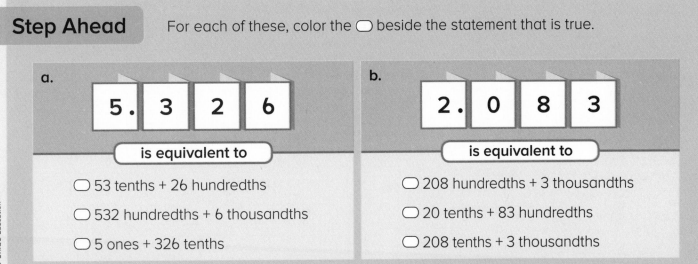

a.

| 5. | 3 | 2 | 6 |

is equivalent to

◯ 53 tenths + 26 hundredths

◯ 532 hundredths + 6 thousandths

◯ 5 ones + 326 tenths

b.

| 2. | 0 | 8 | 3 |

is equivalent to

◯ 208 hundredths + 3 thousandths

◯ 20 tenths + 83 hundredths

◯ 208 tenths + 3 thousandths

Computation Practice

Which insect has a stronger sense of smell than a dog?

★ Complete the equations. Find each answer in the grid below and cross out the letter above. Then write the remaining letters at the bottom of the page.

380 – 210 =

460 + 280 =

630 – 440 =

560 + 370 =

410 – 150 =

550 + 180 =

450 – 170 =

290 + 560 =

420 – 280 =

340 + 180 =

850 – 370 =

280 + 360 =

660 – 150 =

240 + 460 =

750 – 340 =

170 + 430 =

520 – 180 =

260 + 510 =

570 + 390 =

350 – 230 =

450 + 380 =

780 – 530 =

280 + 470 =

430 – 280 =

460 + 480 =

✳

F	L	E	A	M	A	N	T	I	D
930	170	700	270	520	960	710	260	410	480
W	**A**	**S**	**P**	**H**	**O**	**R**	**N**	**E**	**T**
250	610	730	740	510	120	280	360	150	830
M	**O**	**T**	**H**	**B**	**E**	**E**	**T**	**L**	**E**
340	850	750	600	640	940	190	580	140	770

Write the letters in order from the ✳ to the bottom-right corner.

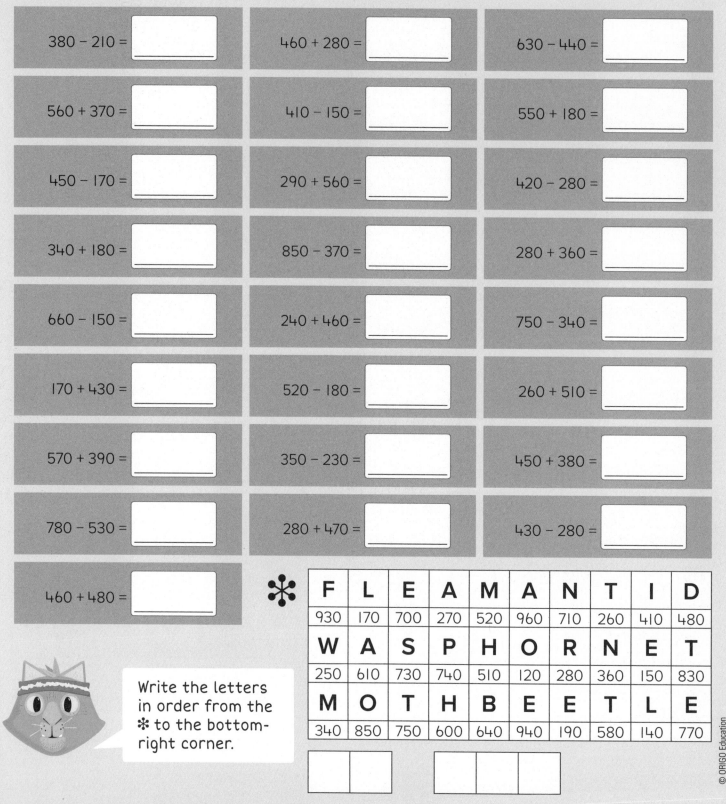

© ORIGO Education

1. Use the standard addition algorithm to calculate each total.

a. There were 3,605 senior tickets, 14,034 adult tickets, and 23,762 student tickets sold at the gate. How many tickets were sold in all?

b. Felipe flew 1,827 miles to Los Angeles, then 7,461 miles to Sydney, and then 2,051 miles to Perth, Australia. How far did he fly?

FROM 4.2.7

2. Complete the missing parts.

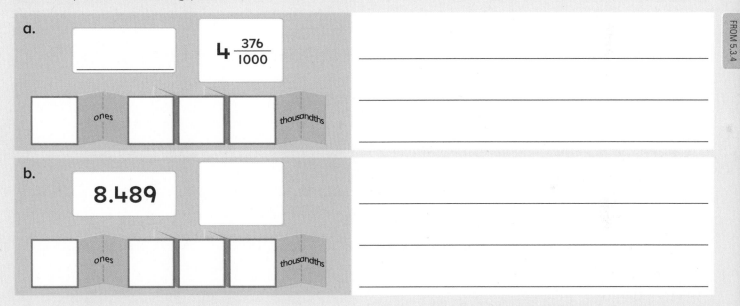

a.

$4\frac{376}{1000}$

ones   thousandths

_____

_____

_____

FROM 5.3.4

b.

8.489

ones   thousandths

_____

_____

_____

Each large shape is one whole. Write the equivalent mixed number and common fraction that describe the parts that are shaded.

a.

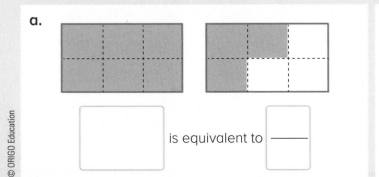

is equivalent to ———

b.

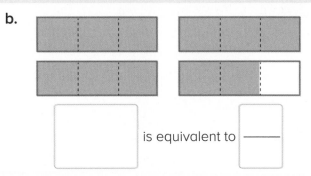

is equivalent to ———

Step In   On each number line, the distance between each whole number is one whole.

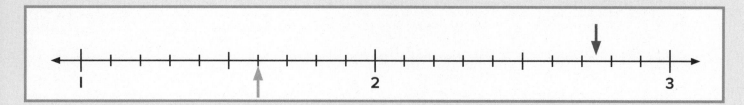

What decimal fraction describes the position marked by the arrow below the line?

How could you figure out the decimal fraction that the arrow above the line is indicating?

> You need to split the number line into smaller parts.

This section of the same number line has been split into hundredths.

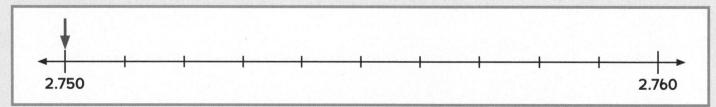

What decimal fraction describes the position marked by the arrow? How do you know?

This section of the same number line has been split into thousandths.
Why can 2.75 be rewritten as 2.750?

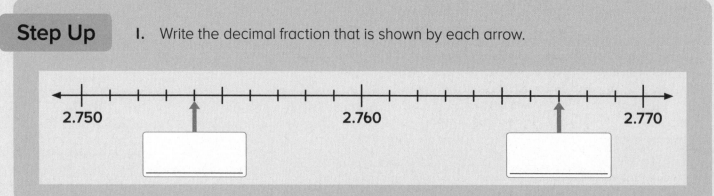

2.750   2.760

What are some decimal fractions between 2.750 and 2.760?

Step Up   I.   Write the decimal fraction that is shown by each arrow.

2. Write the decimal fraction that is shown by each arrow.

a.

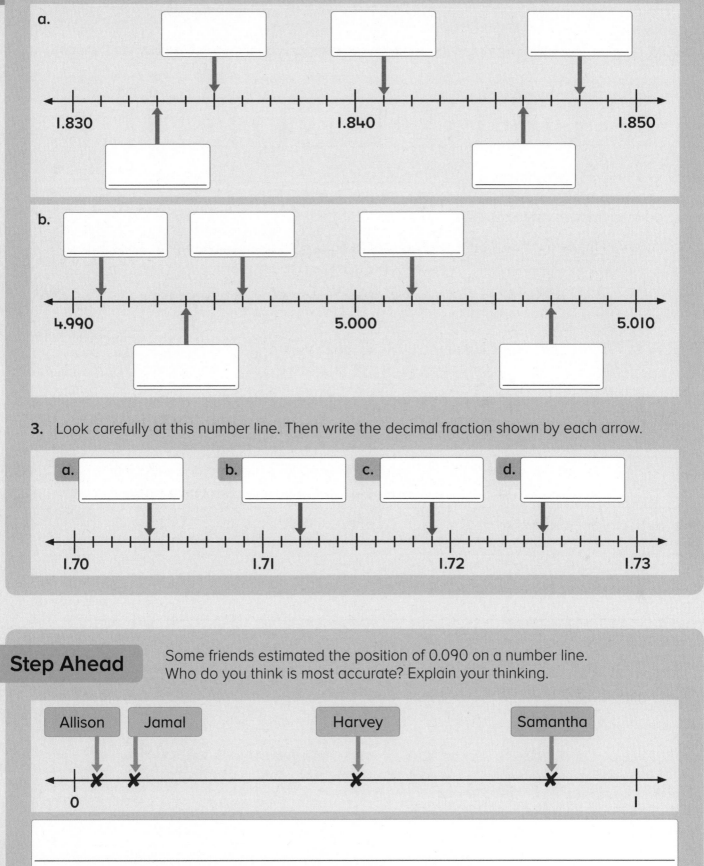

b.

3. Look carefully at this number line. Then write the decimal fraction shown by each arrow.

| a. | b. | c. | d. |

Step Ahead

Some friends estimated the position of 0.090 on a number line. Who do you think is most accurate? Explain your thinking.

Allison   Jamal   Harvey   Samantha

0   1

Step In

How do you say each of these decimal fractions?

| 0. | 5 | 3 | 0 | | 0. | 7 | 0 | 5 |

How could you compare the two decimal fractions to figure out which is greater?

You could shade each fraction on a thousandths square. Then compare the amounts that are shaded.

I would start with the ones and compare the digits in each place.

Estimate the position of each decimal fraction on this number line.

0   1

How did you figure out each estimate?

How do you tell which fraction is greater on the number line?

Step Up

1. Draw an arrow to show the approximate position of each number on the number line.

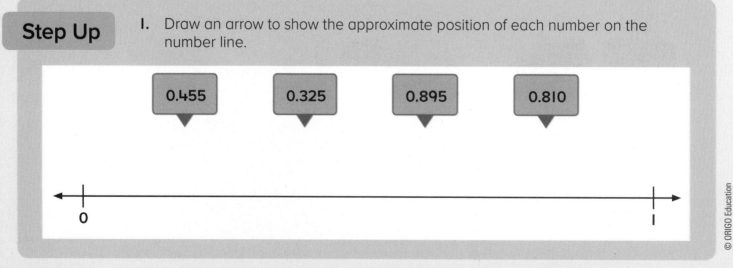

0.455   0.325   0.895   0.810

0   1

2. In each group, circle the **greatest** fraction.

a.

| 0.435 | 0.800 | 0.590 |

b.

| 0.605 | 0.650 | 0.065 |

c.

| 0.795 | 0.957 | 0.597 |

d.

| 0.002 | 0.020 | 0.102 |

3. Write **<** or **>** to make each statement true.

a. 0.505 ◯ 0.055

b. 0.189 ◯ 0.198

c. 0.065 ◯ 0.056

d. 0.021 ◯ 0.102

e. 0.110 ◯ 0.011

f. 0.900 ◯ 0.099

4. Write each group of fractions in order from **least** to **greatest**. Use the number line to help you.

a.

| 0.505 | 0.890 | 0.550 | 0.915 |

0 ———————————————————— 1

b.

| 0.075 | 0.210 | 0.740 | 0.501 |

0 ———————————————————— 1

Step Ahead   Write digits to make true comparison statements.

a. 3.561 ◯< 3._____49

b. 0.014 ◯> 0.0_____9

c. 4.05 _____ ◯> _____.053

Think and Solve

THINK TANK

Each of these nine shapes is made from squares with sides of 2 cm.

What is the area of the square that can be made using all these shapes?

_____ cm²

Words at Work

Write a word problem involving thousandths.
Then write how you solve the problem.

© ORIGO Education

Ongoing Practice

1. Use this number line to help you write the differences.

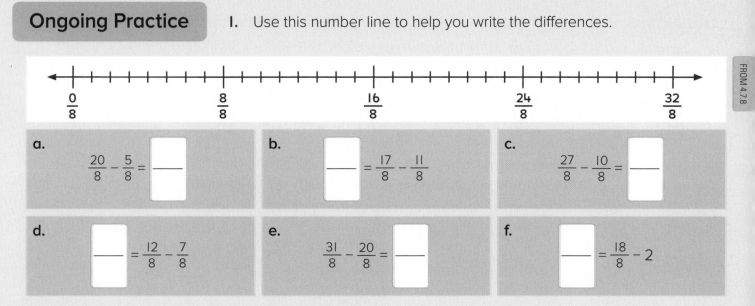

a.
$$\frac{20}{8} - \frac{5}{8} = \boxed{}$$

b.
$$\boxed{} = \frac{17}{8} - \frac{11}{8}$$

c.
$$\frac{27}{8} - \frac{10}{8} = \boxed{}$$

d.
$$\boxed{} = \frac{12}{8} - \frac{7}{8}$$

e.
$$\frac{31}{8} - \frac{20}{8} = \boxed{}$$

f.
$$\boxed{} = \frac{18}{8} - 2$$

2. Write each decimal fraction in expanded form.

a. 4.762 _____

b. 8.016 _____

Preparing for Module 4

Solve each problem. Draw a picture to prove your answer is correct.

a. Nadia needs $\frac{2}{3}$ cup of flour for a honey cake and $\frac{2}{6}$ for a carrot cake. Which cake uses more flour?

_____ cake

b. Archie ran $\frac{1}{6}$ of a mile and Alisa ran $\frac{1}{3}$ of a mile. Who ran the greater distance?

FROM 4.7.8

FROM 5.3.6

Step In

Where would you show this decimal fraction on the number line?

0.52

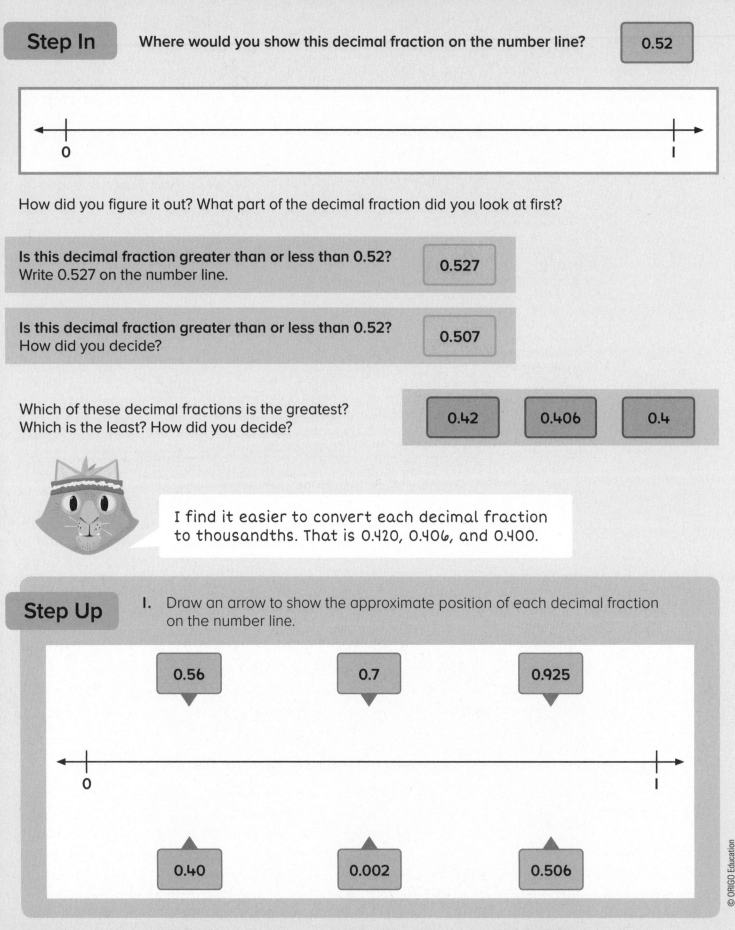

0

1

How did you figure it out? What part of the decimal fraction did you look at first?

Is this decimal fraction greater than or less than 0.52?
Write 0.527 on the number line.

0.527

Is this decimal fraction greater than or less than 0.52?
How did you decide?

0.507

Which of these decimal fractions is the greatest?
Which is the least? How did you decide?

0.42   0.406   0.4

I find it easier to convert each decimal fraction to thousandths. That is 0.420, 0.406, and 0.400.

Step Up

1. Draw an arrow to show the approximate position of each decimal fraction on the number line.

0.56   0.7   0.925

0

1

0.40   0.002   0.506

2. Write **<**, **>**, or **=** to make each statement true.

a.
0.5 ◯ 0.425

b.
0.099 ◯ 0.02

c.
0.06 ◯ 0.016

d.
0.109 ◯ 0.19

e.
0.2 ◯ 0.200

f.
0.411 ◯ 0.46

g.
0.740 ◯ 0.74

h.
0 ◯ 0.1

i.
0.99 ◯ 0.998

3. Write each group of decimal fractions in order from **least** to **greatest**.

a.
| 0.32 | 0.03 | 0.375 | 0.505 |

b.
| 0.786 | 0.065 | 0.7 | 0.65 |

c.
| 0.51 | 0.005 | 0.79 | 0.703 |

4. Write these in order from **greatest** to **least**.

| 0.5 | 0.425 | 0.475 | 0.45 | 0.54 | 0.505 |

Step Ahead Write six decimal fractions that are greater than 0.497, but less than 0.51.

© ORIGO Education

Step In

The number line below shows thousandths.
Write the numbers to match the marks that are between 1.39 and 1.40.

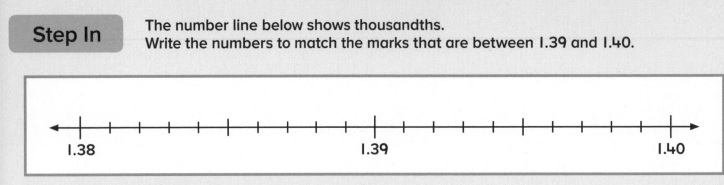

What hundredth is nearest to 1.391? How did you decide?

Mark 1.391 on this number line. Be as accurate as possible.

What is the nearest tenth? How do you know?

On this number line, the distance between each whole number is one whole.
Where would you show 1.391?

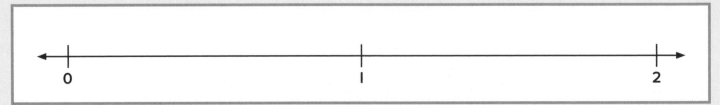

What is the nearest whole number? How do you know?

Step Up

1. Draw an arrow to show the exact position of each number on the number line.
   Then write the nearest **hundredth**.

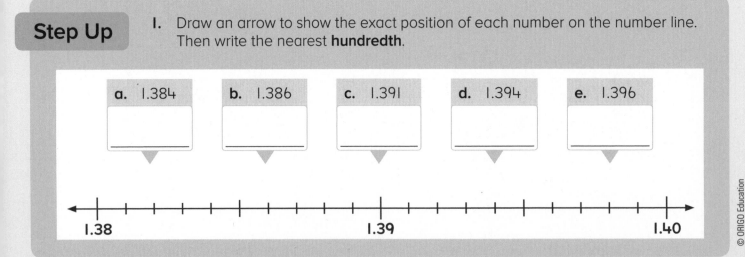

a. 1.384   b. 1.386   c. 1.391   d. 1.394   e. 1.396

2. Draw an arrow to show the approximate position of each number on the number line. Then write the nearest **tenth**.

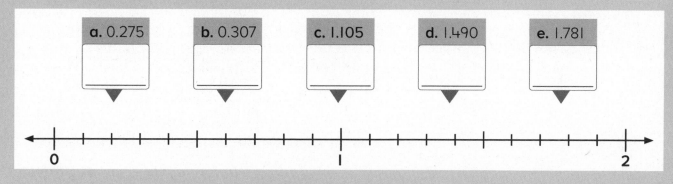

a. 0.275   b. 0.307   c. 1.105   d. 1.490   e. 1.781

3. Draw an arrow to show the approximate position of each number on the number line. Then write the nearest **whole number**.

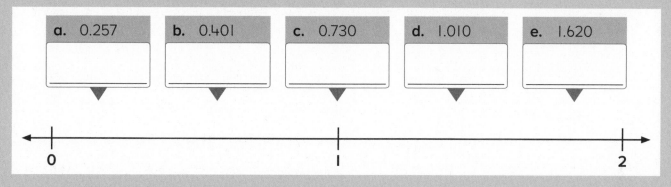

a. 0.257   b. 0.401   c. 0.730   d. 1.010   e. 1.620

4. Round each number to the nearest whole number, and then tenth. Use the number line to help.

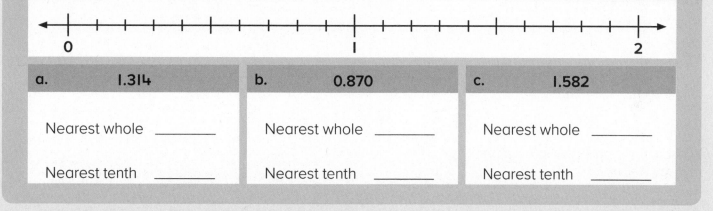

a.	1.314	b.	0.870	c.	1.582
Nearest whole _____		Nearest whole _____		Nearest whole _____	
Nearest tenth _____		Nearest tenth _____		Nearest tenth _____	

Step Ahead

Franco pays for lunch for three friends. The lunches cost $3.14, $2.45, and $3.23. His friends tell Franco to round the total amount to the nearest whole dollar, and then split the total amount equally among three.

What amount should each friend pay Franco?

$_____

Computation Practice

⭐ Complete the equations. Then write each letter above its matching quotient at the bottom of the page. Some letters appear more than once.

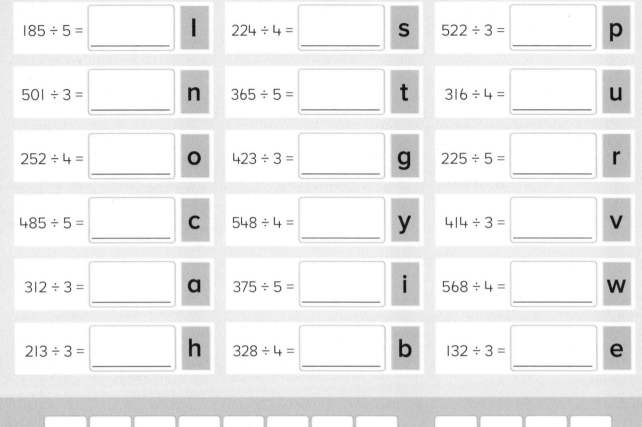

$185 \div 5 =$ ____ **l**

$224 \div 4 =$ ____ **s**

$522 \div 3 =$ ____ **p**

$501 \div 3 =$ ____ **n**

$365 \div 5 =$ ____ **t**

$316 \div 4 =$ ____ **u**

$252 \div 4 =$ ____ **o**

$423 \div 3 =$ ____ **g**

$225 \div 5 =$ ____ **r**

$485 \div 5 =$ ____ **c**

$548 \div 4 =$ ____ **y**

$414 \div 3 =$ ____ **v**

$312 \div 3 =$ ____ **a**

$375 \div 5 =$ ____ **i**

$568 \div 4 =$ ____ **w**

$213 \div 3 =$ ____ **h**

$328 \div 4 =$ ____ **b**

$132 \div 3 =$ ____ **e**

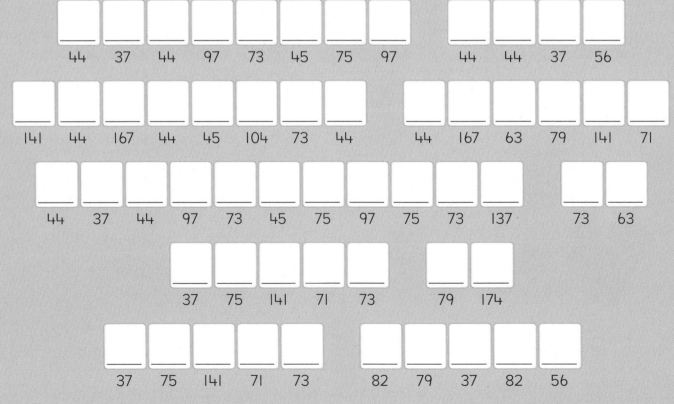

44 37 44 97 73 45 75 97   44 44 37 56

141 44 167 44 45 104 73 44   44 167 63 79 141 71

44 37 44 97 73 45 75 97 75 73 137   73 63

37 75 141 71 73   79 174

37 75 141 71 73   82 79 37 82 56

Ongoing Practice

1. Calculate the difference. Draw jumps on the number line to show your thinking.

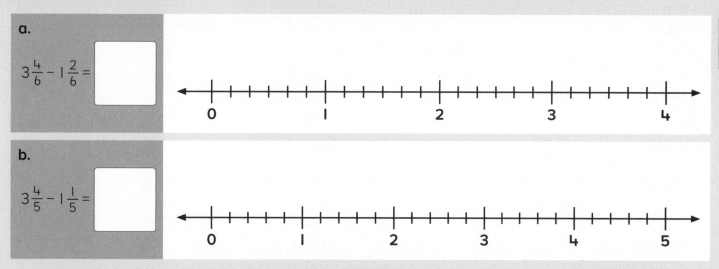

a.

$3\frac{4}{6} - 1\frac{2}{6} =$ ⬜

b.

$3\frac{4}{5} - 1\frac{1}{5} =$ ⬜

2. Write **<**, **>**, or **=** to make each statement true.

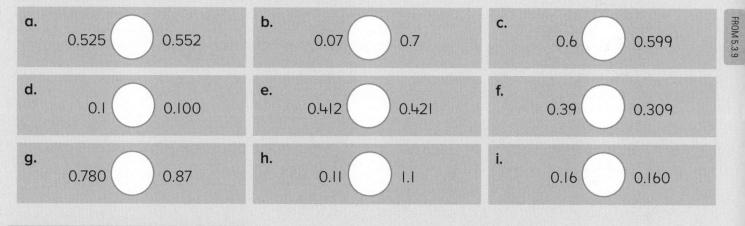

a. 0.525 ◯ 0.552

b. 0.07 ◯ 0.7

c. 0.6 ◯ 0.599

d. 0.1 ◯ 0.100

e. 0.412 ◯ 0.421

f. 0.39 ◯ 0.309

g. 0.780 ◯ 0.87

h. 0.11 ◯ 1.1

i. 0.16 ◯ 0.160

Preparing for Module 4

Solve each problem. Show your thinking.

a. Bella's drink bottle holds 2 quarts. Jayden's bottle holds 40 fl oz. How much more does Bella's bottle hold than Jayden's bottle?

_____ fl oz

b. A leaking faucet loses 34 fl oz each day. How much water is lost after one week?

_____ gal and _____ fl oz

Step In   Callum's arm span measures 1.417 m, and Leila's arm span measures 1.471 m.

How could you round each length to give approximate lengths?

Should you round to the nearest whole number or to the nearest tenth? Why?

How would you round each length to the nearest tenth of a meter?

What digits will you look at to help you round each length?

Victoria follows these steps to round the length of Callum's arm span to the nearest tenth of a meter.

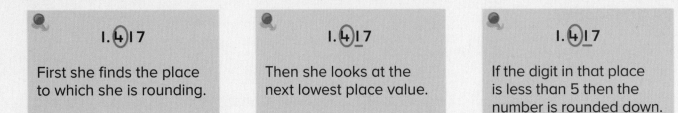

1.④17	1.④1̲7	1.④1̲7
First she finds the place to which she is rounding.	Then she looks at the next lowest place value.	If the digit in that place is less than 5 then the number is rounded down.

What length is Callum's arm span rounded to?

How could you use Victoria's strategy to round the length of Leila's arm span to the nearest tenth of a meter?

How would you round each arm span to the nearest hundredth of a meter?

Step Up   1.   Round each decimal fraction to the nearest **whole number**.

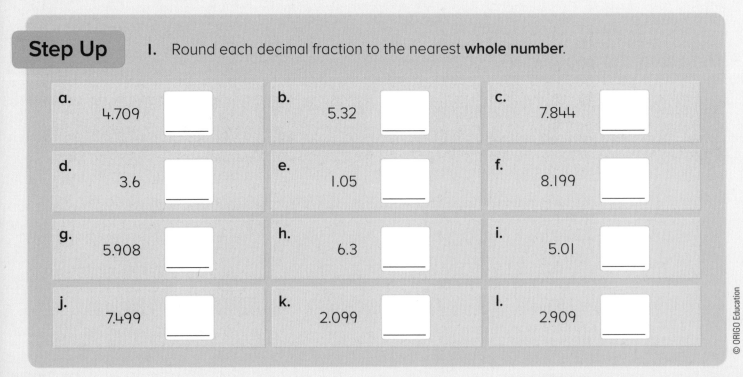

a. 4.709 ☐

b. 5.32 ☐

c. 7.844 ☐

d. 3.6 ☐

e. 1.05 ☐

f. 8.199 ☐

g. 5.908 ☐

h. 6.3 ☐

i. 5.01 ☐

j. 7.499 ☐

k. 2.099 ☐

l. 2.909 ☐

2. Round each decimal fraction to the nearest **tenth**.

a.
4.38 ☐
_____

b.
2.095 ☐
_____

c.
6.54 ☐
_____

d.
0.809 ☐
_____

e.
3.45 ☐
_____

f.
1.511 ☐
_____

3. Round each decimal fraction to the nearest **hundredth**.

a.
7.514 ☐
_____

b.
0.879 ☐
_____

c.
3.052 ☐
_____

d.
1.935 ☐
_____

e.
4.888 ☐
_____

f.
2.005 ☐
_____

4. Read the number on the expander. Then round each number to the nearest whole number, tenth, and hundredth.

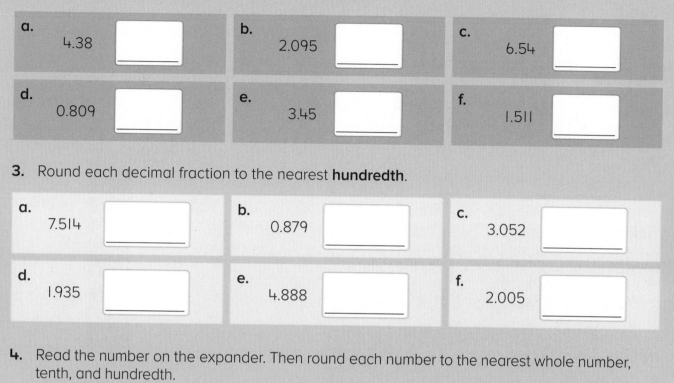

	Nearest whole number	Nearest tenth	Nearest hundredth
a. 3. 8 7 2			
b. 5. 2 1 9			
c. 2. 0 8 5			
d. 0. 8 5 7			

Step Ahead   Circle the decimal fractions that you would round to 1.3.

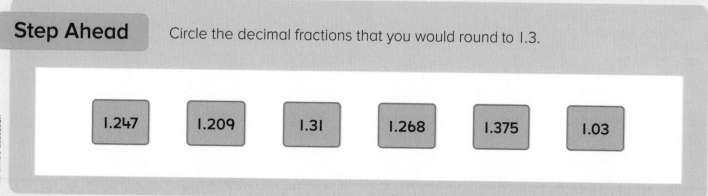

1.247   1.209   1.31   1.268   1.375   1.03

Step In

Read this experiment.

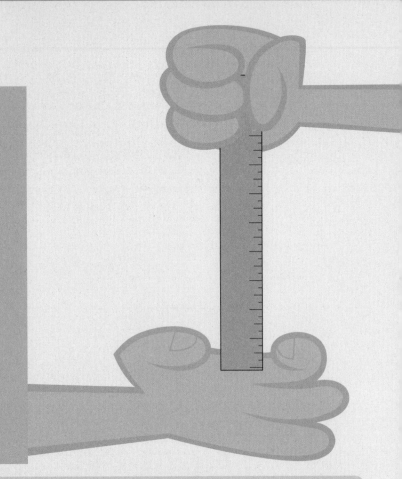

THE EXPERIMENT

Step 1

One student holds a foot-long ruler by one end so it hangs vertically.

Step 2

At the other end of the ruler, a second student places their thumb and forefinger about half an inch from either side of the ruler.

Step 3

When the student holding the ruler releases it without warning, the second student must try to catch it.

Step 4

The speed of the student's reaction is measured from 0 to where it is caught (rounded to the nearest 0.5 inch).

Step Up

1. Work with another student to conduct the experiment ten times. Record **your** results in the table below.

Trial	Result (in)	Trial	Result (in)
1		6	
2		7	
3		8	
4		9	
5		10	

2. What was your best (shortest) result? _____

3. Work with your teacher to find out the best result for each student in your class. Record each result on page 115.

4. Complete this line plot to show the data you collected in Question 3.

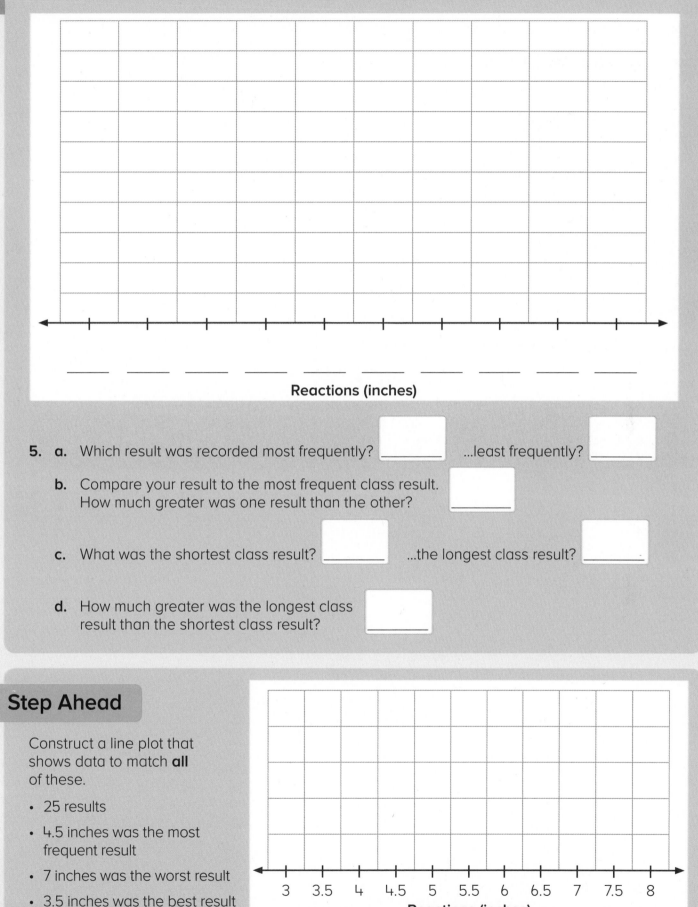

_____ _____ _____ _____ _____ _____ _____ _____ _____ _____ _____

Reactions (inches)

5. a. Which result was recorded most frequently? _____ ...least frequently? _____

b. Compare your result to the most frequent class result. How much greater was one result than the other? _____

c. What was the shortest class result? _____ ...the longest class result? _____

d. How much greater was the longest class result than the shortest class result? _____

Step Ahead

Construct a line plot that shows data to match **all** of these.

• 25 results

• 4.5 inches was the most frequent result

• 7 inches was the worst result

• 3.5 inches was the best result

3   3.5   4   4.5   5   5.5   6   6.5   7   7.5   8

Reactions (inches)

Think and Solve

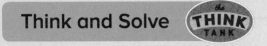

Use the clues and each of the numbers on the sign to complete the grid.

Clues

- All four numbers in a row must have a common factor greater than 1.

- Pairs of numbers in a column must have a common factor greater than 1.

7   10   35
28   12
16   14

	21		

Words at Work

Evan and Ruby each wrote a decimal fraction involving thousandths. Read the clues and write a possible number for Evan and Ruby. Write in words how you figured it out.

CLUES

Evan's number rounded to the nearest tenth is greater than Ruby's number rounded to the nearest hundredth. Ruby's number rounded to the nearest tenth is greater than Evan's number rounded to the nearest hundredth. When Evan and Ruby round their numbers to the nearest whole number, they both get the same number. Ruby's number is greater than Evan's number.

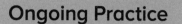

Ongoing Practice

1. Calculate the difference. Draw jumps on the number line to show your thinking.

FROM 4.7.10

a.

$4\frac{1}{4} - 2\frac{3}{4} =$ ☐

0   1   2   3   4   5

b.

$3\frac{2}{5} - 1\frac{4}{5} =$ ☐

0   1   2   3   4

2. For each number, draw an arrow to show its approximate position on the number line. Then round it to the nearest tenth and write the tenth.

FROM 5.3.10

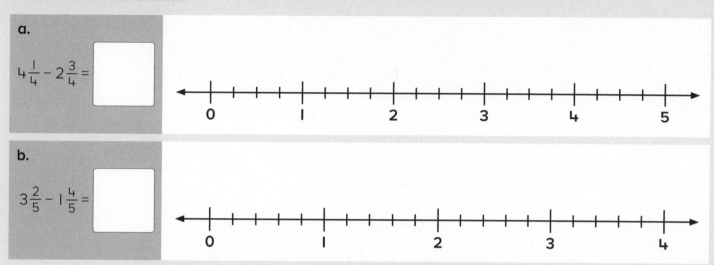

a. 0.21   **b.** 0.435   **c.** 0.97   **d.** 1.08   **e.** 1.49   **f.** 1.905

0   1   2

Preparing for Module 4   Solve each problem. Show your thinking.

a. Mom split 3 lb of ground meat equally into 2 bags. How much meat is in each bag?

____ OZ

b. Dad bought $2\frac{1}{2}$ lb of flour and 12 oz of sugar. What was the total mass of his purchase?

____ OZ

© ORIGO Education

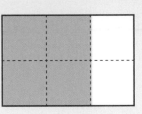

Step In

Laura's dad has a rectangular garden bed split into equal areas.

The shaded part of this diagram shows how much of the garden has been planted.

What fraction of the garden has been planted?

Laura's dad decides to split the garden bed into a different number of equal parts. The same amount of the garden has been planted.

Look at this diagram. How did he split the garden bed?

Write the fraction of the garden that is planted.

What do you notice about the two fractions you wrote?

I can see that the value of the denominator in the second fraction is double the value of the denominator in the first fraction. The value of the numerator is also double.

Fractions are **equivalent** if they cover the same area of each shape.

Complete this diagram to show how the fractions are related.

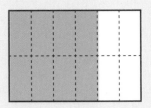

Imagine Laura's dad planted the whole garden. Color more parts of the two diagrams above to show the change.

What fraction would you write to match the total amount that is planted in the first diagram? What whole number would you write?

What fraction would you write to match the total amount that is planted in the second diagram? What whole number would you write?

What do you notice?

Think about how you would compare $\frac{3}{8}$ and $\frac{4}{16}$.

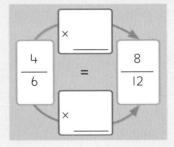

What do you need to do first?
How could you use this diagram to help you?

Which amount is greater?

1. Complete these to show equivalent fractions.

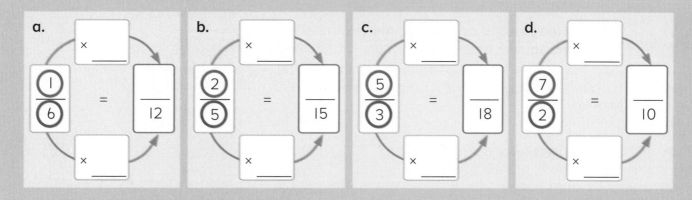

a.

$$\frac{1}{6} = \frac{}{12}$$

× ____   × ____

b.

$$\frac{2}{5} = \frac{}{15}$$

× ____   × ____

c.

$$\frac{5}{3} = \frac{}{18}$$

× ____   × ____

d.

$$\frac{7}{2} = \frac{}{10}$$

× ____   × ____

2. For each of these, write the fraction, and then write four fractions that are equivalent.

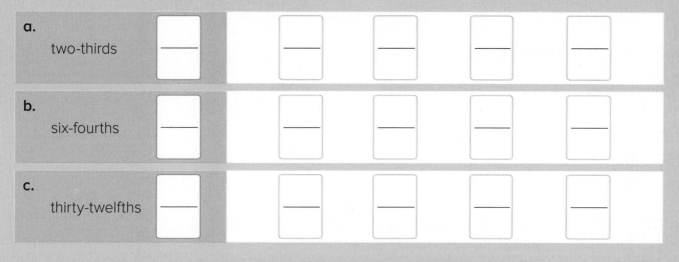

a. two-thirds

b. six-fourths

c. thirty-twelfths

3. Change one fraction in each pair so they have the same denominator. Then rewrite the fractions.

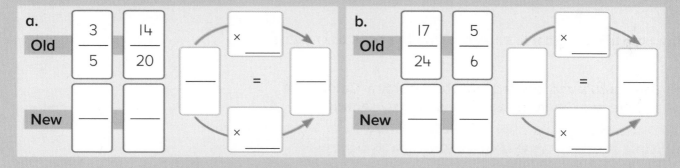

a.

Old $\frac{3}{5}$ $\frac{14}{20}$

New   ____ ____

$$\frac{}{} = \frac{}{}$$

× ____   × ____

b.

Old $\frac{17}{24}$ $\frac{5}{6}$

New   ____ ____

$$\frac{}{} = \frac{}{}$$

× ____   × ____

Step Ahead   Use each number only once to write three pairs of equivalent fractions.

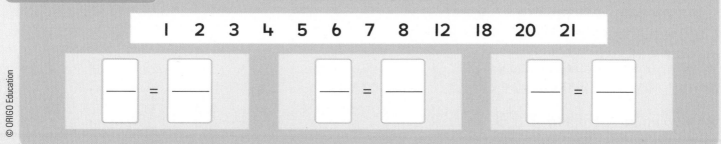

| 1 | 2 | 3 | 4 | 5 | 6 | 7 | 8 | 12 | 18 | 20 | 21 |

$$\frac{}{} = \frac{}{}$$ $$\frac{}{} = \frac{}{}$$ $$\frac{}{} = \frac{}{}$$

Step In

Look at this multiplication chart.

Choose one row of numbers.
What do you notice about the numbers in the blue parts of that row?

Imagine the green parts were cut off the grid and the remaining parts were cut horizontally into 10 separate strips.

These two strips have been placed one above the other. What do you notice?

3	6	9	12	15	18	21	24	27	30
8	16	24	32	40	48	56	64	72	80

×	1	2	3	4	5	6	7	8	9	10
1	1	2	3	4	5	6	7	8	9	10
2	2	4	6	8	10	12	14	16	18	20
3	3	6	9	12	15	18	21	24	27	30
4	4	8	12	16	20	24	28	32	36	40
5	5	10	15	20	25	30	35	40	45	50
6	6	12	18	24	30	36	42	48	54	60
7	7	14	21	28	35	42	49	56	63	70
8	8	16	24	32	40	48	56	64	72	80
9	9	18	27	36	45	54	63	72	81	90
10	10	20	30	40	50	60	70	80	90	100

The first two numbers look like the fraction $\frac{3}{8}$ and the second two look like the fraction $\frac{6}{16}$.

What other fractions can you see in the two strips? Write two of them.

What do you notice about all four fractions?

All of these fractions are equivalent to $\frac{3}{8}$.

Complete this diagram to show how $\frac{3}{8}$ is equivalent to $\frac{15}{40}$.

What do you notice?

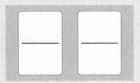

How could you figure out which is greater, $\frac{4}{5}$ or $\frac{3}{4}$?

What is a denominator they have in common?

How could you use the rows of the multiplication chart to help you?

Try multiplying both denominators together.
What do you notice?

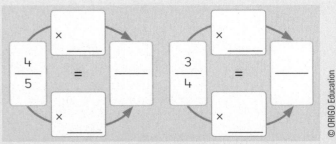

Step Up

1. For each pair of fractions, write equivalent fractions that have the same denominator. Write the missing factors to show your thinking.

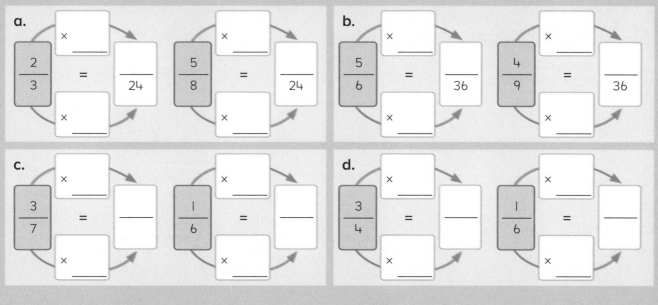

a.
$\dfrac{2}{3} = \dfrac{}{24}$ $\dfrac{5}{8} = \dfrac{}{24}$

b.
$\dfrac{5}{6} = \dfrac{}{36}$ $\dfrac{4}{9} = \dfrac{}{36}$

c.
$\dfrac{3}{7} = \dfrac{}{}$ $\dfrac{1}{6} = \dfrac{}{}$

d.
$\dfrac{3}{4} = \dfrac{}{}$ $\dfrac{1}{6} = \dfrac{}{}$

2. Rewrite both fractions so the denominators are the same.

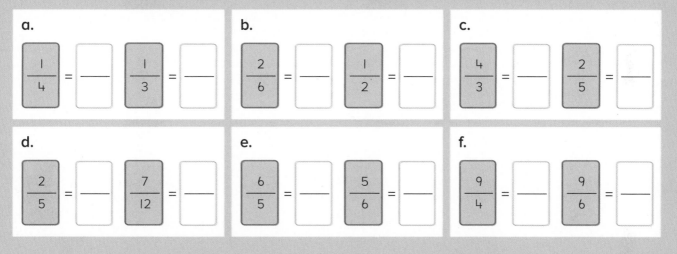

a.
$\dfrac{1}{4} = \dfrac{}{}$ $\dfrac{1}{3} = \dfrac{}{}$

b.
$\dfrac{2}{6} = \dfrac{}{}$ $\dfrac{1}{2} = \dfrac{}{}$

c.
$\dfrac{4}{3} = \dfrac{}{}$ $\dfrac{2}{5} = \dfrac{}{}$

d.
$\dfrac{2}{5} = \dfrac{}{}$ $\dfrac{7}{12} = \dfrac{}{}$

e.
$\dfrac{6}{5} = \dfrac{}{}$ $\dfrac{5}{6} = \dfrac{}{}$

f.
$\dfrac{9}{4} = \dfrac{}{}$ $\dfrac{9}{6} = \dfrac{}{}$

3. Look at the fractions in the shaded boxes in Questions 1 and 2 above. Circle the greater fraction in each pair.

Step Ahead

Write chains of equivalent fractions to match what is given. Do not use the same fraction more than once.

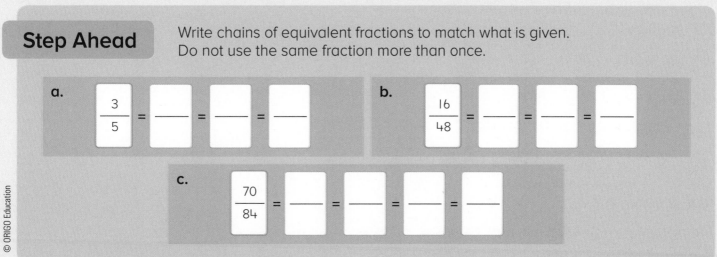

a.
$\dfrac{3}{5} = \dfrac{}{} = \dfrac{}{} = \dfrac{}{}$

b.
$\dfrac{16}{48} = \dfrac{}{} = \dfrac{}{} = \dfrac{}{}$

c.
$\dfrac{70}{84} = \dfrac{}{} = \dfrac{}{} = \dfrac{}{} = \dfrac{}{}$

Computation Practice

★ Complete the equations. Write each letter above its matching product at the bottom of the page.

5 × 11 = ☐ **h**

5 × 49 = ☐ **i**

5 × 35 = ☐ **f**

5 × 37 = ☐ **n**

5 × 33 = ☐ **d**

5 × 39 = ☐ **s**

5 × 47 = ☐ **e**

5 × 83 = ☐ **o**

5 × 23 = ☐ **t**

5 × 65 = ☐ **l**

5 × 17 = ☐ **c**

5 × 41 = ☐ **y**

5 × 19 = ☐ **w**

5 × 27 = ☐ **b**

Some letters appear more than once.

☐ ☐ ☐ ☐ ☐ ☐ ☐ ☐
115 55 235   135 325 415 415 165

☐ ☐ ☐ ☐ ☐ ☐ ☐ ☐ ☐
415 175   245 185 195 235 85 115 195

☐ ☐ ☐ ☐ ☐ ☐ ☐ ☐
245 195   205 235 325 325 415 95

Ongoing Practice

I. Show the time on the analog and digital clocks.

a. 20 minutes to 4

b. 15 minutes to 11

c. 8 minutes to 5

d. 25 minutes to 12

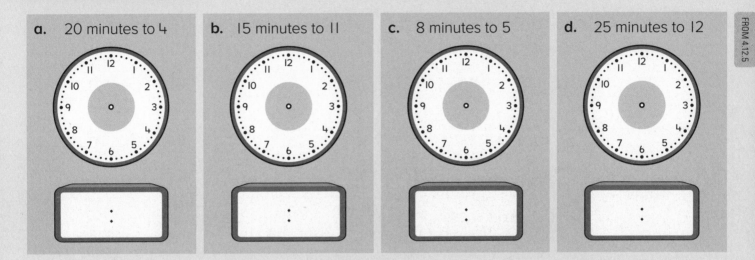

2. Complete each of these to find an equivalent fraction.

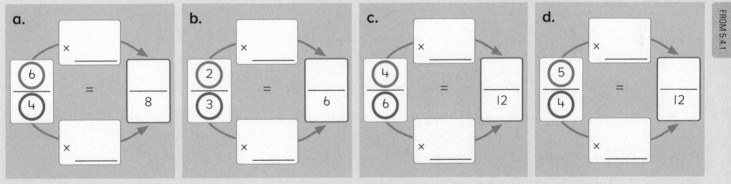

a.
$$\frac{6}{4} = \frac{}{8}$$

b.
$$\frac{2}{3} = \frac{}{6}$$

c.
$$\frac{4}{6} = \frac{}{12}$$

d.
$$\frac{5}{4} = \frac{}{12}$$

Preparing for Module 5

Write the total cost. Show your thinking.

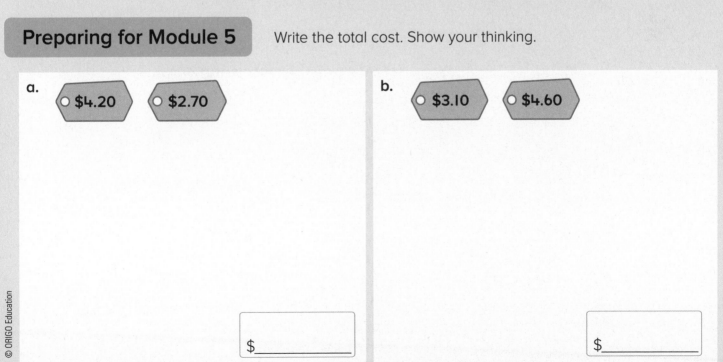

a. $4.20 $2.70

$_____

b. $3.10 $4.60

$_____

Step In On each number line, the distance between each whole number represents one mile.

These students each marked the distance they live from school on the number lines below.

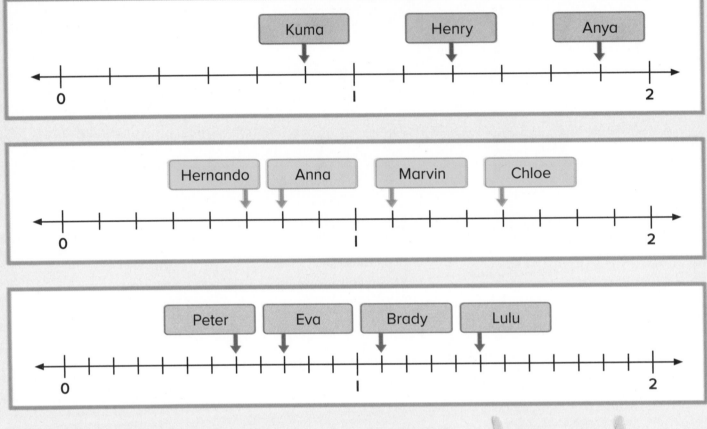

What types of numbers could be used to record these distances?

The distances must be shown as some type of fraction.

What distance do you think Kuma recorded? How do you know?

Which students marked distances that were a little more than one mile? How do you know?
What distance do you think each of these students marked?

Look at the distance Chloe lives from the school.

Why could this distance be written more than one way?

Choose two other students who marked a distance that could be written in more than one way.
What are the different ways you could write the distances for these students?

I. Draw a line from each common fraction and mixed number to show its position on the number line.

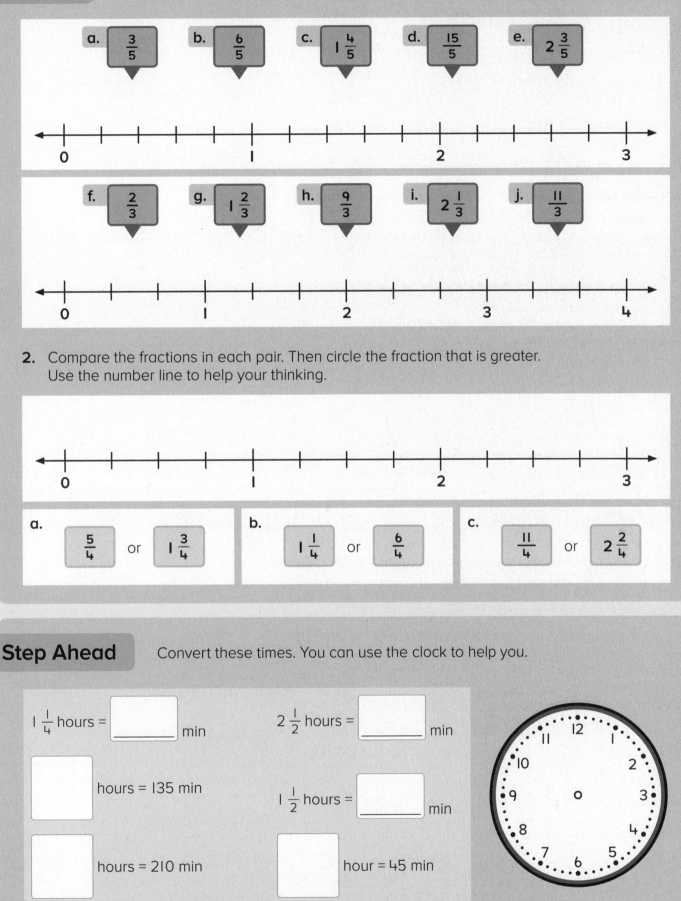

a. $\dfrac{3}{5}$ b. $\dfrac{6}{5}$ c. $1\dfrac{4}{5}$ d. $\dfrac{15}{5}$ e. $2\dfrac{3}{5}$

0   1   2   3

f. $\dfrac{2}{3}$ g. $1\dfrac{2}{3}$ h. $\dfrac{9}{3}$ i. $2\dfrac{1}{3}$ j. $\dfrac{11}{3}$

0   1   2   3   4

2. Compare the fractions in each pair. Then circle the fraction that is greater. Use the number line to help your thinking.

0   1   2   3

a. $\dfrac{5}{4}$ or $1\dfrac{3}{4}$

b. $1\dfrac{1}{4}$ or $\dfrac{6}{4}$

c. $\dfrac{11}{4}$ or $2\dfrac{2}{4}$

Convert these times. You can use the clock to help you.

$1\dfrac{1}{4}$ hours = _____ min

$2\dfrac{1}{2}$ hours = _____ min

_____ hours = 135 min

$1\dfrac{1}{2}$ hours = _____ min

_____ hours = 210 min

_____ hour = 45 min

Step In

A recipe uses $\frac{3}{4}$ cup of milk to make one batch of eight pancakes.

Manuel wants to make six batches of pancakes, so he will need $6 \times \frac{3}{4}$ or $\frac{18}{4}$ cups of milk.

How many whole cups of milk will he need?

How could you figure it out?

> I know that 4 one-fourths makes one whole, and 8 one-fourths makes two wholes. I need to find out how many wholes I can make with 18 one-fourths.

> I think there might be a remainder involved.

How do you write $\frac{18}{4}$ as a mixed number?

> A **proper fraction** has a numerator that is less than its denominator. An **improper fraction** has a numerator that is equal to or greater than its denominator.

Step Up

1. Write each improper fraction as a mixed number. Show your thinking.

a.
$\frac{9}{4}$ is equivalent to   ⟶ ☐

b.
$\frac{5}{2}$ is equivalent to   ⟶ ☐

c.
$\frac{8}{3}$ is equivalent to   ⟶ ☐

d.
$\frac{15}{8}$ is equivalent to   ⟶ ☐

2. Write each improper fraction as a mixed number. Show your thinking.

a.

$\frac{14}{6}$ is equivalent to ⟶ ☐

b.

$\frac{32}{10}$ is equivalent to ⟶ ☐

c.

$\frac{34}{5}$ is equivalent to ⟶ ☐

d.

$\frac{27}{12}$ is equivalent to ⟶ ☐

3. Read each story and write the total as a **mixed number**. Show your thinking.

a. One box weighs $\frac{3}{4}$ pound. Nine of those boxes together weigh $\frac{27}{4}$ pounds.

☐ lb

b. One hair ribbon is $\frac{5}{6}$ of a yard long. To make 7 ribbons, $\frac{35}{6}$ yd of ribbon is needed.

☐ yd

Step Ahead   Circle the greater amount in each pair.

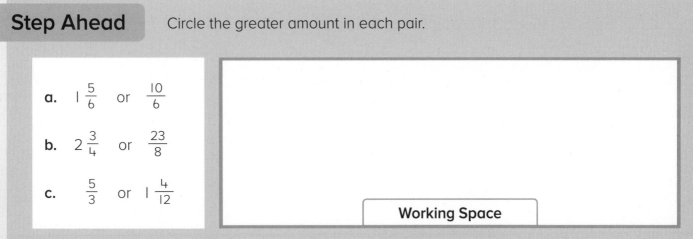

a. $1\frac{5}{6}$ or $\frac{10}{6}$

b. $2\frac{3}{4}$ or $\frac{23}{8}$

c. $\frac{5}{3}$ or $1\frac{4}{12}$

Working Space

Think and Solve

THINK TANK

What is the mystery 4-digit number?

CLUES

When it is right-side up, the digit in the hundreds place is greater than 7.

When it is rotated 180 degrees, the difference between the number that is right-side up and the rotated number is 210.

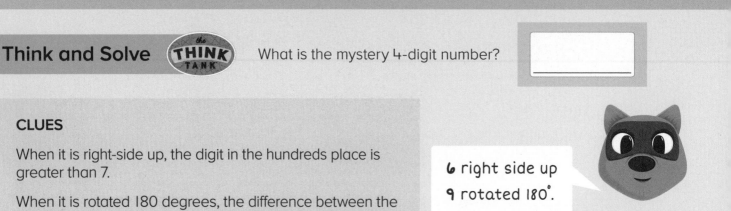

6 right side up
9 rotated 180°.

Words at Work

Imagine another student was away from school when you were learning how to convert improper fractions to mixed numbers. Write in words how you would explain the steps to them.

_____
_____
_____
_____
_____
_____
_____
_____
_____
_____
_____
_____

Ongoing Practice

I. Calculate the total number of minutes. Then write the total another way.

a.

| Washed mom's car | 37 minutes |
| Washed dad's car | 45 minutes |

☐ minutes

☐ hour ☐ minutes

b.

| Watched TV | 58 minutes |
| Did homework | 49 minutes |

☐ minutes

☐ hour ☐ minutes

2. For each pair of fractions, write equivalent fractions that have the same denominator. Write the missing factors to show your thinking.

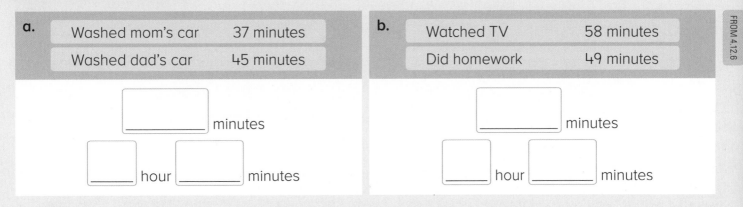

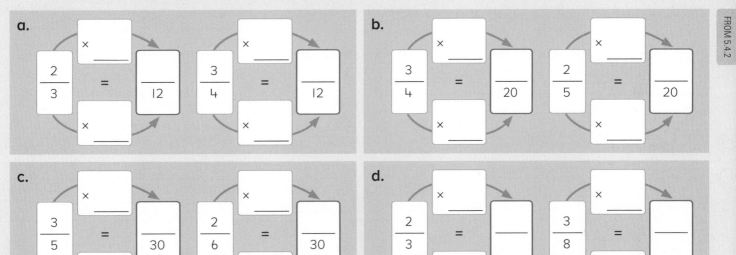

Preparing for Module 5

Estimate each total. Then use the standard addition algorithm to calculate the exact total.

a. Estimate

☐

```
    3   1   7
+   2   3   2
_____
```

b. Estimate

☐

```
    4   9   5
+   3   3   3
_____
```

c. Estimate

☐

```
    5   7   6
+       6   5
_____
```

d. Estimate

☐

```
    2   6   2
+   1   3   9
_____
```

Step In

Kyle changed $2\frac{4}{5}$ to an improper fraction. He drew this picture to show his thinking.

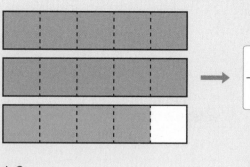

$$2\frac{4}{5} \rightarrow \quad \rightarrow \quad \rightarrow \frac{14}{5}$$

What does the picture tell you? What steps were made?

What equations could explain what was done?

> The denominator tells me that we are working with fifths.
> I need to think about how many one-fifths are equal to 2 wholes.

Brianna showed her thinking this way.

$$2\frac{4}{5} \rightarrow 2+\frac{4}{5} \rightarrow 1+1\frac{4}{5} \rightarrow \frac{5}{5}+\frac{5}{5}+\frac{4}{5} \rightarrow \frac{10}{5}+\frac{4}{5} \rightarrow \frac{14}{5}$$

Jose showed his thinking like this.

$$2\frac{4}{5} \rightarrow 2+\frac{4}{5} \rightarrow \frac{2\times5}{5}+\frac{4}{5} \rightarrow \frac{10}{5}+\frac{4}{5} \rightarrow \frac{14}{5}$$

How do Brianna's and Jose's methods relate to the picture Kyle drew?

How do they relate to each other?

How could you use these methods to change $5\frac{2}{6}$ to an improper fraction?

Step Up

1. Adjust this picture to show how $2\frac{3}{4}$ is equivalent to $\frac{11}{4}$.

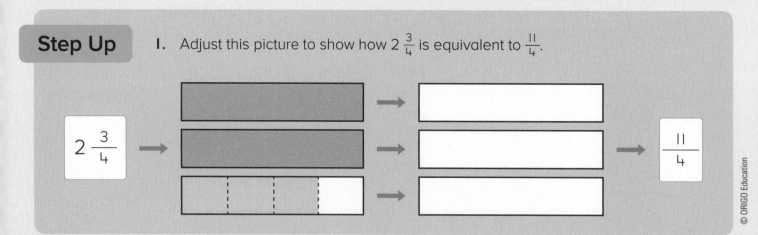

2. Write each mixed number as an improper fraction. Show your thinking.

a.

$4\frac{2}{3}$ is equivalent to ➡️ $\frac{}{}$

b.

$5\frac{2}{6}$ is equivalent to ➡️ $\frac{}{}$

c.

$2\frac{1}{4}$ is equivalent to ➡️ $\frac{}{}$

d.

$4\frac{1}{4}$ is equivalent to ➡️ $\frac{}{}$

e.

$6\frac{3}{10}$ is equivalent to ➡️ $\frac{}{}$

Step Ahead

Carol used these steps to rewrite $3\frac{2}{5}$ as an improper fraction. What mistake did she make?

$$3\frac{2}{5} \rightarrow 3+\frac{2}{5} \rightarrow \frac{3\times5}{5}+\frac{3\times2}{5} \rightarrow \frac{15}{5}+\frac{6}{5} \rightarrow \frac{21}{5}$$

Step In

The results of a class quiz are distributed to the students.

QUIZ

Emma looks at her result, and says she answered $\frac{3}{5}$ of the questions correctly. Terek says $\frac{4}{6}$ of his answers are correct.

How could you figure out who answered more questions correctly?

To compare the two fractions, I need to find a denominator that they each share.

What denominator do the two fractions have in common?

How could you use this diagram to help compare the two fractions?

Who answered more questions correctly?

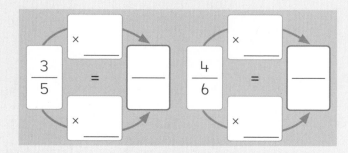

Terek and Emma compare their results. They notice that they each got this question wrong.

How would you solve this problem?

Two friends compare the distance they cycle to school each day. Karen says she cycles $2\frac{1}{4}$ miles. Ramon says he cycles $\frac{5}{2}$ miles. Who cycles the greater distance?

Step Up

1. Solve each problem. Show your thinking.

a. Two friends are reading the same book. Julia has read $\frac{3}{5}$ of the book. Samuru has read $\frac{4}{10}$ of the book. Who has read fewer pages?

b. 7 packs of meat are put in Bag A. Each pack weighs $\frac{1}{2}$ lb. One box of laundry powder is put in Bag B. The box weighs 2 lb. Which shopping bag is heavier?

2. Solve each problem. Show your thinking.

a. Natalie uses $\frac{1}{4}$ cup of detergent for each load of laundry. She does 7 loads of laundry. Dwane uses $\frac{1}{3}$ of a cup of detergent for each load of laundry. He does 5 loads. Who uses more detergent?

b. Gloria has $3\frac{1}{2}$ loaves of bread in her freezer. Liam has 13 partial loaves in his freezer. Each part is $\frac{1}{4}$ of a loaf. Who has more bread?

c. Two athletes compare the distance they swim each week. Reece swims $1\frac{1}{2}$ miles in total. Terri swims $\frac{1}{4}$ mile each day, for 5 days. Who swims the greater distance?

d. Lisa has 2 red apples and 2 green apples. She cuts the red apples into fourths, and the green apples into eighths. She eats 2 pieces of red apple and 3 pieces of green apple. Which color of apple has more left over?

Step Ahead

a. Write a comparison word problem. Use different denominators.

b. Exchange problems with another student and write the answer to **their** problem below.

Computation Practice

★ Complete the equations. Then write each letter above its matching total at the bottom of the page.

70 + 344 = ____	**l**
493 + 90 = ____	**i**
50 + 286 = ____	**a**
582 + 70 = ____	**a**
90 + 684 = ____	**a**
337 + 90 = ____	**i**
466 + 60 = ____	**o**
70 + 299 = ____	**c**
555 + 90 = ____	**b**
40 + 671 = ____	**b**
377 + 70 = ____	**p**

538 + 80 = ____	**n**
60 + 685 = ____	**e**
393 + 40 = ____	**s**
471 + 50 = ____	**s**
80 + 249 = ____	**r**
579 + 60 = ____	**l**
687 + 80 = ____	**s**
50 + 365 = ____	**a**
474 + 60 = ____	**r**
30 + 282 = ____	**k**
523 + 90 = ____	**k**

										'
652	447	526	414	774	534	711	745	415	329	433

521	613	427	618		583	767		645	639	336	369	312

© ORIGO Education

Ongoing Practice

1. Write the missing times.

a.

4 hours before					
Time	8:45 a.m.	10:04 a.m.	6:25 a.m.	7:20 p.m.	3:50 a.m.
4 hours after					

b.

5 minutes before					
Time	8:45 a.m.	10:04 a.m.	6:25 a.m.	7:20 p.m.	3:50 a.m.
5 minutes after					

2. Write each improper fraction as a mixed number. Show your thinking.

a. $\frac{48}{5}$ **is equivalent to**

b. $\frac{44}{3}$ **is equivalent to**

c. $\frac{59}{6}$ **is equivalent to**

d. $\frac{28}{9}$ **is equivalent to**

Preparing for Module 5

Estimate the difference. Then use the standard subtraction algorithm to calculate the exact difference.

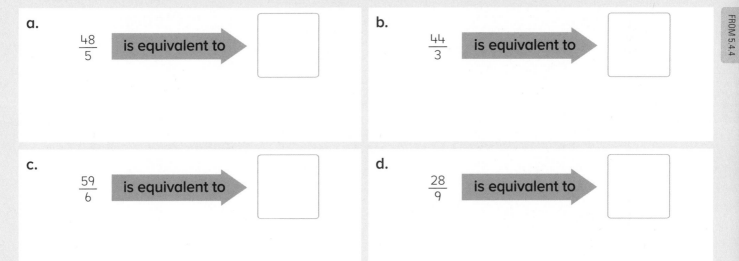

a. Estimate

```
    3  7  4
 -  1  6  3
_____
```

b. Estimate

```
    5  9  3
 -  2  6  7
_____
```

c. Estimate

```
    6  3  9
 -  4  0  7
_____
```

d. Estimate

```
    4  4  2
 -  3  1  5
_____
```

Step In   This picture shows the height of three record floods.

2005
7.5 feet

What can you tell about the height of each flood?

How would you say each of these in inches?

1963
6.9 feet

I would convert the feet to inches.
I know there are 12 inches in 1 ft.

How could you calculate the number of inches in half a foot?

1984
6 feet

Complete these statements.

[   ] inches   **is equivalent to**   1 ft.

[   ] inches   **is equivalent to** $\frac{1}{2}$ ft **or** 0.5 ft.

It's difficult to convert decimal fractions like 0.9 feet into inches.

[   ] inches   **is equivalent to** $\frac{1}{4}$ ft **or** 0.25 ft.

[   ] inches   **is equivalent to** $\frac{3}{4}$ ft **or** 0.75 ft.

Step Up   1.   Convert inches into feet to complete these.

a. 14 inches = [   ] ft [   ] in

b. 28 inches = [   ] ft [   ] in

c. 20 inches = [   ] ft [   ] in

d. 33 inches = [   ] ft [   ] in

e. 48 inches = [   ] ft [   ] in

f. 39 inches = [   ] ft [   ] in

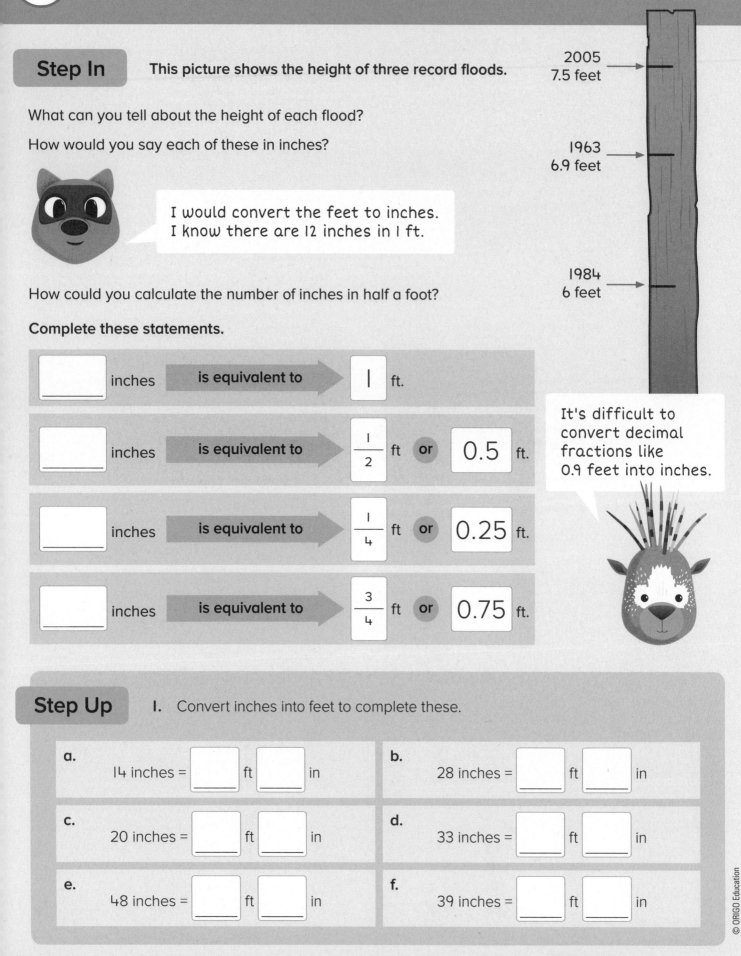

2. Convert feet to inches to complete these. Show your thinking.

a.
4.5 ft = [____] in

b.
3.25 ft = [____] in

c.
6.5 ft = [____] in

d.
5.75 ft = [____] in

e.
$7\frac{1}{2}$ ft = [____] in

f.
$8\frac{3}{4}$ ft = [____] in

3. Solve each problem. Show your thinking.

a. 15 inches of rain is recorded in July. This is 4 inches more than the month before. What is the total rainfall for June and July?

[____] ft [____] in

b. This year's record flood is 8 inches higher than the previous record of 7.5 feet. What is the height of this year's flood?

[____] ft [____] in

Step Ahead

The record flood level in Lillian's town is 8.5 ft. The 2008 flood was 9 inches lower. Write the height of the 2008 flood beside the tide mark.

8.5 ft ⟶ 2012

[____] ft ⟶ 2008

Working Space

Step In

Two friends play a game of golf. At the first hole, Maka's ball stops 4 yards from the hole. Ruth's ball stops 15 feet from the hole.

Whose ball is closer to the hole? How do you know?

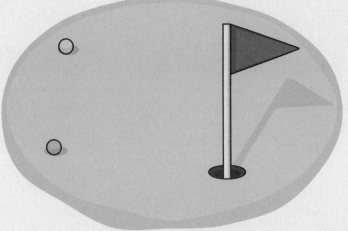

I know there are 3 feet in 1 yard.

Maka misses his first putt.

His ball is now $2\frac{1}{3}$ yards from the hole.

How could you say this distance in feet?

Think about how you converted the distance from yards to feet. What expression could you write to show what you did?

What do you know about the relationship between yards and miles ?

How many yards are equivalent to half a mile?
How do you know?

How could you calculate the number of yards that are equivalent to $1\frac{1}{4}$ miles?

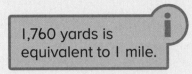

1,760 yards is equivalent to 1 mile.

Step Up 1. Write the missing numbers in this table.

Yards	7	5			3	10		4	
Feet		15	27	60			45	12	3

© ORIGO Education

2. Solve each problem. Show your thinking.

a. Deon's ball stops $7\frac{2}{3}$ yards from the hole. Kylie's ball stops 16 feet from the hole. How much closer is Kylie's ball to the hole?

_____ ft

b. Selena's ball stops $1\frac{3}{4}$ feet from the hole. Jamar's ball is 2 inches closer to the hole. How far is Jamar's ball from the hole?

_____ in

c. The fifth hole is 186 yards in length. Connor's first shot stops 12 feet from the hole. What is the length of his first shot?

_____ yd

d. A half-mile road is being resurfaced. At the end of the first day, there is still 840 yd to resurface. What length of road was resurfaced on the first day?

_____ yd

Step Ahead

The 18th hole is 324 yards long. The first shot stops 135 yards from the hole. The second shot stops 9 feet from the hole.

What was the length of each shot?   1st shot _____ yd   2nd shot _____ yd

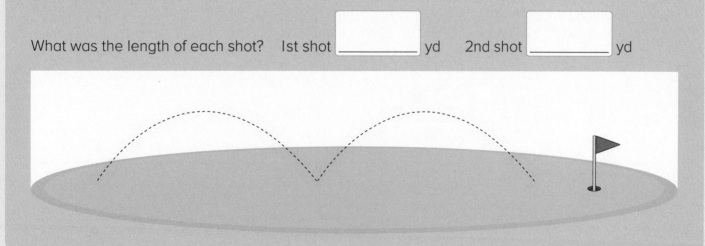

Think and Solve THINK TANK

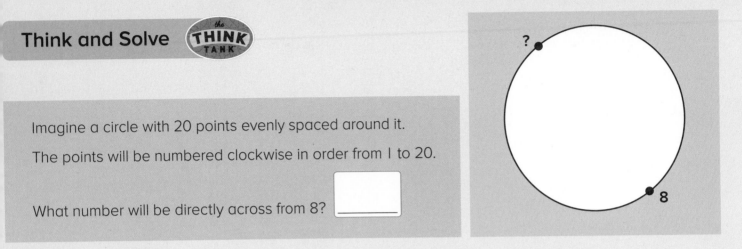

Imagine a circle with 20 points evenly spaced around it.

The points will be numbered clockwise in order from 1 to 20.

What number will be directly across from 8? _____

Words at Work   Explain in words how you could convert 220 yards to miles, feet, and then inches.

Ongoing Practice

1. Draw marbles in each empty bag to match the label.

a. Bag A has 4 times as many marbles as Bag B.　　**b.** Bag C has 3 times as many marbles as Bag D.

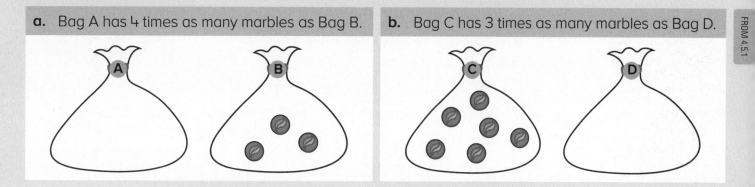

2. Write each mixed number as an improper fraction. Show your thinking.

a.

$3\frac{4}{5}$ **is equivalent to** ⬚

b.

$6\frac{7}{10}$ **is equivalent to** ⬚

c.

$4\frac{5}{6}$ **is equivalent to** ⬚

d.

$5\frac{3}{4}$ **is equivalent to** ⬚

Preparing for Module 5

Use a ruler to draw each shape.

a.　　a non-square rectangle

b.　　a rhombus

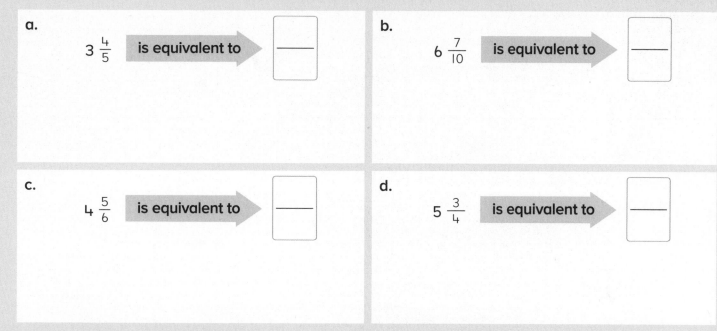

Step In

This pitcher holds 1 quart of water.

How many pitchers would you need to fill a 2-gallon container? How do you know?

Imagine this pitcher is used to fill the empty bottles with water.

How many bottles can be filled from one full pitcher?

How many pitchers of water are needed to fill six of these bottles?

There are 32 fl oz in 1 quart.

Complete these statements.

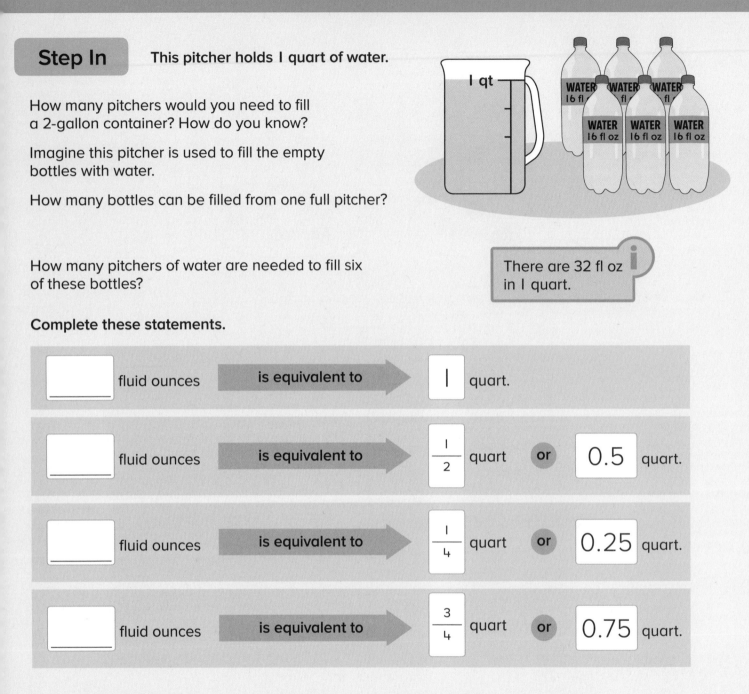

	fluid ounces	is equivalent to	1 quart.		
	fluid ounces	is equivalent to	$\frac{1}{2}$ quart	or	0.5 quart.
	fluid ounces	is equivalent to	$\frac{1}{4}$ quart	or	0.25 quart.
	fluid ounces	is equivalent to	$\frac{3}{4}$ quart	or	0.75 quart.

How would you calculate the number of fluid ounces that are equivalent to 1 gallon?

Step Up

1. Write the missing numbers in the table.

Gallons			3	10	8		15		
Quarts	8	20	12	40		36		100	48

2. Convert each amount to quarts. Write equations to show your thinking.

a.

4.5 gal = [ ] qt

b.

6.75 gal = [ ] qt

3. Convert each amount to fluid ounces. Show your thinking.

a.

5 qt = [ ] fl oz

b.

4.75 qt = [ ] fl oz

c.

3.5 qt = [ ] fl oz

d.

6.25 qt = [ ] fl oz

Step Ahead

Look at the price of the quart of milk. Then write a price for the bottle of milk. Explain how you calculated the price.

○ $1.90

MILK
I quart

○ $_____

MILK
I gallon

Step In

What is the mass of each package?

How could you calculate the difference in mass between these two packages?

12 oz

$2\frac{1}{2}$ lb

How could you calculate the number of ounces in one-half of a pound?

There are 16 oz in 1 pound.

Complete these statements.

| | ounces | is equivalent to | 1 pound. |

| | ounces | is equivalent to | $\frac{1}{2}$ pound **or** 0.5 pound. |

| | ounces | is equivalent to | $\frac{1}{4}$ pound **or** 0.25 pound. |

| | ounces | is equivalent to | $\frac{3}{4}$ pound **or** 0.75 pound. |

What are some other statements you could write?

How many pounds are equivalent to 40 ounces? How do you know?

I wonder how many ounces are in $\frac{1}{8}$ of a pound?

Step Up

1. Write the missing numbers in the table.

Pounds		3		8	9	5	10		7
Ounces	64	48	32			80		96	

© ORIGO Education

2. Convert pounds to ounces to complete these. Show your thinking.

a.
3.5 lb = _____ oz

b.
2.75 lb = _____ oz

c.
4.25 lb = _____ oz

d.
5.5 lb = _____ oz

e.
10.75 lb = _____ oz

f.
6.25 lb = _____ oz

3. Write the missing mass to make each balance picture true.

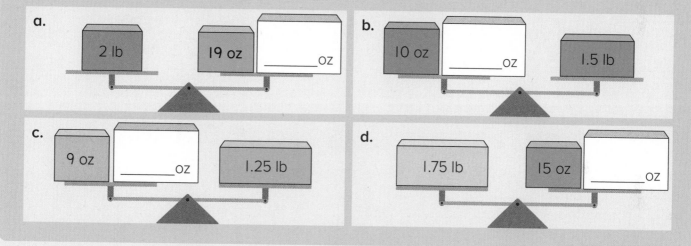

a. 2 lb | 19 oz | _____ oz

b. 10 oz | _____ oz | 1.5 lb

c. 9 oz | _____ oz | 1.25 lb

d. 1.75 lb | 15 oz | _____ oz

Step Ahead

The total mass of these items is 3.25 lb. One item is 2 lb. Write a possible mass for each other item.

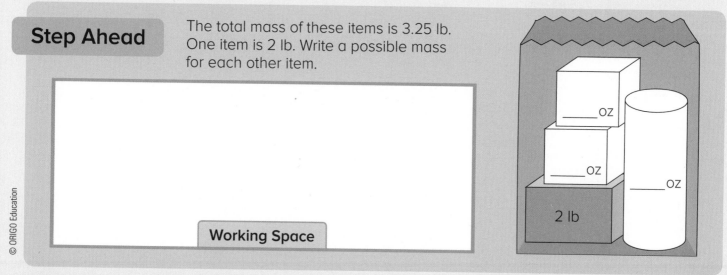

_____ oz

_____ oz

_____ oz

2 lb

Working Space

Computation Practice

Why should you not tell jokes when you are ice skating?

★ Complete the equations. Then write each letter above its matching product below. Some letters appear more than once.

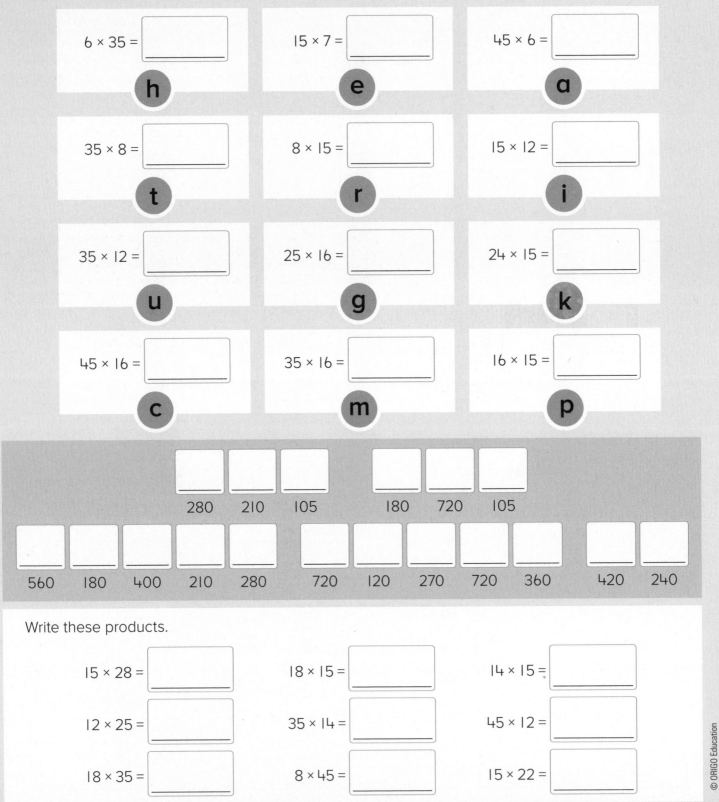

$6 \times 35 =$ ____ **h**

$15 \times 7 =$ ____ **e**

$45 \times 6 =$ ____ **a**

$35 \times 8 =$ ____ **t**

$8 \times 15 =$ ____ **r**

$15 \times 12 =$ ____ **i**

$35 \times 12 =$ ____ **u**

$25 \times 16 =$ ____ **g**

$24 \times 15 =$ ____ **k**

$45 \times 16 =$ ____ **c**

$35 \times 16 =$ ____ **m**

$16 \times 15 =$ ____ **p**

280   210   105   180   720   105

560   180   400   210   280   720   120   270   720   360   420   240

Write these products.

$15 \times 28 =$ ____

$18 \times 15 =$ ____

$14 \times 15 =$ ____

$12 \times 25 =$ ____

$35 \times 14 =$ ____

$45 \times 12 =$ ____

$18 \times 35 =$ ____

$8 \times 45 =$ ____

$15 \times 22 =$ ____

Ongoing Practice

1. Write an equation to calculate each answer.
Complete the diagram to show the answer.

a. Jacob has saved $1,805. Vishaya has saved $200 more.
How much has Vishaya saved?

Jacob | **$1,805**

_____

Vishaya

b. The price in Store A is $80. The price in Store B is 3 times as much as Store A.
What is the price in Store B?

Store A | **$80**

_____

Store B

2. Write the missing mass to make each balance picture true.

a.

3 lb   34 oz   _____oz

b.

18 oz   _____oz   1.75 lb

Preparing for Module 5

Look at this tree diagram. Write the listed words in the correct parts of the diagram.

rectangle   square   non-square rhombus   quadrilateral   rhombus   non-square rectangle

other quadrilaterals

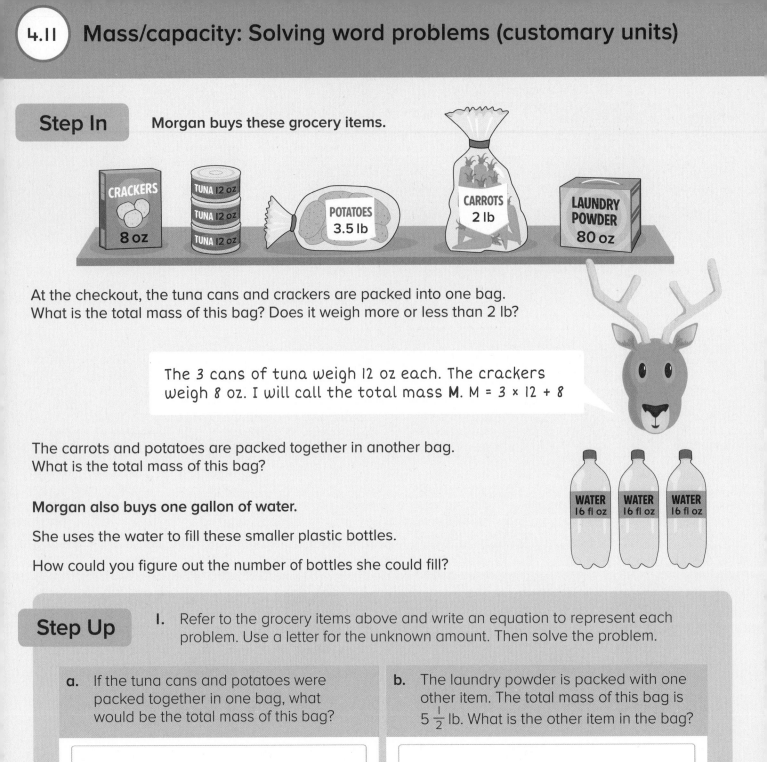

Step In   Morgan buys these grocery items.

At the checkout, the tuna cans and crackers are packed into one bag.
What is the total mass of this bag? Does it weigh more or less than 2 lb?

> The 3 cans of tuna weigh 12 oz each. The crackers weigh 8 oz. I will call the total mass **M**. M = 3 × 12 + 8

The carrots and potatoes are packed together in another bag.
What is the total mass of this bag?

Morgan also buys one gallon of water.

She uses the water to fill these smaller plastic bottles.

How could you figure out the number of bottles she could fill?

Step Up   I.   Refer to the grocery items above and write an equation to represent each problem. Use a letter for the unknown amount. Then solve the problem.

a. If the tuna cans and potatoes were packed together in one bag, what would be the total mass of this bag?	b. The laundry powder is packed with one other item. The total mass of this bag is $5\frac{1}{2}$ lb. What is the other item in the bag?
_____ oz	

2. Solve each problem. Show your thinking.

a. Jie has half a gallon of milk. He buys more milk and now has 0.75 gal. How much milk did he buy?

_____ gal

b. A 2 lb block of cheese is cut into 8 oz pieces. How many pieces are there?

_____ pieces

c. Four glasses each hold 8 fl oz. Their total capacity is 1.75 gallons less than a bucket. How much does the bucket hold?

_____ gal

d. A storekeeper is running low on milk. He counts 4 two-gallon bottles, 3 half-gallon cartons, and 6 quarts. How many gallons of milk does he have in total?

_____ gal

Step Ahead

Antonio buys five bottles of juice for a party. Each bottle holds 64 fl oz. He pours them all into one large bowl to make fruit punch.

At least how many gallons must the bowl hold? _____ gal

Working Space

Step In

Susan bakes and sells loaves of homemade bread. With the recipe she uses, each loaf should weigh 22 oz.

Some loaves seem larger than others, so she decides to investigate.

She decides to weigh each of the loaves that she made that day.

What could she do? How could she carry out the investigation?

The line plot below shows the mass of each loaf.

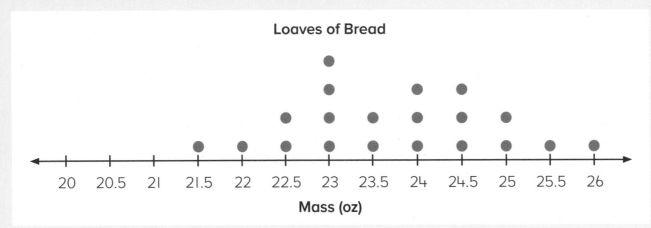

What do you notice?

What does the shape of the line plot tell you about the loaves of bread?

What should she do with the findings?

What changes could she make to the recipe or selling price?

Step Up

Jerome bakes and sells banana bread. Each loaf of banana bread should weigh 30 oz. The line plot below shows the mass of 20 loaves.

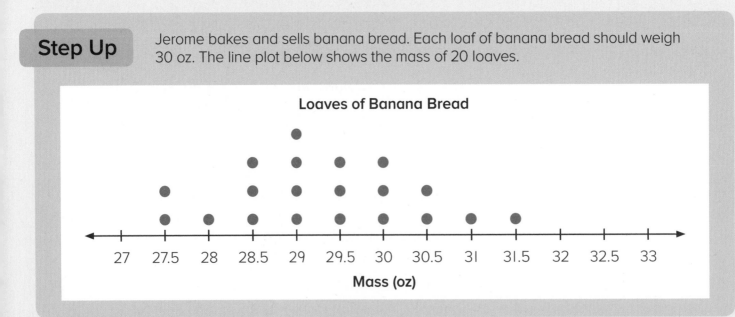

Use the line plot at the bottom of page 152 to answer Questions 1 and 2.

1. a. How many loaves have a mass that is greater than 30 oz?

    _____

    b. How much heavier was the heaviest loaf than the lightest loaf?

    _____ oz

    c. What is the total mass of the loaves that weighed 29.5 oz?

    _____ oz

    d. What is the total mass of the loaves that weighed more than 30 oz?

    _____ oz

2. a. What does the shape of the line plot tell you about the loaves of bread?

    b. Imagine you randomly selected one loaf of banana bread.
        What do you think it would weigh? Explain your thinking.

Step Ahead   The information below was collected at an animal reserve.
Lion cubs typically gain about 25 oz in their first week.

What concerns might the reserve managers have?
Explain why.

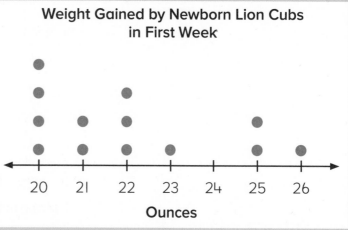

Weight Gained by Newborn Lion Cubs in First Week

Ounces

Think and Solve THINK TANK

The numbers in the circles are the sums of the rows and the columns.

Same shapes are the same numbers. Write the number that each shape represents.

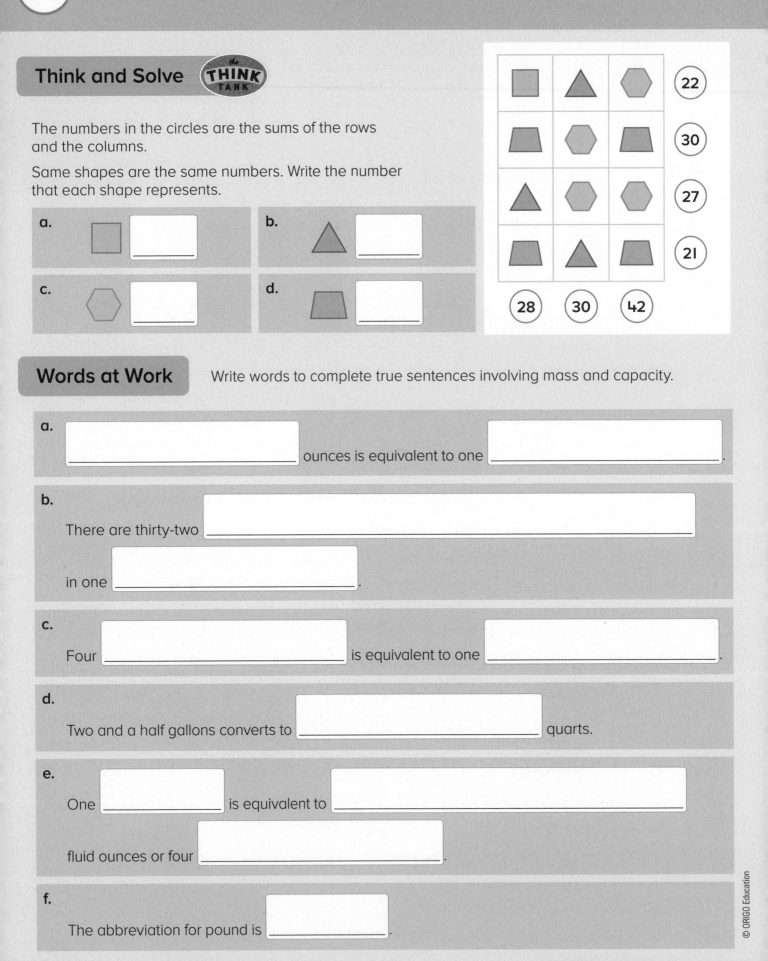

a. [ ] _____

b. [ ] _____

c. [ ] _____

d. [ ] _____

Words at Work

Write words to complete true sentences involving mass and capacity.

a. _____ ounces is equivalent to one _____ .

b. There are thirty-two _____

in one _____ .

c. Four _____ is equivalent to one _____ .

d. Two and a half gallons converts to _____ quarts.

e. One _____ is equivalent to _____

fluid ounces or four _____ .

f. The abbreviation for pound is _____ .

Ongoing Practice

1. Write an equation to calculate each answer.
Complete the diagram to show the answer.

a. Rita is twice the height of her son. She is 168 cm tall. How tall is her son?

Rita | 168 cm

Rita's son | [   ]

b. Robert earns $1,024 in one month. He earned 4 times as much as his friend Amber.
How much did Amber earn?

Robert | $1,024

Amber | [   ]

2. This line plot shows the mass of 20 tiger cubs born over a 12-month period.

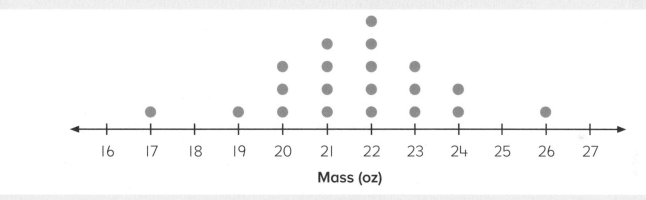

Mass (oz)

What does the shape of the line plot tell you about the mass of the cubs?

[   ]

Preparing for Module 5

Use a ruler to draw lines between vertices to split each shape into triangles. Use as few lines as possible.

a.
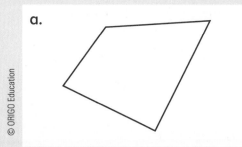

b.
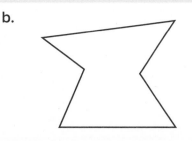

c.
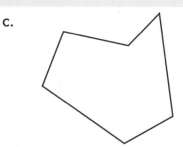

Decimal fractions: Reviewing addition strategies (without composing)

Step In

This table shows the amount of protein in some fast foods.

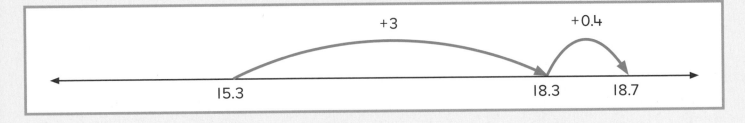

Big Burger Bar	
Lean burger	15.3 g
Fries	3.4 g
Onion rings	5.12 g
Potato skins	1.65 g

Which two items together have about 19 grams of protein?

How could you calculate the total protein for one lean burger and one serving of fries?

Matthew used a number line to calculate the total.

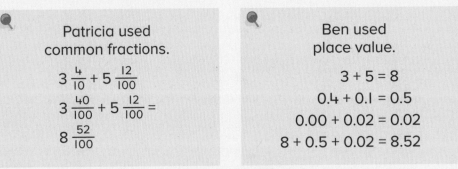

What steps did he follow? What is another way to figure out the total?

How would you calculate the total protein for one serving of fries and one serving of onion rings?

Patricia used
common fractions.

$$3\frac{4}{10} + 5\frac{12}{100}$$
$$3\frac{40}{100} + 5\frac{12}{100} =$$
$$8\frac{52}{100}$$

Ben used
place value.

$$3 + 5 = 8$$
$$0.4 + 0.1 = 0.5$$
$$0.00 + 0.02 = 0.02$$
$$8 + 0.5 + 0.02 = 8.52$$

Describe each strategy. Which strategy do you prefer? Why?

Step Up

1. Draw jumps on the number line to calculate each total.

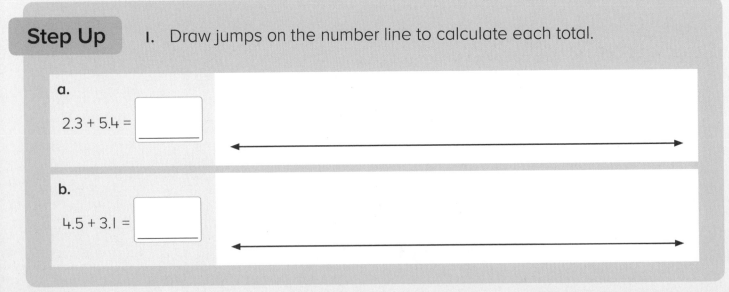

a.

2.3 + 5.4 = ☐

b.

4.5 + 3.1 = ☐

2. Calculate each total. Draw jumps on the number line to show your thinking.

a.

$6.2 + 1.37 =$ ▢

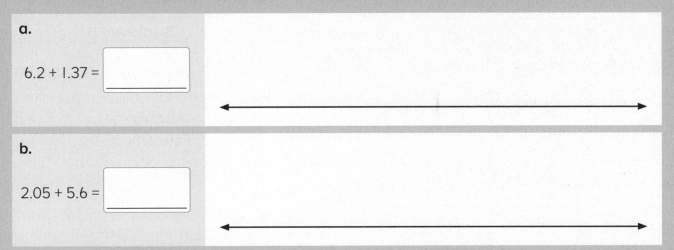

b.

$2.05 + 5.6 =$ ▢

3. Calculate each total. Show your thinking.

a.

$2.45 + 1.32 =$ ▢

b.

$7.3 + 2.53 =$ ▢

c.

$12.09 + 5.3 =$ ▢

d.

$10.71 + 11.06 =$ ▢

Step Ahead

Paige has $3.45 in her purse.
She borrows some money to buy her lunch.
She now has $4.98.

How much money did she borrow?

$ _____

Step In   These students played two rounds of shot put and added the distances.

	Ist Throw	2nd Throw
Dakota	3.5 m	3.7 m
Amy	3.09 m	3.45 m
Norton	4.2 m	3.92 m

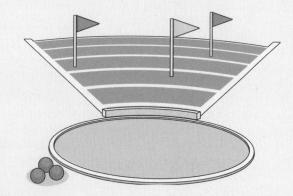

How could you calculate the total distance of Dakota's throws?

How could you calculate the total distance of Amy's throws?

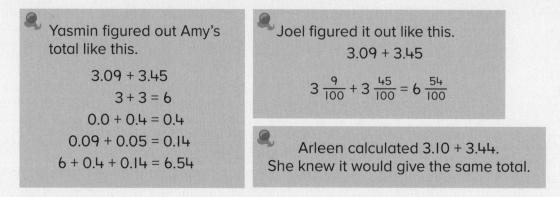

Yasmin figured out Amy's total like this.

$$3.09 + 3.45$$
$$3 + 3 = 6$$
$$0.0 + 0.4 = 0.4$$
$$0.09 + 0.05 = 0.14$$
$$6 + 0.4 + 0.14 = 6.54$$

Joel figured it out like this.

$$3.09 + 3.45$$
$$3\frac{9}{100} + 3\frac{45}{100} = 6\frac{54}{100}$$

Arleen calculated 3.10 + 3.44.
She knew it would give the same total.

What steps does each person follow? Which strategy do you prefer? Why?

Use the strategy you like best to calculate the total length of Norton's throws.

Who threw the greatest total distance?

Step Up   I.   Calculate each total. Show your thinking.

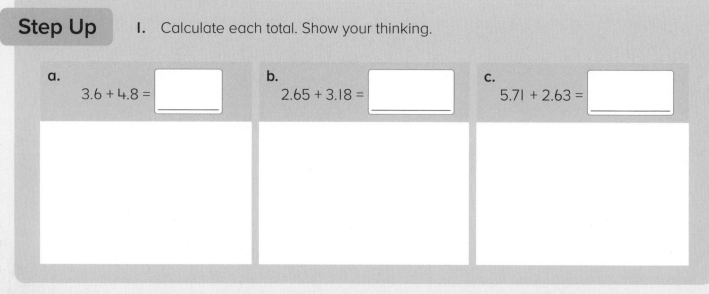

a.   3.6 + 4.8 = _____

b.   2.65 + 3.18 = _____

c.   5.71 + 2.63 = _____

2. Calculate each total. Show your thinking.

a.

○ $3.80   ○ $4.30

$_____

b.

○ $1.90   ○ $5.60

$_____

c.

○ $2.38   ○ $2.45

$_____

d.

○ $7.62   ○ $1.09

$_____

e.

○ $5.40   ○ $1.70

$_____

f.

○ $3.10   ○ $2.90

$_____

Step Ahead   Calculate the missing lengths.

	1st Throw	2nd Throw	Total
Steven	3.5 m	___ m	7.02 m
Sharon	___ m	4.25 m	9.2 m
Emilio	___ m	___ m	8.05 m

3.50 + ? = 7.02

© ORIGO Education

Computation Practice

What is the world's largest dog breed?

★ Complete the equations. Then write each letter above its matching product at the bottom of the page.

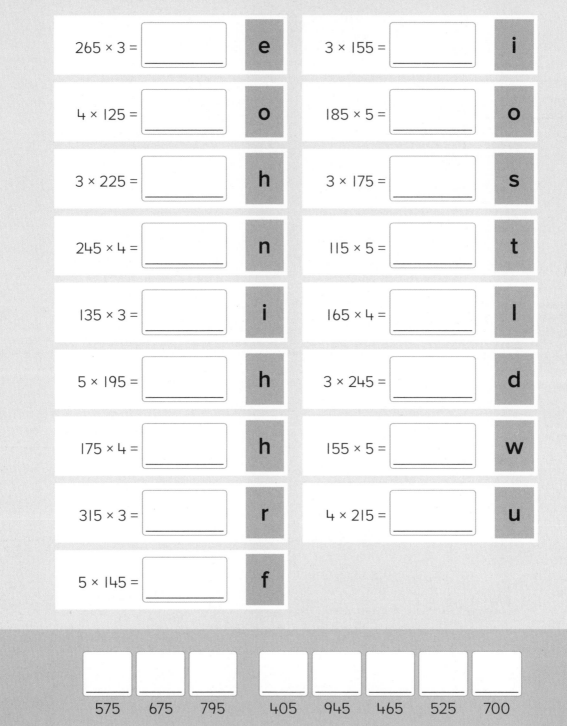

$265 \times 3 =$ ____ **e**

$3 \times 155 =$ ____ **i**

$4 \times 125 =$ ____ **o**

$185 \times 5 =$ ____ **o**

$3 \times 225 =$ ____ **h**

$3 \times 175 =$ ____ **s**

$245 \times 4 =$ ____ **n**

$115 \times 5 =$ ____ **t**

$135 \times 3 =$ ____ **i**

$165 \times 4 =$ ____ **l**

$5 \times 195 =$ ____ **h**

$3 \times 245 =$ ____ **d**

$175 \times 4 =$ ____ **h**

$155 \times 5 =$ ____ **w**

$315 \times 3 =$ ____ **r**

$4 \times 215 =$ ____ **u**

$5 \times 145 =$ ____ **f**

575	675	795	405	945	465	525	700

775	500	660	725	975	925	860	980	735

© ORIGO Education

Ongoing Practice

I. Complete this table. You can use base-10 ones blocks to help.

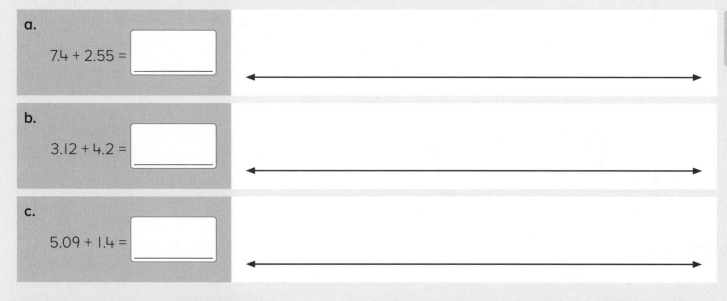

Number of cubes in base	Number of layers	Total number of cubes
7	I	
	3	
	5	
	7	
	9	

2. Calculate each total. Draw jumps on the number line to show your thinking.

a.

$7.4 + 2.55 =$ ☐

⟵──────────────────────⟶

b.

$3.12 + 4.2 =$ ☐

⟵──────────────────────⟶

c.

$5.09 + 1.4 =$ ☐

⟵──────────────────────⟶

Preparing for Module 6

Use what you know about adding fractions to complete each of these.

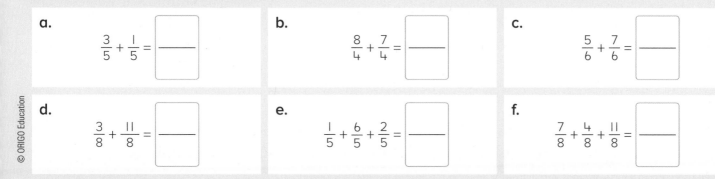

a.
$$\frac{3}{5} + \frac{1}{5} = \underline{\qquad}$$

b.
$$\frac{8}{4} + \frac{7}{4} = \underline{\qquad}$$

c.
$$\frac{5}{6} + \frac{7}{6} = \underline{\qquad}$$

d.
$$\frac{3}{8} + \frac{11}{8} = \underline{\qquad}$$

e.
$$\frac{1}{5} + \frac{6}{5} + \frac{2}{5} = \underline{\qquad}$$

f.
$$\frac{7}{8} + \frac{4}{8} + \frac{11}{8} = \underline{\qquad}$$

Step In

These two packages were weighed in kilograms.

Estimate the mass of the two packages together.

How could you calculate the exact mass of the two packages?

5.72 kg

6.8 kg

These numbers are not easy to add in my head. I need to write them down.

Abigail used the standard addition algorithm to calculate the total. What steps does she follow?

Step 1	Step 2	Step 3

Step 1

T	O	t	h
	6 . 8		
+	5 . 7	2	
	.	2	

Step 2

T	O	t	h
	6 . 8		
+	5 . 7	2	
	. 5	2	

Step 3

T	O	t	h
	6 . 8		
+	5 . 7	2	
1	2 . 5	2	

Abigail wrote 6.8 in the top row. Does the total change if she writes 6.80?

What does the 1 above the 6 represent?

Step Up

1. Estimate the total. Then use the standard algorithm to calculate the exact total.

a.
Estimate _____

T	O	t	h
1	2 . 3	1	
+	6 . 5		
	.		

b.
Estimate _____

T	O	t	h
	8 . 3	4	
+	3 . 2	5	
	.		

c.
Estimate _____

T	O	t	h
1	2 . 4	7	
+	1 4 . 0	8	
	.		

2. Estimate the total mass in your head. Then use the standard algorithm to calculate the exact mass.

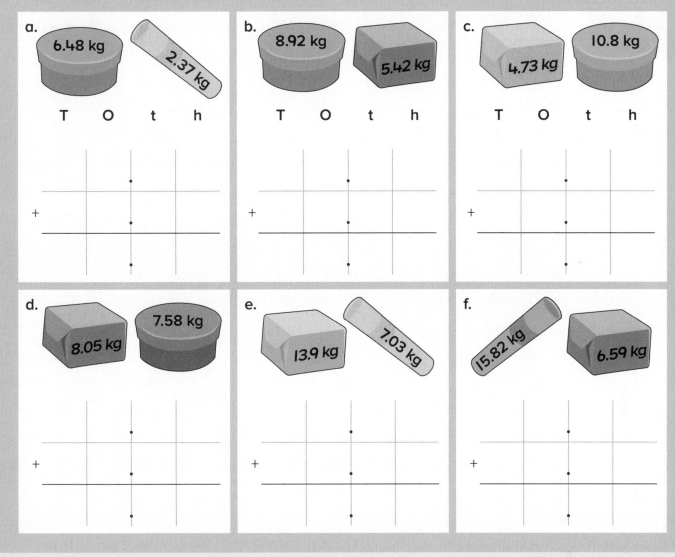

a.

6.48 kg   2.37 kg

T	O	t	h
+			

b.

8.92 kg   5.42 kg

T	O	t	h
+			

c.

4.73 kg   10.8 kg

T	O	t	h
+			

d.

8.05 kg   7.58 kg

+		

e.

13.9 kg   7.03 kg

+		

f.

15.82 kg   6.59 kg

+		

Step Ahead

This student seems to repeat the same error on a test.
Describe the mistake in words.

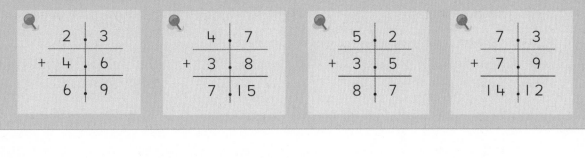

```
    2 . 3            4 . 7            5 . 2            7 . 3
+   4 . 6        +   3 . 8        +   3 . 5        +   7 . 9
─────────        ─────────        ─────────        ─────────
    6 . 9            7 . 15           8 . 7           14 . 12
```

_____

_____

_____

Step In   Estimate the perimeter of this triangle.

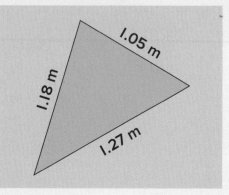

1.18 m
1.05 m
1.27 m

Each side is just over one meter, so the perimeter is between 3 and 4 meters.

How would you calculate the exact perimeter?

Hiro and Beth used different written methods.

Hiro added the hundredths first.

$$\begin{array}{r} \overset{2}{} \\ 1.18 \\ 1.27 \\ + 1.05 \\ \hline 3.50 \end{array}$$

Beth used partial sums. She added the ones first.

$$\begin{array}{r} 1.18 \\ 1.27 \\ + 1.05 \\ \hline 3.00 \\ 0.30 \\ 0.20 \\ \hline 3.50 \end{array}$$

Describe the steps they followed.

Does it matter in what order the side lengths are recorded?

Is there another way you could do it?

Step Up   1. Estimate each total. Then use the standard algorithm to calculate the exact total.

a.
Estimate _____

T	O	t	h
	1 . 2	
	2 . 4	8
+	1 . 3	1

b.
Estimate _____

T	O	t	h
	3 . 2	5
	1 . 0	5
+	5 . 4	1

c.
Estimate _____

T	O	t	h
	6 . 9	2
	0 . 4	5
+	1 . 7	1

2. Estimate the perimeter of each shape in your head. Then use the standard algorithm to calculate the exact perimeter.

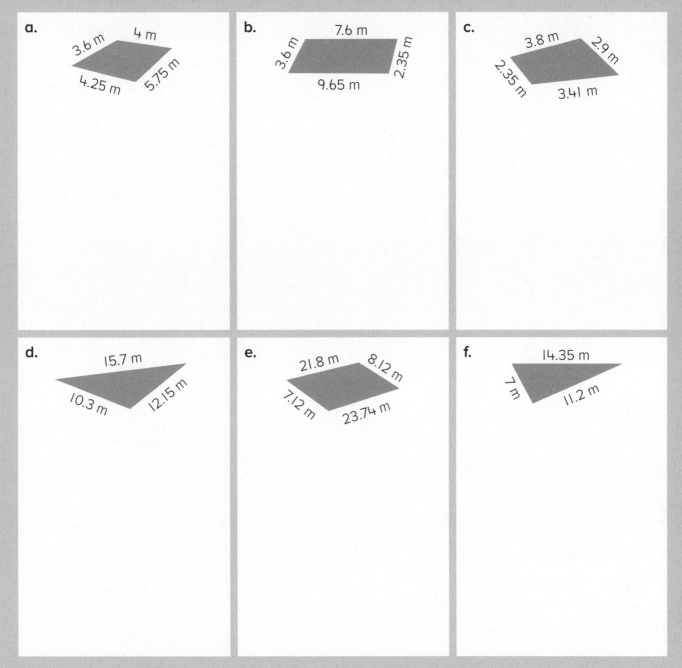

a.
3.6 m
4 m
4.25 m
5.75 m

b.
7.6 m
3.6 m
2.35 m
9.65 m

c.
3.8 m
2.9 m
2.35 m
3.41 m

d.
15.7 m
10.3 m
12.15 m

e.
21.8 m
8.12 m
7.12 m
23.74 m

f.
14.35 m
7 m
11.2 m

Step Ahead

Draw and label a shape that has sides of different length and a perimeter of 10 meters.
Show each side measure as a decimal fraction involving hundredths.

Think and Solve

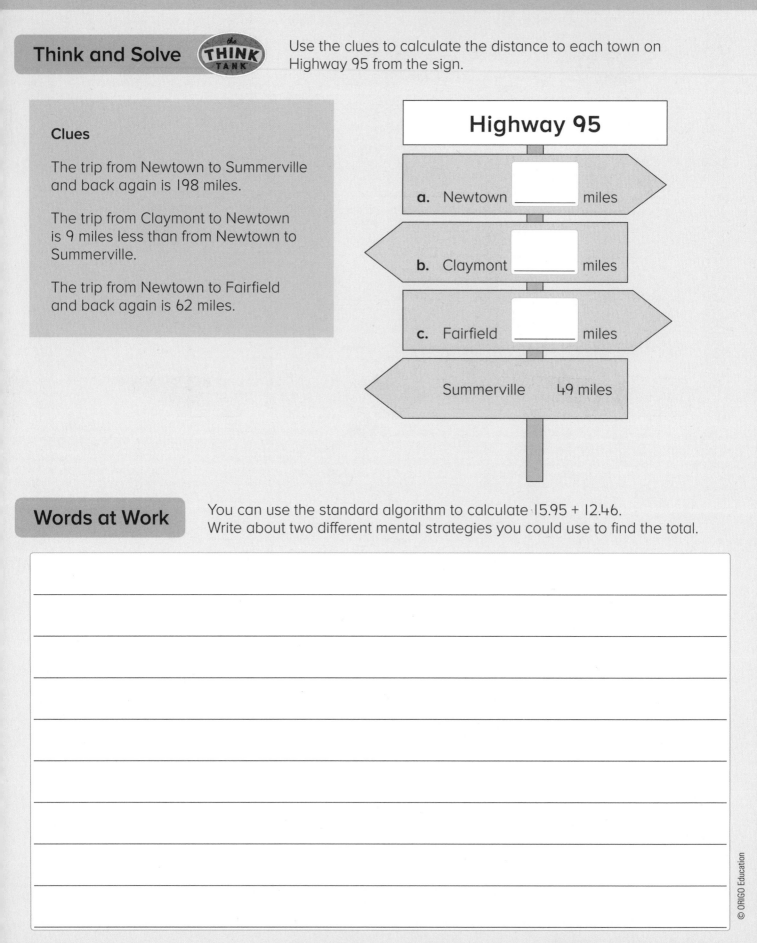

Clues

The trip from Newtown to Summerville and back again is 198 miles.

The trip from Claymont to Newtown is 9 miles less than from Newtown to Summerville.

The trip from Newtown to Fairfield and back again is 62 miles.

Use the clues to calculate the distance to each town on Highway 95 from the sign.

Highway 95

a. Newtown _____ miles

b. Claymont _____ miles

c. Fairfield _____ miles

Summerville 49 miles

Words at Work

You can use the standard algorithm to calculate 15.95 + 12.46. Write about two different mental strategies you could use to find the total.

© ORIGO Education

Ongoing Practice

1. Each prism is made with centimeter cubes. Calculate the volume of each prism. Then write an equation to show the order in which you multiplied.

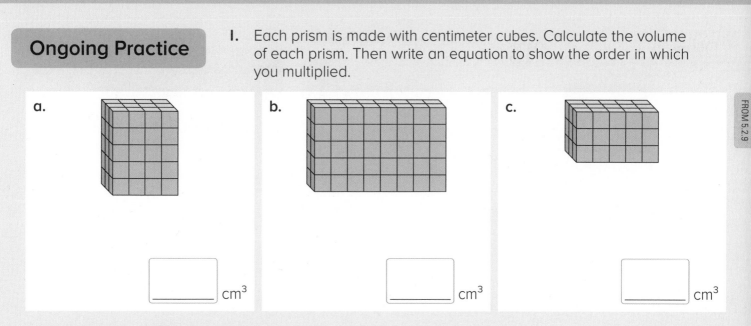

a.

_____ cm³

b.

_____ cm³

c.

_____ cm³

2. Calculate the total. Show your thinking.

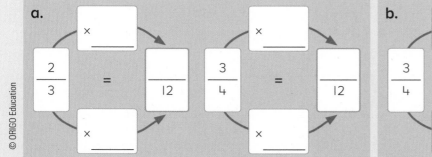

a. ○ $4.60   ○ $3.80

$_____

b. ○ $2.50   ○ $3.70

$_____

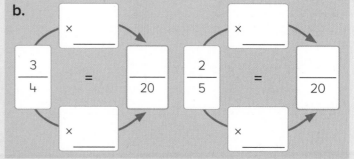

c. ○ $5.19   ○ $3.55

$_____

d. ○ $6.75   ○ $2.15

$_____

Preparing for Module 6

For each pair of fractions, write equivalent fractions that have the same denominator. Write the missing factors to show your thinking.

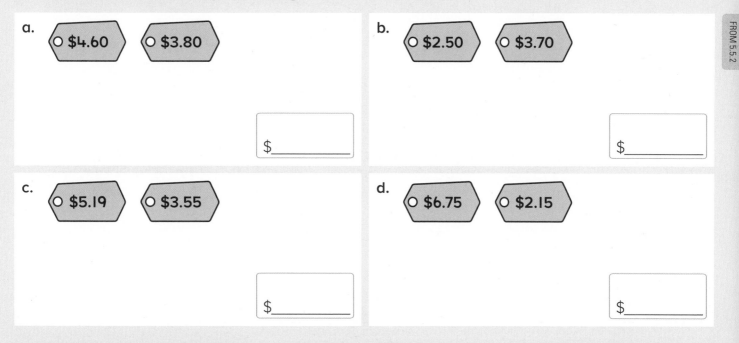

a.

$$\frac{2}{3} = \frac{}{12} \qquad \frac{3}{4} = \frac{}{12}$$

b.

$$\frac{3}{4} = \frac{}{20} \qquad \frac{2}{5} = \frac{}{20}$$

Step In

Olivia is planning a hike. How much farther is Springwood Falls than Hard Rock Valley?

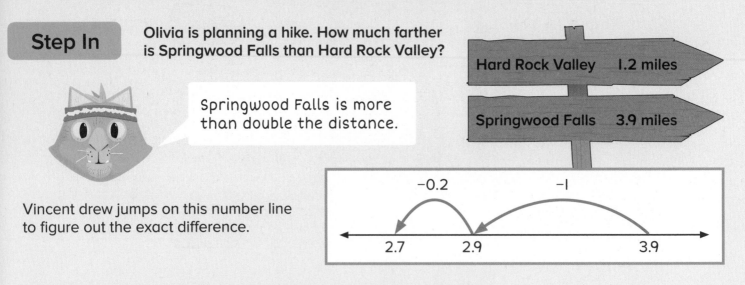

Springwood Falls is more than double the distance.

Hard Rock Valley   1.2 miles

Springwood Falls   3.9 miles

Vincent drew jumps on this number line to figure out the exact difference.

−0.2   −1

2.7   2.9   3.9

What steps did he follow? What is another way to find the difference?

Olivia decides to buy some supplies.

How would you calculate the difference in cost between these two items?

Carmela figured it out like this.

$7.99 − $2.45
$7.99 − $2 = $5.99
$5.99 − $0.40 = $5.59
$5.59 − $0.05 = $5.54

Michael figured it out like this.

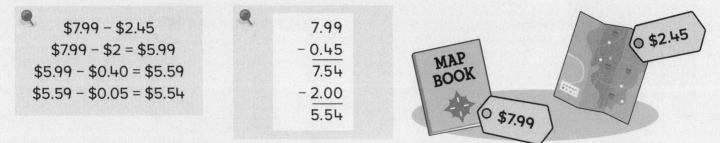

```
   7.99
 − 0.45
   7.54
 − 2.00
   5.54
```

MAP BOOK $7.99

$2.45

What steps did they each follow?

What is another way to calculate the difference?

Step Up

1. Draw jumps on the number line to calculate each difference.

a.

6.5 − 2.3 = ☐

b.

7.8 − 4.1 = ☐

2. Calculate the difference between these prices. Show your thinking.

a.

$3.50 $1.20

$_____

b.

$5.30 $6.70

$_____

c.

$3.30 $8.40

$_____

d.

$4.88 $1.32

$_____

e.

$5.75 $2.52

$_____

f.

$3.47 $6.99

$_____

Step Ahead

A student used this number line to calculate 7.81 − 2.41.
Write the correct difference. Then explain the mistake that was made.

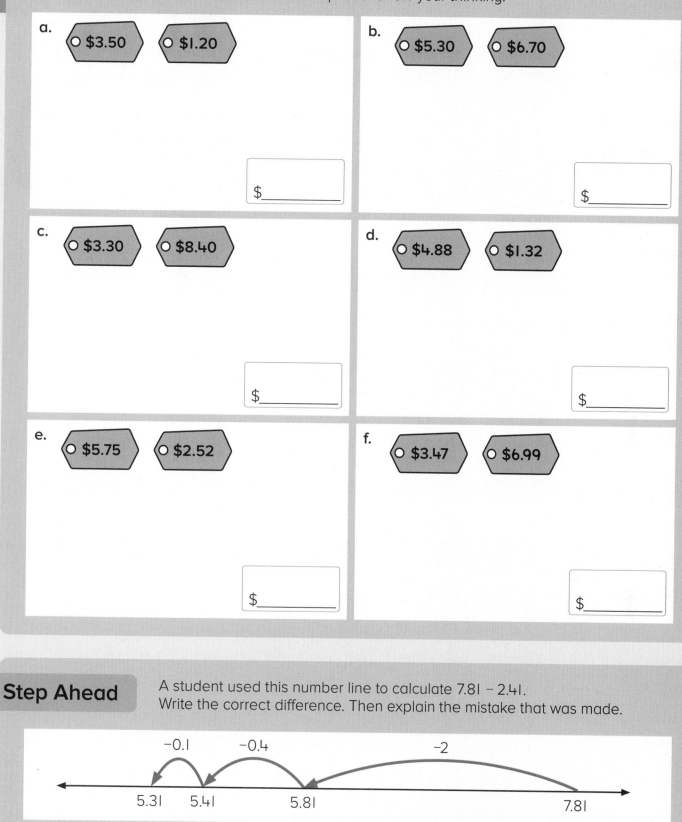

−0.1   −0.4   −2

5.31   5.41   5.81   7.81

Step In How would you estimate the difference in mass between these two dogs?

It must be about 3 kg because 17 − 14 = 3.

14.2 kg   17.65 kg

How would you calculate the exact difference?

Oliver used the standard algorithm, and followed these steps.

Step 1				
T	O	t	h	
1	7 .	6	5	
− 1	4 .	2		
	.		5	

Step 2				
T	O	t	h	
1	7 .	6	5	
− 1	4 .	2		
	.	4	5	

Step 3				
T	O	t	h	
1	7 .	6	5	
− 1	4 .	2		
	3 .	4	5	

How could you calculate the difference in cost between these two items?

$8.68 $3.25

The numbers are a bit messy, so I would use a written method.

Step Up

1. Estimate the difference. Then use the standard algorithm to calculate the exact difference.

a.

Estimate _____

T	O	t	h
	7 .	8	6
−	3 .	4	0
	.		

b.

Estimate _____

T	O	t	h
1	8 .	9	3
−	6 .	5	1
	.		

c.

Estimate _____

T	O	t	h
2	4 .	0	7
− 1	2 .	0	3
	.		

2. Estimate the difference in your head. Then use the standard algorithm to calculate the exact difference.

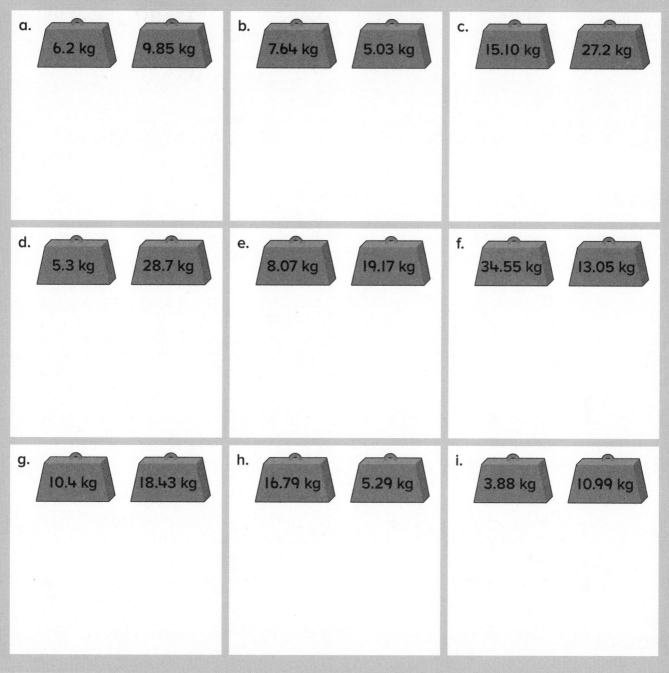

a. 6.2 kg   9.85 kg

b. 7.64 kg   5.03 kg

c. 15.10 kg   27.2 kg

d. 5.3 kg   28.7 kg

e. 8.07 kg   19.17 kg

f. 34.55 kg   13.05 kg

g. 10.4 kg   18.43 kg

h. 16.79 kg   5.29 kg

i. 3.88 kg   10.99 kg

Step Ahead

A student used the standard subtraction algorithm to calculate 16.45 − 3.2. Write the correct answer. Then explain the mistake that was made.

```
    1 6 . 4 5
 -      3 . 2
 ------------
    1 6   1 . 3
```

Computation Practice

★ Use a ruler to draw a straight line to the correct answer. The line will pass through a number and a letter. Write each letter above its matching number at the bottom of the page to discover a fact about the natural world. Some letters appear more than once.

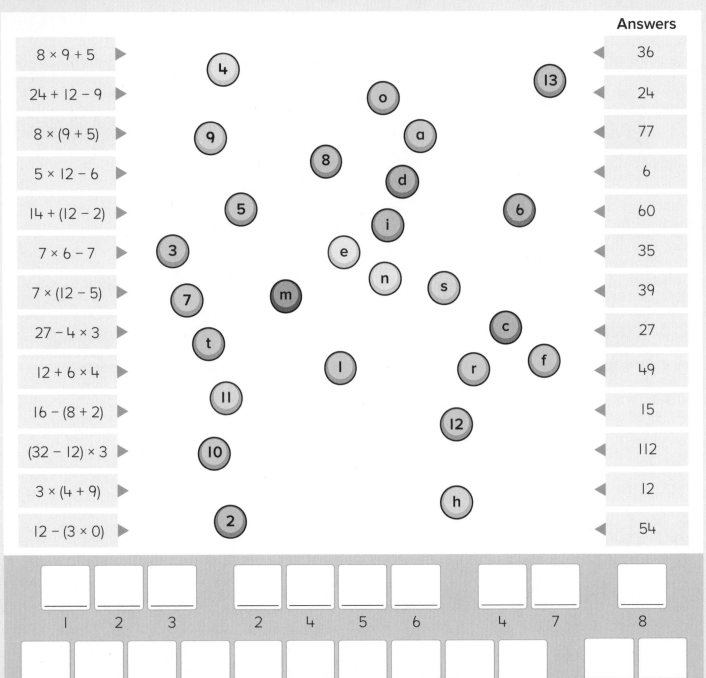

Problem		Answers
8 × 9 + 5 ▶		◀ 36
24 + 12 − 9 ▶		◀ 24
8 × (9 + 5) ▶		◀ 77
5 × 12 − 6 ▶		◀ 6
14 + (12 − 2) ▶		◀ 60
7 × 6 − 7 ▶		◀ 35
7 × (12 − 5) ▶		◀ 39
27 − 4 × 3 ▶		◀ 27
12 + 6 × 4 ▶		◀ 49
16 − (8 + 2) ▶		◀ 15
(32 − 12) × 3 ▶		◀ 112
3 × (4 + 9) ▶		◀ 12
12 − (3 × 0) ▶		◀ 54

1 2 3   2 4 5 6   4 7   8

5 2 9 6 4 10 3 5 4 11   9 11

12 8 13 3   4 7   2 8 9 5

© ORIGO Education

Ongoing Practice

1. Each prism is made with centimeter cubes. Calculate the volume. Show your thinking.

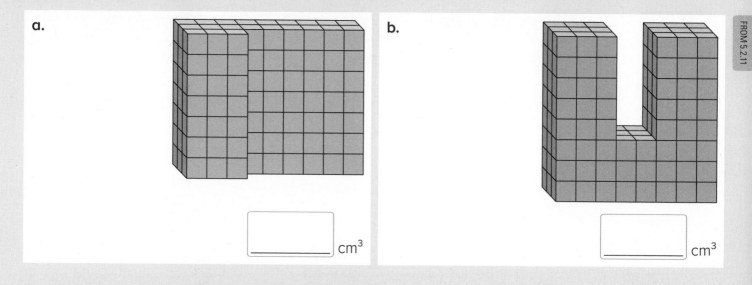

a.

_____ cm³

b.

_____ cm³

2. Calculate the total mass of each pair of packages.

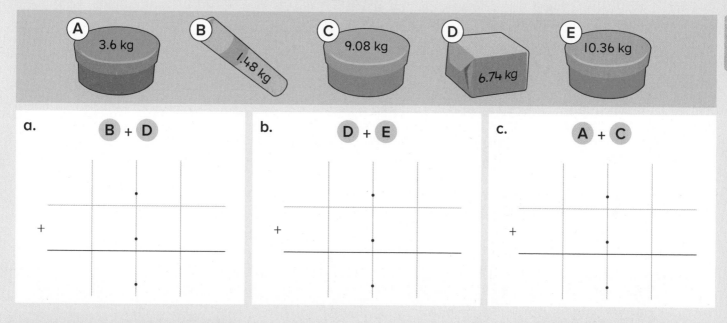

A 3.6 kg   B 1.48 kg   C 9.08 kg   D 6.74 kg   E 10.36 kg

a.   B + D

+

b.   D + E

+

c.   A + C

+

Preparing for Module 6

Split each mixed number into whole numbers and fractions before adding. Then write the total. Show your thinking.

a.
$$4\frac{1}{4} + 3\frac{2}{4} = \boxed{}$$

b.
$$3\frac{5}{6} + 2\frac{2}{6} = \boxed{}$$

c.
$$5\frac{6}{8} + 3\frac{5}{8} = \boxed{}$$

Step In

What do you know about tides? Do tides occur at the same time each day? Look at this table.

Tide Chart				
Day	1st high	2nd high	1st low	2nd low
Monday	9.2 ft	8.4 ft	1.8 ft	0.9 ft
Wednesday	9.3 ft	8.1 ft	1.6 ft	0.8 ft

How could you figure out the difference between the first and second high tides on Monday?

The difference is small so I will count on from 8.4.

What is the difference between the first high tide and the first low tide on Wednesday?

Alexis uses the standard subtraction algorithm to calculate the difference.

What steps does she follow?

Why does she cross out the 9 ones and the 3 tenths?

How can you prove that 8 ones and 13 tenths shows the same number as 9 ones and 3 tenths?

Step 1	Step 2	Step 3
O　t	O　t	O　t
9 . 3	8　13	8　13
− 1 . 6	9 . 3	9 . 3
	− 1 . 6	− 1 . 6
		7 . 7

How could you use the standard subtraction algorithm to calculate the difference between the second high tide and the first low tide on Monday?

Step Up

1. Estimate the difference in your head. Then draw jumps on the number line to calculate the exact difference.

a.

$7.2 - 5.7 =$ ⬚

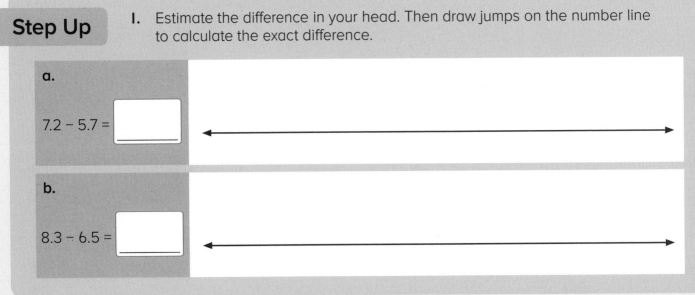

b.

$8.3 - 6.5 =$ ⬚

© ORIGO Education

2. Estimate the difference in your head. Then use the standard algorithm to calculate the exact difference.

a. High tide 7.3 ft	Low tide 1.6 ft

b. High tide 8.2 ft	Low tide 1.9 ft

c. High tide 9.0 ft	Low tide 2.8 ft

d. High tide 8.5 ft	Low tide 3.7 ft

3. Complete each equation. Show your thinking on page 194.

a.
$4.6 - 2.9 =$ _____

b.
$8 - 3.7 =$ _____

c.
$14.2 - 2.5 =$ _____

d.
$9.1 - 6.4 =$ _____

Step Ahead

High tide on Monday was 0.4 ft more than on Tuesday. Thursday's tide was 9.1 ft. This was 0.3 ft more than on Monday, but 0.2 ft less than on Sunday.

Figure out the height of the tide on each day.

Monday _____ ft

Tuesday _____ ft

Thursday _____ ft

Sunday _____ ft

Working Space

Step In

Felix jumped 4.85 meters in the long jump event at school.
Zoe jumped 0.97 meters less than Felix. Anoki jumped 0.29 meters less than Felix.

How could you figure out the length of Zoe's jump?

I would count back and adjust my answer like this.

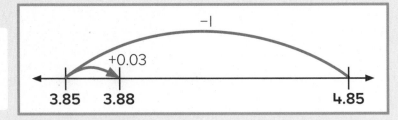

Draw jumps on this number line to show how you could figure out the length of Anoki's jump.

These three written methods were used to figure out the length of Anoki's jump.
What are the steps for each method? Complete the calculations.

4.85 − 0.09 = 4.76

4.76 − 0.20 = _____

Difference is _____

4.85 − 0.29

4 − 0 = 4

$\frac{85}{100} - \frac{\boxed{}}{100} = \frac{\boxed{}}{100}$

Difference is _____

	4	.	8	5
−	0	.	2	9

Which method do you prefer? Why?

Step Up

1. Estimate the difference in your head. Then draw jumps on the number line to calculate the exact difference.

a.

7.65 − 3.26 = [ ]

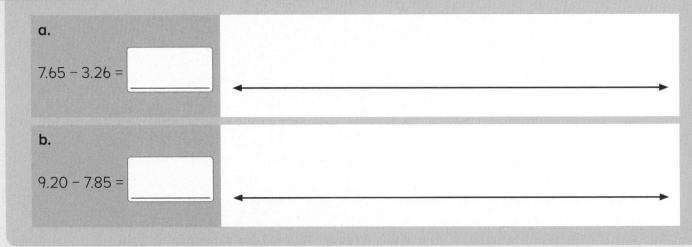

b.

9.20 − 7.85 = [ ]

2. Estimate the difference in your head. Then calculate the exact difference. Show your thinking.

a.

8.46 − 3.18 = _____

b.

9.35 − 5.72 = _____

c.

15.82 − 12.09 = _____

d.

18 − 10.85 = _____

e.

10.72 − 4.27 = _____

f.

21.58 − 17.53 = _____

3. Solve each problem. Show your thinking.

a. A thin rope is 5.78 meters shorter than a thick rope that is 10 meters long. How long is the thin rope?

_____ m

b. Emilia has saved $9.48. Amos has saved $5.72. How much more money has Emilia saved than Amos?

$_____

Step Ahead

Imagine you have this money and you buy both items. How much money will you have left?

$_____

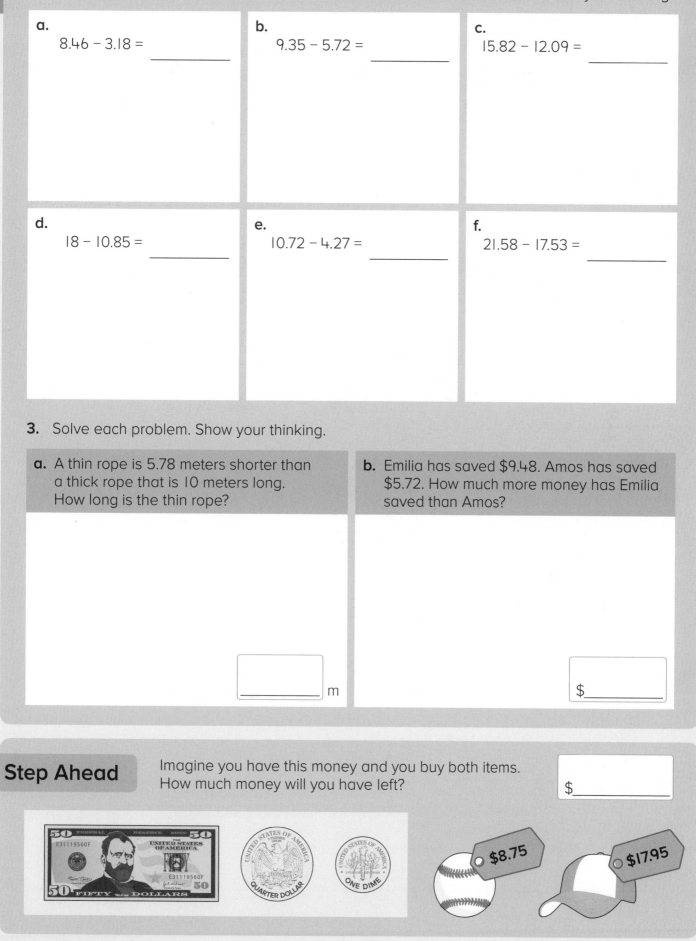

$8.75

$17.95

Think and Solve

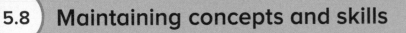

This ⬠ means double the first number and subtract the second number.

$$6 ⬠ 1 = 11$$

Look at these and figure out what ◿ is doing.

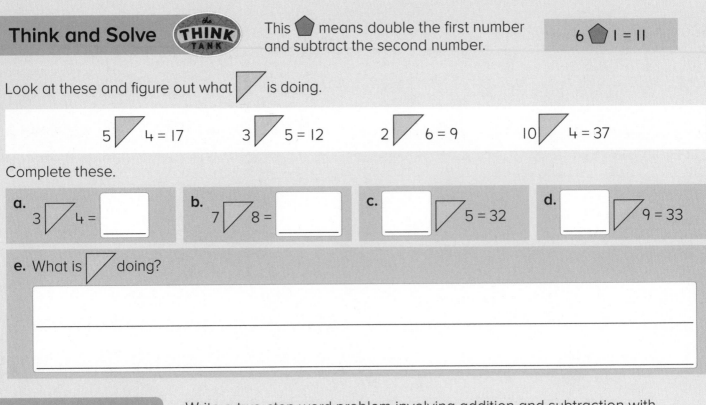

$$5 ◿ 4 = 17 \qquad 3 ◿ 5 = 12 \qquad 2 ◿ 6 = 9 \qquad 10 ◿ 4 = 37$$

Complete these.

a. $3 ◿ 4 = \boxed{}$

b. $7 ◿ 8 = \boxed{}$

c. $\boxed{} ◿ 5 = 32$

d. $\boxed{} ◿ 9 = 33$

e. What is ◿ doing?

Words at Work

Write a two-step word problem involving addition and subtraction with hundredths. Then write how you find the solution.

Ongoing Practice

1. Use the standard multiplication algorithm to calculate the product. Then estimate the product to check your answer makes sense.

a.
```
      5   6
  ×   2   7
  _____
```

b.
```
      7   3
  ×   3   5
  _____
```

c.
```
      6   5
  ×   4   1
  _____
```

d.
```
      8   3
  ×   6   4
  _____
```

2. Estimate each perimeter in your head. Use the standard algorithm to calculate the exact perimeter.

a.
3 m   2.85 m   4.45 m

b.
2.15 m   1.75 m   2.25 m   1.8 m

c.
4.32 m   3.45 m   2.81 m

Preparing for Module 6

Write each answer. Show your thinking.

a.
$86 ÷ 7 =$ _____ remainder _____

b.
$94 ÷ 8 =$ _____ remainder _____

Step In   This table shows the height of some dinosaurs.

Dinosaur	Height (m)
Argentinosaurus	21.4
Diplodocus	7.3
Spinosaurus	2.4
Ultrasaurus	16.27

About how much taller is Ultrasaurus than Diplodocus?

How would you calculate the exact difference in height?

Dallas uses the standard algorithm for subtraction.

What steps does she follow?

The height of Diplodocus is 7.3 meters. Why did Dallas write 7.30 meters? Did she need to record the zero?

Why did she cross out the 6 ones?

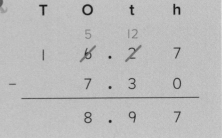

She regrouped I one as I0 tenths.

I6 ones, 2 tenths, and 7 hundredths shows the same number as I5 ones, I2 tenths, and 7 hundredths.

Step Up   I. Use the table at the top of the page to calculate the difference in **height** between these dinosaurs. Show your thinking.

a.   Diplodocus   Spinosaurus

_____ m

b.   Argentinosaurus   Ultrasaurus

_____ m

2. Estimate the difference in **length** between these dinosaurs. Then calculate the exact difference. Show your thinking.

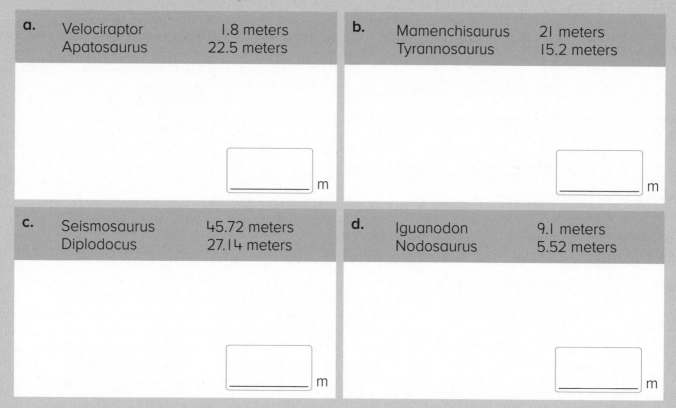

a.
Velociraptor   1.8 meters
Apatosaurus   22.5 meters

_____ m

b.
Mamenchisaurus   21 meters
Tyrannosaurus   15.2 meters

_____ m

c.
Seismosaurus   45.72 meters
Diplodocus   27.14 meters

_____ m

d.
Iguanodon   9.1 meters
Nodosaurus   5.52 meters

_____ m

3. Solve each problem. Show your thinking.

a. $8 \times (15.6 + 2.40)$

b. $0.5 + 48 \div 6 - 5.2$

c. $(21.4 - 3.65) + 5\frac{4}{10}$

Step Ahead

Circle two prices. Calculate the difference in your head, then write the difference. Explain the steps you followed.

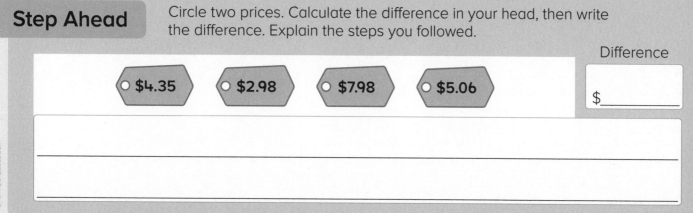

Difference

$ _____

$4.35 $2.98 $7.98 $5.06

Step In

Think about the quadrilaterals you know.

© ORIGO Education

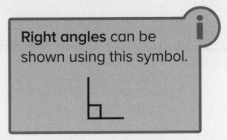

Right angles can be shown using this symbol.

What do you know about the angles of rectangles?

What do you know about the sides of rhombuses?

A square is a type of rectangle and also a type of rhombus. Why?

Parallelograms are quadrilaterals that have two pairs of parallel sides.

What are all the ways of describing each shape below?

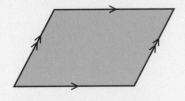
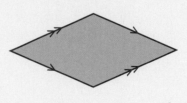
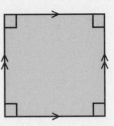

What do you think the arrows mean?

Step Up

Cut out the shapes from the support page.

a. Paste the parallelograms in the space below.

b. Paste the shapes that are not parallelograms in the space below.

c. Look at the parallelograms you pasted on page 184.

Which shapes are also rectangles?

Step Ahead   Draw these shapes.

a.
Another example of a parallelogram

b.
A quadrilateral that is not a parallelogram

Computation Practice

How can you tell which end of a worm is the head?

★ Complete the equations. Then write each letter above its matching quotient at the bottom of the page. Some letters appear more than once.

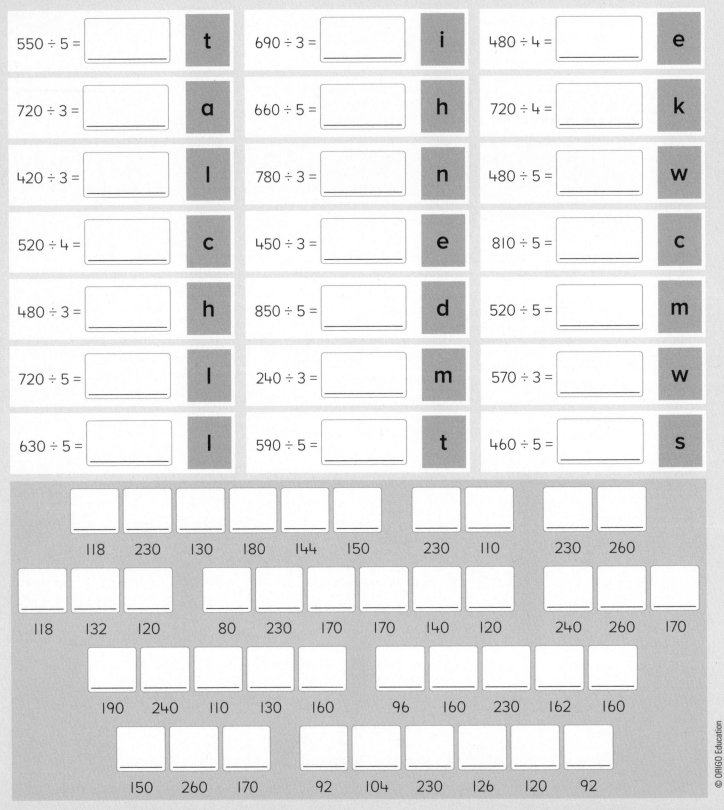

550 ÷ 5 = ___ **t**

720 ÷ 3 = ___ **a**

420 ÷ 3 = ___ **l**

520 ÷ 4 = ___ **c**

480 ÷ 3 = ___ **h**

720 ÷ 5 = ___ **l**

630 ÷ 5 = ___ **l**

690 ÷ 3 = ___ **i**

660 ÷ 5 = ___ **h**

780 ÷ 3 = ___ **n**

450 ÷ 3 = ___ **e**

850 ÷ 5 = ___ **d**

240 ÷ 3 = ___ **m**

590 ÷ 5 = ___ **t**

480 ÷ 4 = ___ **e**

720 ÷ 4 = ___ **k**

480 ÷ 5 = ___ **w**

810 ÷ 5 = ___ **c**

520 ÷ 5 = ___ **m**

570 ÷ 3 = ___ **w**

460 ÷ 5 = ___ **s**

118　230　130　180　144　150　　230　110　　230　260

118　132　120　　80　230　170　170　140　120　　240　260　170

190　240　110　130　160　　96　160　230　162　160

150　260　170　　92　104　230　126　120　92

Ongoing Practice

1. Use the standard multiplication algorithm to calculate the exact product. Then estimate the product to check that your answer makes sense.

a.
```
    2  1  5
  ×    3  4
  _____
```

b.
```
    5  8  5
  ×    3  4
  _____
```

c.
```
    3  6  2
  ×    4  5
  _____
```

FROM 5.2.4

2. Write **P** inside each parallelogram.

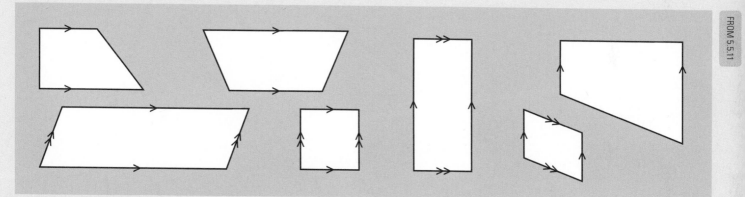

FROM 5.5.11

Preparing for Module 6

Complete these calculations. Show your thinking.

a.
736 ÷ 4 = [ ]

b.
2,343 ÷ 3 = [ ]

c.
1,377 ÷ 9 = [ ]

Step In   **What do you know about the shapes in this tree diagram?**

Draw a shape in each white box to match its label.
Look at the shapes you sorted on pages 184 and 185 to help you.

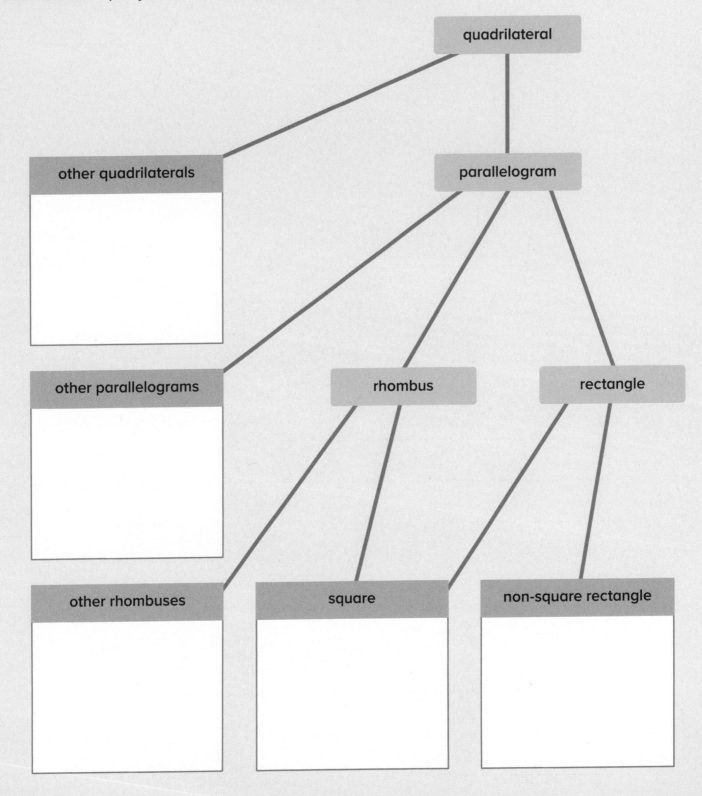

1. Write **P** inside the parallelograms.

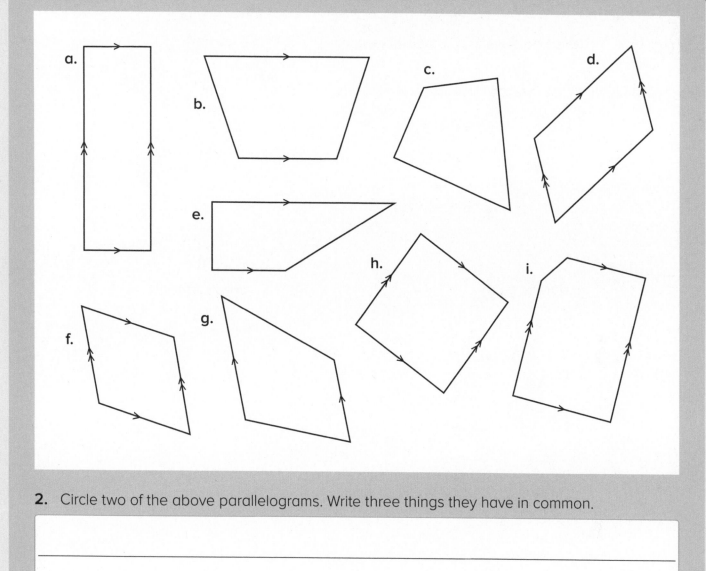

2. Circle two of the above parallelograms. Write three things they have in common.

Step Ahead

Choose one parallelogram and one of the other shapes from Question 1. Write how they are the same, and how they are different.

Step In Measure the sides of these triangles.

Why do you think these are called **equilateral triangles**?

These shapes are called **isosceles triangles**.
How are they all the same?

These shapes are called **scalene triangles**.
How are these different from the other triangles?

Step Up 1. For each triangle below, use the same color to mark the sides that are the same in length. One has been done for you.

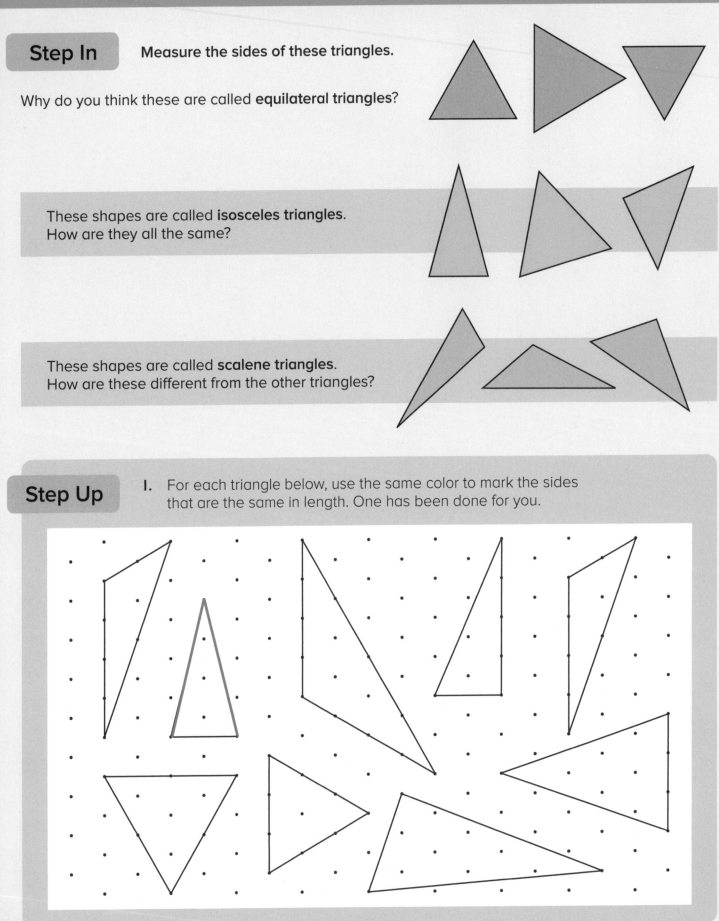

2. Draw and label three equilateral triangles, three isosceles triangles, and three scalene triangles. Make each triangle different.

Step Ahead

a. Use a centimeter ruler to draw two angle arms that are each 8 cm long. Draw a third line to create a triangle.

b. What type of triangle did you make? _____

Think and Solve THINK TANK

Switch the positions of two numbers in the grid so the numbers match the clues. Write all the numbers in the empty grid to show the solution.

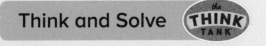

Clues

- All numbers in a row have a common factor greater than one.

- All numbers in a column have a common factor greater than one.

56	35	30
24	21	18
16	20	12

Words at Work

Read the clues. Choose matching words from the list and write them on the grid. Some words are not used.

Clues Across

2. A parallelogram is a quadrilateral that has two pairs of __ sides.

5. A triangle with only __ sides the same length is an isosceles triangle.

6. A triangle with no sides the same length is a __ triangle.

Clues Down

1. The sides of a rhombus are all the same __.

3. A __ is a type of parallelogram.

4. A __ is a type of rhombus and a type of rectangle.

5. A triangle with __ sides the same length is an equilateral triangle.

length
width
triangle
two
scalene
rectangle
parallel
square
rhombus
three
right

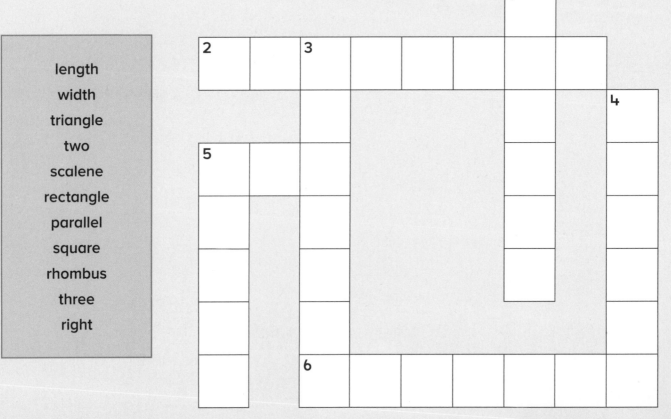

© ORIGO Education

Ongoing Practice

1. Use the standard multiplication algorithm to calculate the exact product. Then estimate the product to check that your answer makes sense.

a.

```
      4  8  1
×     3  4  6
_____
```

b.

```
      4  5  9
×     2  3  8
_____
```

c.

```
   5  3  0  5
×        2  6  7
_____
```

2. Draw and label one equilateral triangle, one isosceles triangle, and one scalene triangle. Mark the sides to show equal lengths.

Preparing for Module 6

Complete the equations to calculate each of these.

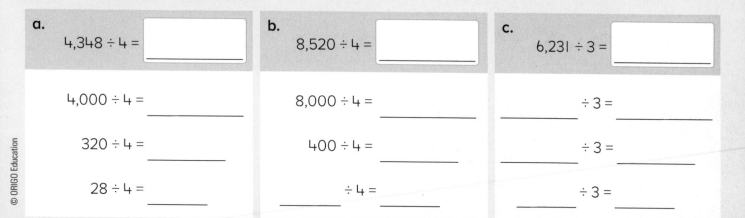

a.

$4,348 \div 4 =$ _____

$4,000 \div 4 =$ _____

$320 \div 4 =$ _____

$28 \div 4 =$ _____

b.

$8,520 \div 4 =$ _____

$8,000 \div 4 =$ _____

$400 \div 4 =$ _____

$\div 4 =$ _____

c.

$6,231 \div 3 =$ _____

$\div 3 =$ _____

$\div 3 =$ _____

$\div 3 =$ _____

Step In Look at these two fractions.

How would you figure out which is greater?

> I know that $\frac{15}{6}$ is greater than 2. The other fraction is less than 2.

> $\frac{1}{6}$ is greater than $\frac{1}{8}$. There are 15 counts of $\frac{1}{6}$, and 15 counts of $\frac{1}{8}$. So, $\frac{15}{6}$ is greater than $\frac{15}{8}$.

What happens if you add the two fractions?

Do you think the total will be closer to 2, 3, or 4? How did you decide?

Circle the pair of fractions that has a total closest to 2.

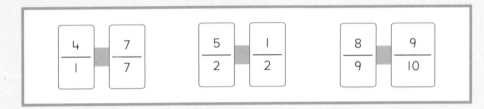

How did you decide which pair of fractions to circle?

Step Up

1. Compare the fractions in each pair. Then write **<**, **>**, or **=** to make a true statement. Explain how you made the comparison.

a. $\frac{5}{8}$ ◯ $\frac{4}{10}$ _____

b. $\frac{3}{3}$ ◯ $\frac{5}{5}$ _____

c. $\frac{5}{6}$ ◯ $\frac{8}{9}$ _____

2. Estimate the sum of each pair of fractions. Then circle the total that is closest.

a.
$\dfrac{3}{2}$ $\dfrac{9}{10}$

2    $2\dfrac{1}{2}$ 3 $3\dfrac{1}{2}$

b.
$\dfrac{2}{5}$ $\dfrac{3}{7}$

1    $1\dfrac{1}{2}$ 2 $2\dfrac{1}{2}$

c.
$\dfrac{5}{6}$ $\dfrac{2}{3}$

$\dfrac{1}{2}$ 1 $1\dfrac{1}{2}$ 2

d.
$\dfrac{7}{4}$ $\dfrac{2}{8}$

1    $1\dfrac{1}{2}$ 2 $2\dfrac{1}{2}$

e.
$\dfrac{1}{10}$ $\dfrac{1}{2}$

$\dfrac{1}{2}$ 1 $1\dfrac{1}{2}$ 2

f.
$\dfrac{4}{7}$ $\dfrac{9}{9}$

$\dfrac{1}{2}$ 1 $1\dfrac{1}{2}$ 2

3. Use estimates to solve each problem. You do not have to calculate the exact answer.

a. Daniel is baking for a fundraiser. He needs $\dfrac{1}{2}$ of a bag of flour to make pancakes, $\dfrac{1}{3}$ of a bag of flour to make muffins, and another $\dfrac{3}{4}$ of a bag of flour to make some cakes.

How many bags of flour should he buy?

____ bags

b. Beatrice runs $\dfrac{3}{4}$ of a mile on Monday, Tuesday, and Wednesday. She then runs $\dfrac{1}{2}$ of a mile on Friday.

About how many miles did she run?

____ miles

Step Ahead   Gabriel lays three of these straws end-to-end on the floor. The total length of the straws is about $5\dfrac{1}{2}$ inches. Color the three straws that he chose.

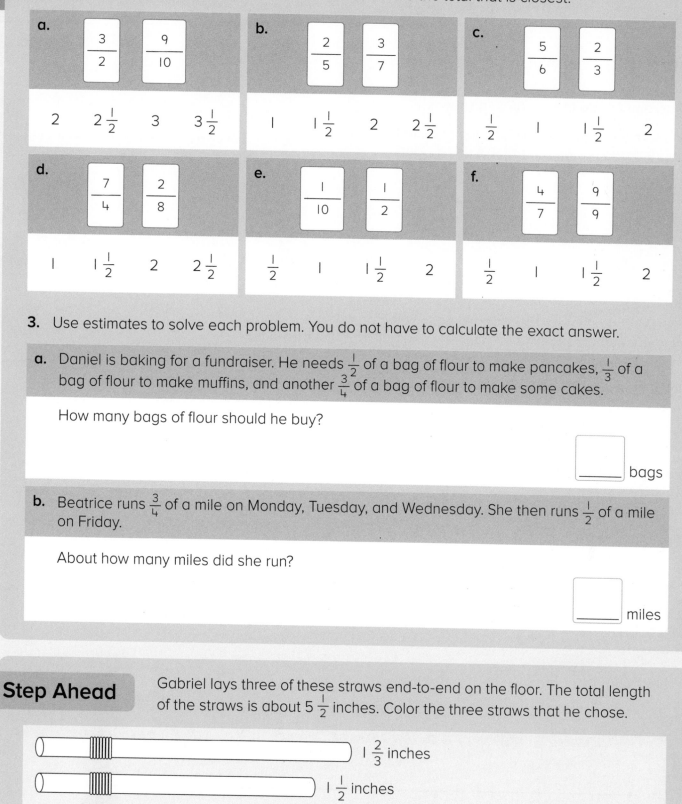

$1\dfrac{2}{3}$ inches

$1\dfrac{1}{2}$ inches

$2\dfrac{1}{10}$ inches

$1\dfrac{3}{4}$ inches

$1\dfrac{4}{5}$ inches

Step In   Each of these large squares shows one whole.

Divide and shade the squares to show $\frac{4}{3}$.

Complete this equation to show the amount that is shaded and the amount that is not shaded.

$$\frac{4}{3} + \boxed{} = \boxed{}$$

Can you think of another way to make $\frac{6}{3}$ by shading the two squares?

When you add common fractions with the same denominator, what do you notice about the denominator? What do you notice about the numerator?

Ashley knows a different way to make 2. She shows her thinking on a number line.

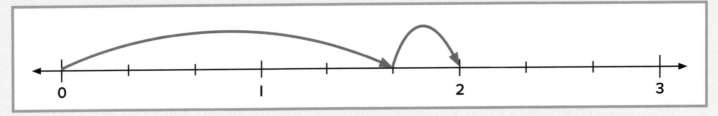

What common fractions does she add? How do you know?

What mixed number did she start with?

Step Up   1. Write fractions to complete true equations. The fractions in each equation should have the same denominators. You can use the number line to help.

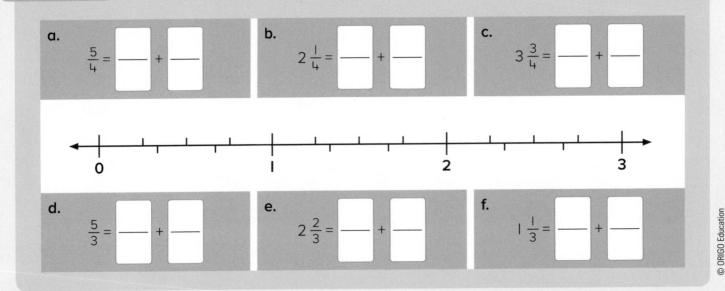

a. $\frac{5}{4} = \boxed{} + \boxed{}$

b. $2\frac{1}{4} = \boxed{} + \boxed{}$

c. $3\frac{3}{4} = \boxed{} + \boxed{}$

d. $\frac{5}{3} = \boxed{} + \boxed{}$

e. $2\frac{2}{3} = \boxed{} + \boxed{}$

f. $1\frac{1}{3} = \boxed{} + \boxed{}$

2. Write the total amount of the ingredients as a common fraction or mixed number. Show your thinking.

Corn Muffins

$\frac{1}{4}$ cup oil

1 $\frac{1}{4}$ cups cornmeal

$\frac{1}{4}$ cup canned corn

$\frac{3}{4}$ cup flour

1 cup milk

1 egg

a. oil, flour, and canned corn

☐ cups

b. cornmeal, milk, and oil

☐ cups

Apple Oatmeal

$\frac{1}{3}$ cup apple juice

$\frac{2}{3}$ cup water

$\frac{2}{3}$ cup oats

cinnamon to taste

c. apple juice, water, and oats

☐ cups

Apple Muffins

1 $\frac{1}{4}$ cups finely chopped apples

$\frac{1}{4}$ cup walnuts

2 $\frac{1}{4}$ cups flour

$\frac{1}{4}$ cup milk

1 egg

d. apples, walnuts, and milk

☐ cups

e. apples and flour

☐ cups

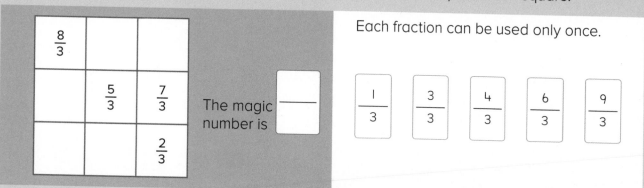

Step Ahead   In a magic square, the numbers in each row, column, and diagonal have the same total, which is called the magic number.

This is a fraction magic square. The fractions in each square have the same denominators. Figure out and write the magic number. Then write fractions to complete each square.

Each fraction can be used only once.

The magic number is ☐

$\frac{8}{3}$		
	$\frac{5}{3}$	$\frac{7}{3}$
		$\frac{2}{3}$

$\frac{1}{3}$ $\frac{3}{3}$ $\frac{4}{3}$ $\frac{6}{3}$ $\frac{9}{3}$

Computation Practice

Two of my three sides are equal in length and two of my angles are equal. What shape am I?

⭐ Complete the equations. Then write each letter above its matching product at the bottom of the page.

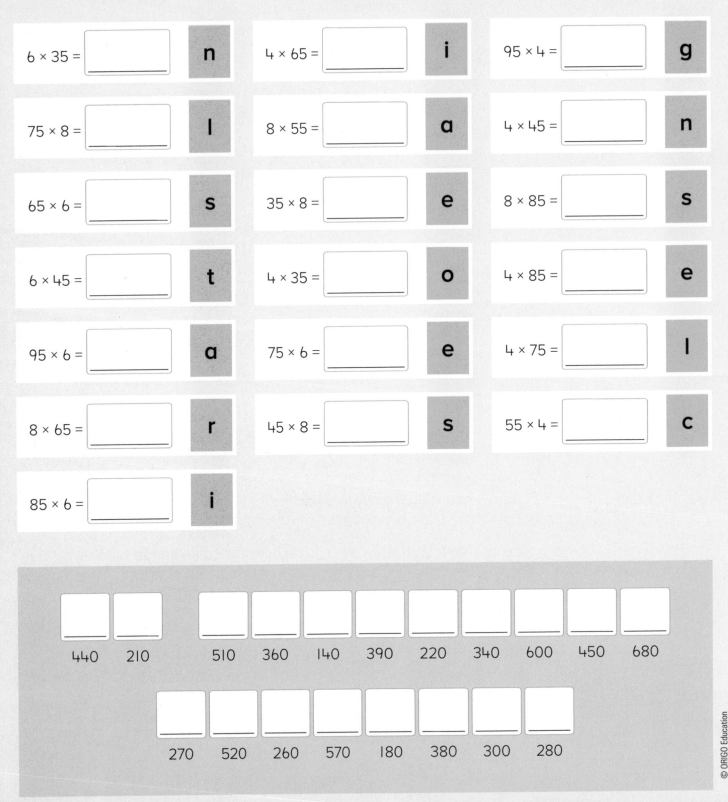

$6 \times 35 =$ ___ **n**

$4 \times 65 =$ ___ **i**

$95 \times 4 =$ ___ **g**

$75 \times 8 =$ ___ **l**

$8 \times 55 =$ ___ **a**

$4 \times 45 =$ ___ **n**

$65 \times 6 =$ ___ **s**

$35 \times 8 =$ ___ **e**

$8 \times 85 =$ ___ **s**

$6 \times 45 =$ ___ **t**

$4 \times 35 =$ ___ **o**

$4 \times 85 =$ ___ **e**

$95 \times 6 =$ ___ **a**

$75 \times 6 =$ ___ **e**

$4 \times 75 =$ ___ **l**

$8 \times 65 =$ ___ **r**

$45 \times 8 =$ ___ **s**

$55 \times 4 =$ ___ **c**

$85 \times 6 =$ ___ **i**

440   210   510   360   140   390   220   340   600   450   680

270   520   260   570   180   380   300   280

© ORIGO Education

Ongoing Practice

I. Circle the part that you would do first in each of these expressions.

a.

$$32 + 4 + 2$$

b.

$$32 \times 4 + 2$$

c.

$$32 \div 4 - 2$$

d.

$$32 + 4 \times 2$$

e.

$$16 \div 8 \times 2$$

f.

$$16 \div 8 + 2$$

g.

$$16 - 8 \times 2$$

h.

$$16 + 8 \div 2$$

2. Write fractions to complete true equations. The fractions in each equation should have the **same denominator**. Use the number line to help.

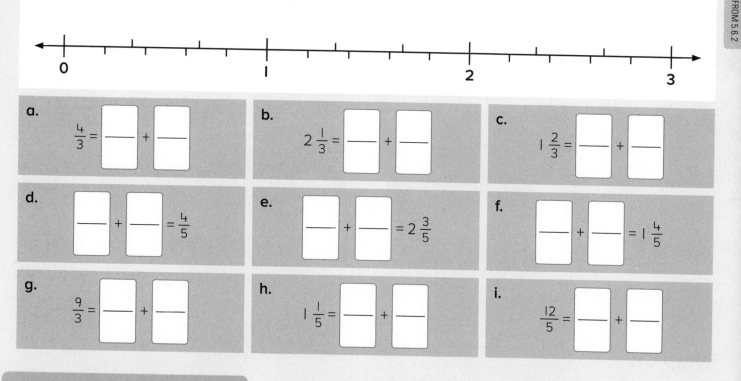

a. $\dfrac{4}{3} = \boxed{} + \boxed{}$

b. $2\dfrac{1}{3} = \boxed{} + \boxed{}$

c. $1\dfrac{2}{3} = \boxed{} + \boxed{}$

d. $\boxed{} + \boxed{} = \dfrac{4}{5}$

e. $\boxed{} + \boxed{} = 2\dfrac{3}{5}$

f. $\boxed{} + \boxed{} = 1\dfrac{4}{5}$

g. $\dfrac{9}{3} = \boxed{} + \boxed{}$

h. $1\dfrac{1}{5} = \boxed{} + \boxed{}$

i. $\dfrac{12}{5} = \boxed{} + \boxed{}$

Preparing for Module 7

Use what you know about subtracting fractions to calculate the difference between each pair of numbers.

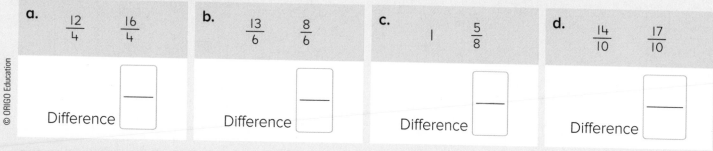

a. $\dfrac{12}{4}$ $\dfrac{16}{4}$

Difference $\boxed{}$

b. $\dfrac{13}{6}$ $\dfrac{8}{6}$

Difference $\boxed{}$

c. 1 $\dfrac{5}{8}$

Difference $\boxed{}$

d. $\dfrac{14}{10}$ $\dfrac{17}{10}$

Difference $\boxed{}$

Step In   These pizzas were left over after a party.

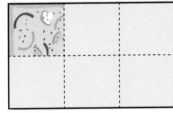
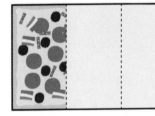
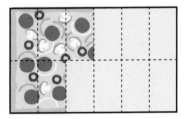

Very Veggie   Mostly Meat   Super Supreme

Choose two types of pizza to take home. What are the possible combinations you could choose?

How much pizza is there in each of these combinations?

$$\frac{1}{3} + \frac{1}{6} = \underline{\qquad}$$

$$\frac{5}{12} + \frac{1}{6} = \underline{\qquad}$$

$$\frac{1}{3} + \frac{5}{12} = \underline{\qquad}$$

What do you notice about the relationship between the denominators in each pair?

Use this diagram to help calculate $\frac{1}{3} + \frac{5}{12}$.

Complete the equation to calculate the total.

$$\underline{\qquad} + \frac{5}{12} = \underline{\qquad}$$

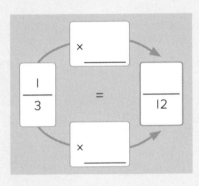

What other totals for the leftover pizza can you calculate?

Step Up   I.   Write the fractions so the denominators are the same. Use the diagram to help. Then write the total.

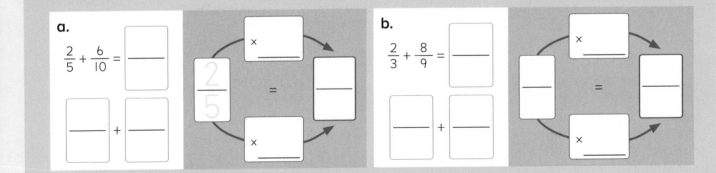

a.
$$\frac{2}{5} + \frac{6}{10} = \underline{\qquad}$$

$$\underline{\qquad} + \underline{\qquad}$$

b.
$$\frac{2}{3} + \frac{8}{9} = \underline{\qquad}$$

$$\underline{\qquad} + \underline{\qquad}$$

2. Write the fractions so the denominators are the same. Then write the total.

a.
$$\frac{1}{3} + \frac{5}{9} = \boxed{} \; \underline{}$$

b.
$$\frac{5}{8} + \frac{3}{16} = \boxed{} \; \underline{}$$

c.
$$\frac{7}{5} + \frac{3}{10} = \boxed{} \; \underline{}$$

d.
$$\frac{1}{4} + \frac{7}{16} = \boxed{} \; \underline{}$$

e.
$$\frac{3}{5} + \frac{11}{15} = \boxed{} \; \underline{}$$

f.
$$\frac{3}{12} + \frac{2}{3} = \boxed{} \; \underline{}$$

3. Color the ⬭ beside the best description of the total. Show your thinking.

a.
$$\frac{1}{2} + \frac{1}{4} + \frac{1}{8}$$

- ⬭ more than I
- ⬭ equal to I
- ⬭ less than I

b.
$$\frac{1}{2} + \frac{1}{3} + \frac{1}{6}$$

- ⬭ more than I
- ⬭ equal to I
- ⬭ less than I

Step Ahead Write numerators to complete each equation.

a.
$$\frac{\boxed{}}{4} + \frac{\boxed{}}{8} = 2$$

b.
$$\frac{\boxed{}}{9} + \frac{\boxed{}}{3} = 1$$

c.
$$\frac{\boxed{}}{9} + \frac{4}{12} = 3$$

d.
$$\frac{\boxed{}}{8} + \frac{2}{2} = 1$$

e.
$$\frac{11}{5} + \frac{\boxed{}}{10} = 3$$

f.
$$\frac{\boxed{}}{6} + \frac{4}{3} = 2$$

Step In

Shiro ran $\frac{4}{5}$ of a mile on Saturday and $\frac{2}{3}$ of a mile on Sunday.

What is your estimate for the total distance he ran?

How did you form your estimate?

How would you calculate the exact distance?

What denominator do the two fractions have in common?

Complete the diagram to find equivalent fractions that share a common denominator.

Complete the equation to calculate the total distance he ran.

I will have to change both denominators to find a denominator they each have in common.

Shiro ran $\frac{22}{15}$ of a mile.
That is equivalent to $1\frac{7}{15}$ miles,
which is a little bit less than $1\frac{1}{2}$ miles.

$$\frac{}{15} + \frac{}{15} = \frac{}{15}$$

Step Up

I. Use the diagram to find equivalent fractions that share a common denominator. Rewrite the equation. Then write the totals.

a.

$$\frac{1}{3} + \frac{3}{4} = \frac{}{}$$

$$\frac{}{} + \frac{}{} = \frac{}{}$$

b.

$$\frac{2}{5} + \frac{1}{4} = \frac{}{}$$

$$\frac{}{} + \frac{}{} = \frac{}{}$$

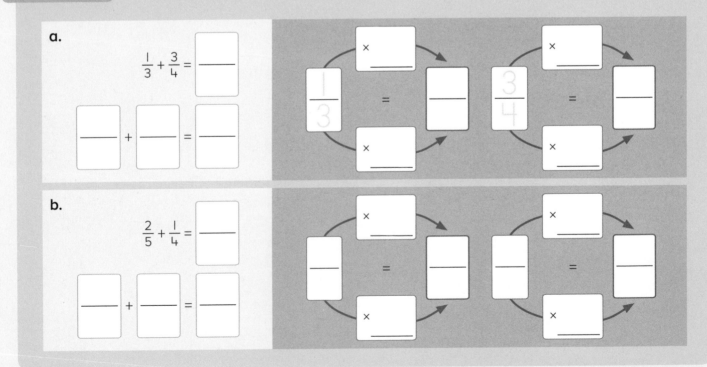

© ORIGO Education

2. Estimate the sum before writing both fractions so the denominators are the same.
Then write the sum.

a.

$\frac{1}{3} + \frac{3}{5} = \underline{\quad}$

b.

$\frac{4}{3} + \frac{3}{8} = \underline{\quad}$

c.

$\frac{3}{5} + \frac{1}{12} = \underline{\quad}$

d.

$\frac{1}{4} + \frac{1}{6} = \underline{\quad}$

e.

$\frac{3}{8} + \frac{1}{3} = \underline{\quad}$

f.

$\frac{4}{9} + \frac{10}{8} = \underline{\quad}$

3. Solve each problem. Show your thinking.

a. Grace, Aston, and Teena live on the same road. Aston's house is between Grace and Teena. Grace lives $\frac{3}{8}$ mile from Aston and he lives $\frac{2}{3}$ mile from Teena. How far is it from Grace's house to Teena's house?

miles

b. Parcel A weighs $\frac{7}{10}$ kg, Parcel B weighs $\frac{4}{5}$ kg, and Parcel C weighs $\frac{1}{4}$ kg. How much less than 2 kg is the total mass of all the parcels?

kg

Step Ahead

Use common fractions with different denominators to complete each equation.

Show your thinking on page 232.

a.

$\underline{\quad} + \underline{\quad} = 1\frac{1}{4}$

b.

$\underline{\quad} + \underline{\quad} = 1\frac{1}{4}$

c.

$\underline{\quad} + \underline{\quad} = 1\frac{1}{4}$

Think and Solve

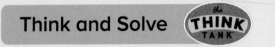

The numbers on the lines are the sums of the numbers in the circles.

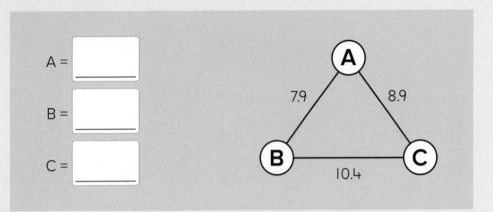

A = ____

B = ____

C = ____

Words at Work

Write about when you or someone you know would need to estimate a total of two or more common fractions outside of school. Write at least three sentences to describe your example.

1. Draw parentheses if they are needed to make an equation true.

a.

$16 - 8 \times 3 = 24$

b.

$4 = 2 \times 16 \div 8$

c.

$7 + 5 \times 2 \div 12 = 2$

d.

$42 + 18 + 15 = 75$

e.

$7 + 4 \times 6 = 66$

f.

$200 = 100 \div 2 \times 4$

g.

$3 + 8 \times 9 - 6 = 33$

h.

$100 \div 5 \times 4 + 15 = 20$

i.

$20 = 15 + 35 - 10 \div 2$

2. Write both fractions so they have the same denominator. Then write the total.

a.

$\frac{1}{4} + \frac{3}{5} = $ ☐

b.

$\frac{2}{3} + \frac{1}{5} = $ ☐

c.

$\frac{3}{4} + \frac{1}{6} = $ ☐

Preparing for Module 7

For each pair of fractions, write equivalent fractions that have the same denominator. Write the missing factors to show your thinking.

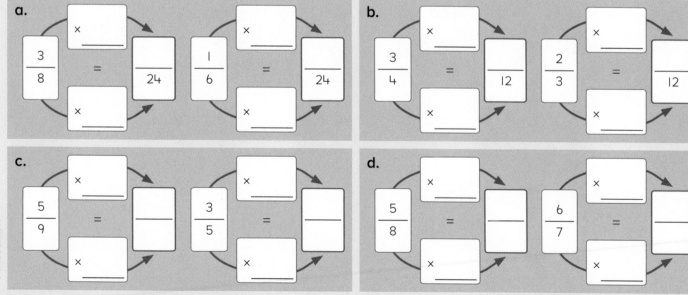

a.

$\frac{3}{8} = \frac{}{24}$ $\frac{1}{6} = \frac{}{24}$

b.

$\frac{3}{4} = \frac{}{12}$ $\frac{2}{3} = \frac{}{12}$

c.

$\frac{5}{9} = $ $\frac{3}{5} = $

d.

$\frac{5}{8} = $ $\frac{6}{7} = $

Step In   Owen bought these two strips of wood for a picture frame.

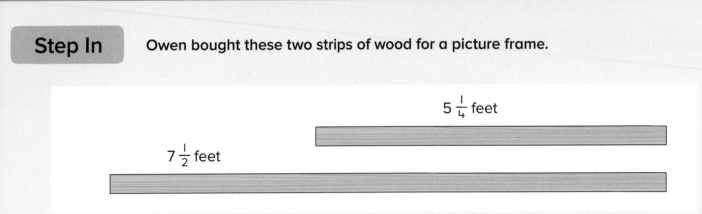

$5\frac{1}{4}$ feet

$7\frac{1}{2}$ feet

How would you calculate the total length?

Look at these students' methods.

Fiona thought it would be easier to add the lengths using improper fractions. This is what she wrote.

$$\frac{15}{2} + \frac{21}{4} = \underline{\quad\quad}$$

Allan added the whole numbers and then the fractions.

$$7 + 5 + \frac{1}{2} + \frac{1}{4} = \boxed{}$$

The denominators have to be the same, so they will need to change one of them.

Before they add, what will they need to do with the fractions?

How do you think they will figure out the total?

Step Up   1.   Calculate each total using improper fractions. Show your thinking.

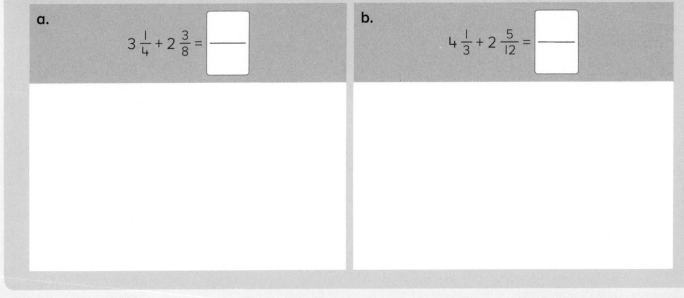

a.

$$3\frac{1}{4} + 2\frac{3}{8} = \underline{\quad\quad}$$

b.

$$4\frac{1}{3} + 2\frac{5}{12} = \underline{\quad\quad}$$

2. Calculate each total using mixed numbers. Show your thinking.

a.

$$1\frac{4}{15} + 4\frac{2}{5} = \boxed{}$$

b.

$$2\frac{3}{8} + 1\frac{5}{24} = \boxed{}$$

3. Use a method of your choice to calculate each total. Show your thinking.

a.

$$1\frac{3}{4} + 3\frac{1}{8} = \boxed{}$$

b.

$$2\frac{1}{3} + 3\frac{6}{12} = \boxed{}$$

Step Ahead

Calculate the perimeter of the mirror frame.
Write the answer as a mixed number. Show your thinking.

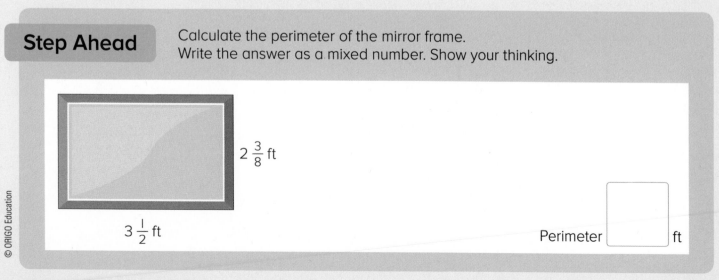

$2\frac{3}{8}$ ft

$3\frac{1}{2}$ ft

Perimeter $\boxed{}$ ft

Common fractions: Adding mixed numbers (unrelated denominators)

Step In

How would you calculate the total amount of juice and water in this apple cake recipe?

Apple Cake

$1\frac{2}{3}$ cups apple juice

$1\frac{1}{4}$ cups water

$1\frac{1}{3}$ cups oats

$1\frac{1}{2}$ cups flour

Hugo changed the amounts to improper fractions to add.	Charlotte used mixed numbers.
$\frac{5}{3} + \frac{5}{4} = \boxed{}$	$1\frac{2}{3} + 1\frac{1}{4} = \boxed{}$

What will Hugo and Charlotte need to do before they can add?

How should Hugo rewrite the fractions to add?
What steps will he follow to calculate the total?

How should Charlotte rewrite the fractions to add?
What steps could Charlotte follow to add the mixed numbers?
What different ways could Charlotte use calculate the total?

> How would you check that the total in Hugo's method is equivalent to the total in Charlotte's method?

Step Up

1. Estimate then calculate each total using improper fractions. Show your thinking.

a.

$$1\frac{1}{4} + 2\frac{1}{3} = \boxed{}$$

b.

$$2\frac{1}{3} + 3\frac{2}{5} = \boxed{}$$

2. Calculate each total using mixed numbers. Show your thinking.

a.

$$2\frac{3}{5} + 3\frac{1}{4} = \boxed{}$$

b.

$$3\frac{3}{4} + 2\frac{1}{6} = \boxed{}$$

3. Use a method of your choice to calculate each total. Show your thinking.

a.

$$2\frac{2}{3} + 1\frac{1}{5} = \boxed{}$$

b.

$$1\frac{2}{10} + 4\frac{3}{4} = \boxed{}$$

Step Ahead

Calculate the total number of hours that were worked. Then write the answer as a mixed number.

Cathy's Timesheet

Monday	$1\frac{1}{4}$ hr
Tuesday	$3\frac{1}{2}$ hr
Wednesday	2 hr
Thursday	0 hr
Friday	$2\frac{1}{3}$ hr

Working Space

$\boxed{}$ hr

Computation Practice

It start raining, and three tall men only had one umbrella between them. None of them got wet. How could that be?

★ Complete the equations. Then write each letter above its matching total at the bottom of the page. Some letters appear more than once.

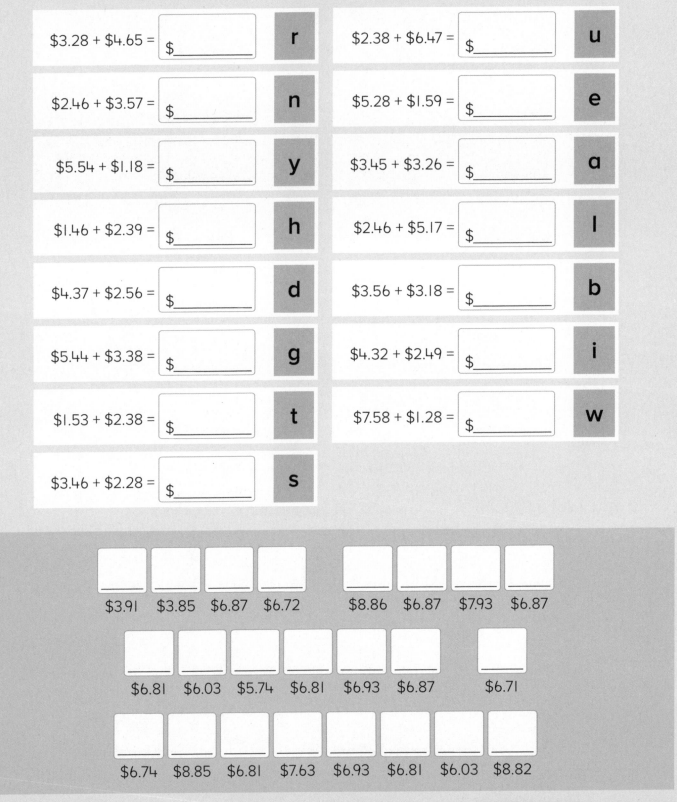

$3.28 + $4.65 = $_____ **r**

$2.38 + $6.47 = $_____ **u**

$2.46 + $3.57 = $_____ **n**

$5.28 + $1.59 = $_____ **e**

$5.54 + $1.18 = $_____ **y**

$3.45 + $3.26 = $_____ **a**

$1.46 + $2.39 = $_____ **h**

$2.46 + $5.17 = $_____ **l**

$4.37 + $2.56 = $_____ **d**

$3.56 + $3.18 = $_____ **b**

$5.44 + $3.38 = $_____ **g**

$4.32 + $2.49 = $_____ **i**

$1.53 + $2.38 = $_____ **t**

$7.58 + $1.28 = $_____ **w**

$3.46 + $2.28 = $_____ **s**

$3.91 $3.85 $6.87 $6.72 $8.86 $6.87 $7.93 $6.87

$6.81 $6.03 $5.74 $6.81 $6.93 $6.87 $6.71

$6.74 $8.85 $6.81 $7.63 $6.93 $6.81 $6.03 $8.82

Ongoing Practice

I. Convert these measurements.

FROM 5.4.7

a.
18 inches = ☐ ft ☐ in

b.
15 inches = ☐ ft ☐ in

c.
23 inches = ☐ ft ☐ in

d.
32 inches = ☐ ft ☐ in

e.
2.5 feet = ☐ in

f.
3.75 feet = ☐ in

2. Estimate, then calculate each total using improper fractions. Show your thinking.

FROM 5.6.5

a.
$$3\frac{2}{6} + 1\frac{1}{3} = \underline{\hspace{1cm}}$$

b.
$$2\frac{3}{6} + 4\frac{1}{4} = \underline{\hspace{1cm}}$$

Preparing for Module 7

Calculate the difference. Show your thinking.

a.
$$4\frac{4}{5} - 1\frac{1}{5} = \boxed{}$$

b.
$$5\frac{8}{12} - 3\frac{7}{12} = \boxed{}$$

c.
$$3\frac{6}{8} - 3\frac{2}{8} = \boxed{}$$

© ORIGO Education

Step In

How would you calculate the total of these two amounts?

$1\frac{2}{3}$ cups $1\frac{3}{4}$ cups

The fractional part of both numbers has to be rewritten before you can add.

What denominator do these two fractions have in common?

Write the missing numerators.

$$1\frac{2}{3} + 1\frac{3}{4} = 1\frac{}{12} + 1\frac{}{12}$$

How would you figure out the total?

What mixed number would you write?

I would add the whole numbers, then the fractions. That is $1 + 1 + \frac{17}{12}$. The total is $3\frac{5}{12}$.

Write an equation to add these two fractions. Try to calculate the total in your head.

$$1\frac{3}{5} + 3\frac{1}{2} = \boxed{} + \boxed{}$$

Step Up

1. For each of these, rewrite the mixed numbers so the fractions have the same denominators. Then show how you add to calculate the total.

a.
$$1\frac{2}{3} + 1\frac{3}{4} = \boxed{}$$

b.
$$2\frac{2}{3} + 1\frac{3}{5} = \boxed{}$$

2. Calculate each total. Show your thinking.

a.

$1 \frac{5}{6} + 2 \frac{3}{4} = \boxed{}$

b.

$2 \frac{5}{6} + 1 \frac{9}{24} = \boxed{}$

3. Estimate then solve each problem. Show your thinking.

a. Awan has two lengths of lumber. One piece is $2 \frac{1}{2}$ yards long and another is $\frac{3}{4}$ yards long. He needs a total length of $4 \frac{1}{3}$ yards. What length of lumber does he need to buy?

$\boxed{}$ yards

b. Jennifer is cooking rice. In one pot she has $1 \frac{1}{2}$ cups of white rice, and in another she has $\frac{3}{4}$ cup of brown rice. In a third pot, Jennifer has $\frac{1}{3}$ cup more of jasmine rice than she has in the pot of white rice. How much rice is being cooked in total?

$\boxed{}$ cups

Step Ahead

Write different mixed numbers to make each equation true. Make the denominators of the fractions different. Show your thinking on page 232.

a. $\boxed{} + \boxed{} + \boxed{} = 6$

b. $\boxed{} + \boxed{} + \boxed{} = 7 \frac{3}{4}$

Step In

Cary bought a cell phone for $369.
He paid for it in three equal monthly payments.

Do you think his monthly payment is more or less than $100?
How did you decide?

How would you calculate the exact amount?

Carmen follows these steps to calculate the exact amount.

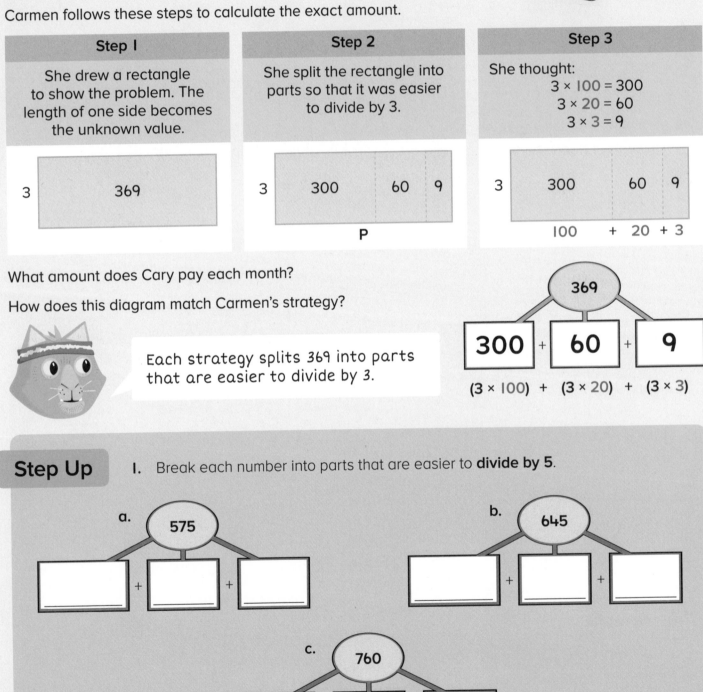

Step 1	Step 2	Step 3
She drew a rectangle to show the problem. The length of one side becomes the unknown value.	She split the rectangle into parts so that it was easier to divide by 3.	She thought: $3 \times 100 = 300$ $3 \times 20 = 60$ $3 \times 3 = 9$

What amount does Cary pay each month?

How does this diagram match Carmen's strategy?

Each strategy splits 369 into parts that are easier to divide by 3.

369
300 + 60 + 9
$(3 \times 100) + (3 \times 20) + (3 \times 3)$

Step Up

1. Break each number into parts that are easier to **divide by 5**.

a. 575

___ + ___ + ___

b. 645

___ + ___ + ___

c. 760

___ + ___ + ___

2. Use a strategy of your choice to complete these equations. Show your thinking.

a.

$693 \div 3 =$ ⬚

b.

$530 \div 5 =$ ⬚

c.

$742 \div 7 =$ ⬚

d.

$612 \div 6 =$ ⬚

e.

$3,906 \div 3 =$ ⬚

f.

$8,420 \div 4 =$ ⬚

Step Ahead   Solve the word problem. Show your thinking on page 232.

Ethan buys a cell phone for $456. He makes equal payments over 6 months for the phone. Jacinta pays $504 for her cell phone. She makes equal payments over 4 months.

a. Who pays more money each month? _____

b. What is the difference between the amounts that they pay each month? $ _____

Think and Solve

THINK TANK

Same shapes are the same number of kilograms.

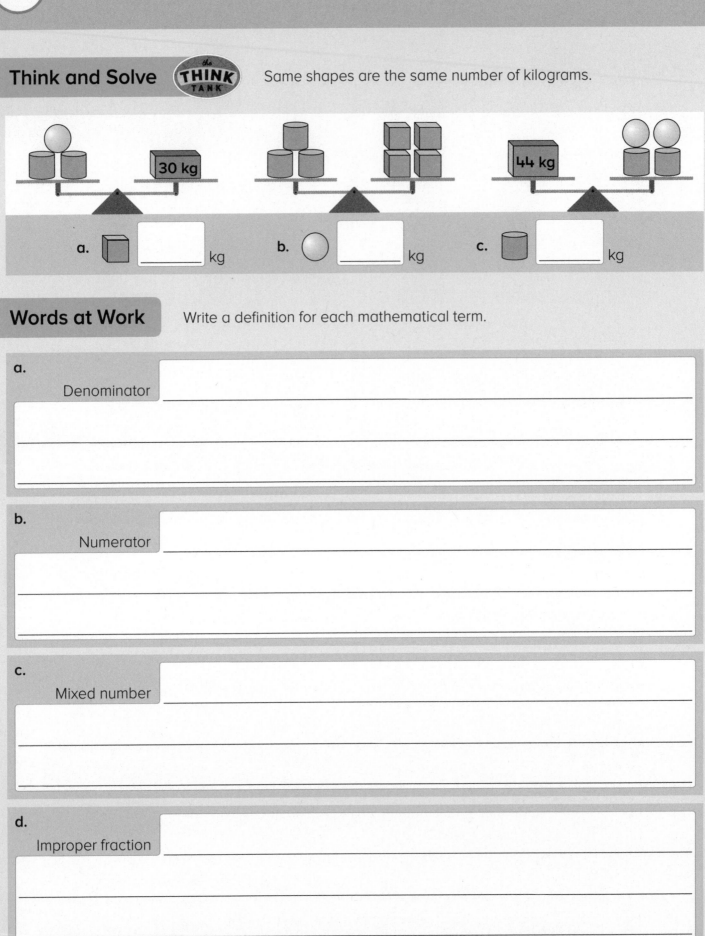

a. ⬜ ☐ kg

b. ◯ ☐ kg

c. ⬭ ☐ kg

Words at Work

Write a definition for each mathematical term.

a. Denominator

b. Numerator

c. Mixed number

d. Improper fraction

Ongoing Practice

1. Convert these measurements.

a.

4 yd = ⬚ ft

b.

8 yd = ⬚ ft

c.

$6\frac{1}{2}$ yd = ⬚ ft

d.

11 yd = ⬚ ft

e.

15 yd = ⬚ ft

f.

$18\frac{1}{2}$ yd = ⬚ ft

g.

⬚ yd = 12 ft

h.

⬚ yd = 9 ft

i.

⬚ yd = 27 ft

j.

⬚ yd = 39 ft

k.

⬚ yd = 21 ft

l.

⬚ yd = 45 ft

2. Write both numbers so the fractions have the same denominator. Then write the total.

a.

$2\frac{1}{3} + 3\frac{2}{4} =$ ⬚

b.

$1\frac{1}{3} + 3\frac{1}{2} =$ ⬚

c.

$4\frac{2}{6} + 2\frac{1}{4} =$ ⬚

Preparing for Module 7

Calculate the difference. Show your thinking.

a.

$4\frac{3}{8} - 1\frac{5}{8} =$ ⬚

b.

⬚ $= 5\frac{1}{4} - 3\frac{3}{4}$

c.

$7\frac{2}{6} - 4\frac{3}{6} =$ ⬚

FROM 5.6.6

Step In It costs $252 to stay at a hotel for three nights.

How would you calculate the cost of staying for one night?

Do you think that it will cost more or less than $100?
How do you know?

To calculate the cost, Emily splits $252 into parts that are
easier to divide by 3.

> I know that 3 × 50 = 150. I don't know
> the number of 3s in 102, so I will
> break down this number some more.

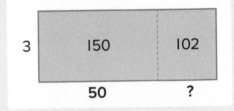

Emily splits $102 into parts that are easier to divide by 3.

How does this diagram help to calculate the cost of staying
at the hotel for one night?

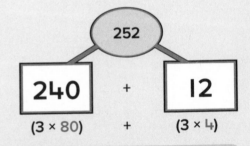

Harvey uses this diagram to calculate the cost.

How does he partition the total amount to make it easier to divide?

Which method do you prefer? Why?

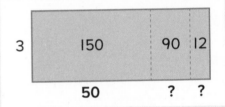

Step Up I. Complete the equation. Partition the rectangle to show your thinking.

708 ÷ 4 = _____

| 4 | 400 | | |

100

2. Split each number into **3 parts** to make it easier to divide. Then complete the equation.

a.

$645 ÷ 5 =$ [____]

645

[____] + [____] + [____]

b.

$1,320 ÷ 4 =$ [____]

1,320

[____] + [____] + [____]

3. Split each number into parts to make it easier to divide. Then complete the equation.

a.

$1,536 ÷ 6 =$ [____]

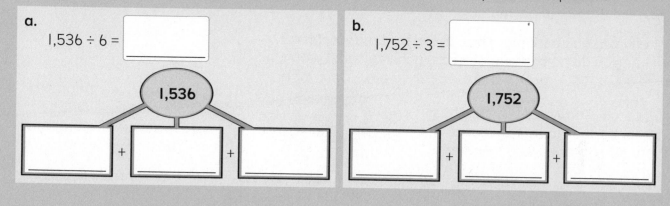

1,536

[____] + [____] + [____]

b.

$1,752 ÷ 3 =$ [____]

1,752

[____] + [____] + [____]

4. Use a strategy of your choice to complete these. Show your thinking on page 232.

a.

$904 ÷ 8 =$ [____]

b.

$1,380 ÷ 5 =$ [____]

c.

$192 ÷ 3 =$ [____]

d.

$1,568 ÷ 7 =$ [____]

Step Ahead

It costs $475 to stay at a hotel for three nights.
Juan decides to stay at the hotel for four nights.

What is the total amount you think he will pay?

$ [____]

Step In

Read each problem.

Michelle buys 250 roses at the markets.

She then puts them into bunches of six to sell. How many whole bunches can she make?

Ringo has 250 kg of compost.

He is going to put the same amount on each of six fruit trees. About how much compost will each tree get?

How are the two problems the same? How are they different?
What is the answer to each problem?

What can you do about the remainder in the roses problem?
What can you do about the remainder in the compost problem?

I can only have whole bunches of roses, so I can only write how many roses are remaining.

I can split up the remaining compost. Each tree will get a whole number of kilograms plus a fraction of a kilogram.

Kayla drew a picture to show her thinking about the remainder in the compost problem.

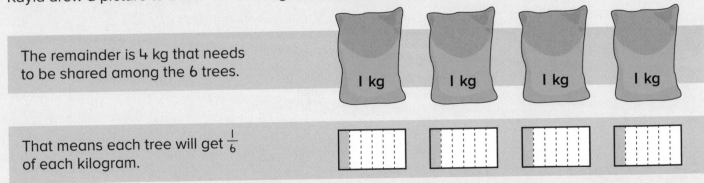

The remainder is 4 kg that needs to be shared among the 6 trees.

1 kg   1 kg   1 kg   1 kg

That means each tree will get $\frac{1}{6}$ of each kilogram.

If each tree gets $\frac{1}{6}$ of the remaining kilograms of compost, what total amount will each tree get?

Step Up

1. Complete each equation, writing each remainder as a whole number. Show your thinking.

a.
$$418 \div 3 = \underline{\hspace{2cm}} \text{ remainder } \underline{\hspace{1cm}}$$

b.
$$2{,}037 \div 5 = \underline{\hspace{2cm}} \text{ remainder } \underline{\hspace{1cm}}$$

2. Solve each problem, and write an answer that makes sense of the remainder. Show your thinking.

a. Fatima has 518 megabytes of storage left on her USB. She wants to download some photos. Each photo uses 3 megabytes of storage space. How many photos can she download?

b. Corey has some garden edging that is 177 inches long and 12 inches wide. If he cuts it into 4 equal pieces, what will be the length of each piece?

c. 1,250 scouts are going on a camping trip. The organizers decide that 4 scouts will sleep in each tent. How many tents do they need to provide for the scouts?

d. A low-pressure faucet lets out 5 gallons of water every hour. How many hours will it take to let out 318 gallons of water?

Step Ahead

1. Write a division equation that has a remainder of 5. Divide a three-digit number by a one-digit number.

$\underline{\hspace{3cm}}$ = $\underline{\hspace{2cm}}$ remainder 5

2. Write an equation that has a mixed number quotient. Divide a three-digit number by a one-digit number.

$\underline{\hspace{3cm}}$ = $\underline{\hspace{2cm}}$

Working Space

Computation Practice

⭐ Use a ruler to draw a straight line to the correct total. The line will pass through a letter. Write each letter above its matching total at the bottom of the page to find a fact about the natural world. Some letters appear more than once.

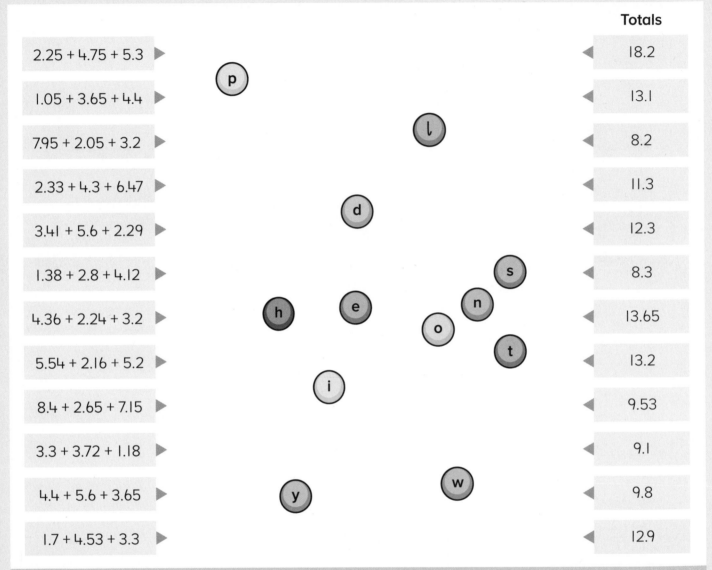

Totals

Expression		Total
2.25 + 4.75 + 5.3	▶	18.2
1.05 + 3.65 + 4.4	▶	13.1
7.95 + 2.05 + 3.2	▶	8.2
2.33 + 4.3 + 6.47	▶	11.3
3.41 + 5.6 + 2.29	▶	12.3
1.38 + 2.8 + 4.12	▶	8.3
4.36 + 2.24 + 3.2	▶	13.65
5.54 + 2.16 + 5.2	▶	13.2
8.4 + 2.65 + 7.15	▶	9.53
3.3 + 3.72 + 1.18	▶	9.1
4.4 + 5.6 + 3.65	▶	9.8
1.7 + 4.53 + 3.3	▶	12.9

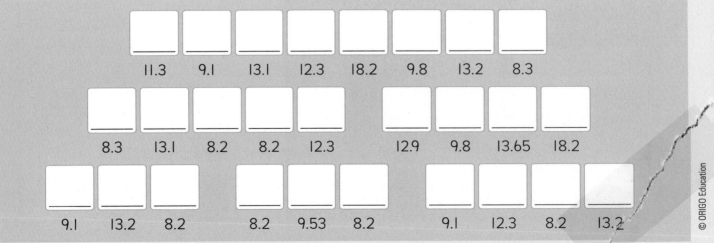

11.3	9.1	13.1	12.3	18.2	9.8	13.2	8.3

8.3	13.1	8.2	8.2	12.3		12.9	9.8	13.65	18.2

9.1	13.2	8.2		8.2	9.53	8.2		9.1	12.3	8.2	13.2

Ongoing Practice

I. Write the missing amount so each balance picture is true.

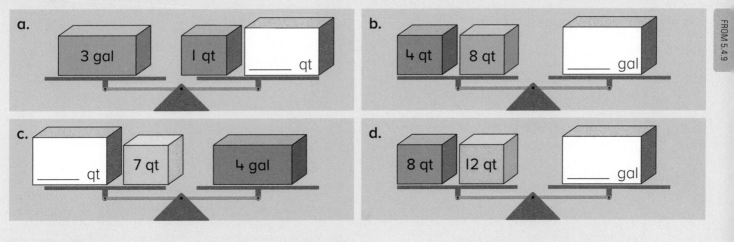

a.
3 gal | I qt | _____ qt

b.
4 qt | 8 qt | _____ gal

c.
_____ qt | 7 qt | 4 gal

d.
8 qt | 12 qt | _____ gal

2. Complete these equations. Show your thinking.

a.
$7{,}524 \div 4 =$ _____

b.
$7{,}449 \div 3 =$ _____

c.
$9{,}615 \div 5 =$ _____

Preparing for Module 7

Use a pattern to help you complete these equations.

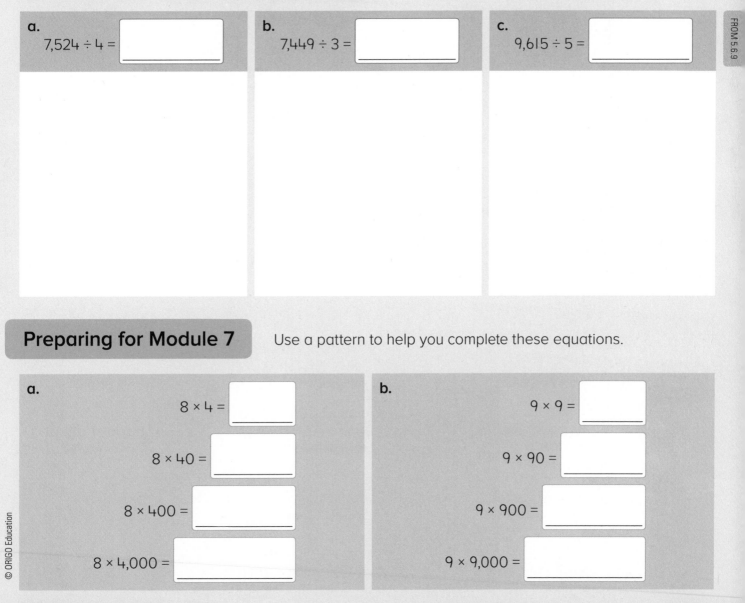

a.

$8 \times 4 =$ _____

$8 \times 40 =$ _____

$8 \times 400 =$ _____

$8 \times 4{,}000 =$ _____

b.

$9 \times 9 =$ _____

$9 \times 90 =$ _____

$9 \times 900 =$ _____

$9 \times 9{,}000 =$ _____

Step In

Some hospitals hold a fundraising event and raise $1,450.
The hospitals decide to share the money raised equally.
There are 10 hospitals.

How could you calculate the amount they should each receive?

I could calculate the amount by finding one-tenth of $1,450.

Some schools hold a fundraising event and raise $3,240.
The schools also share the money raised equally. There are 20 schools.

What amount should they each receive?

Blake uses factors of 20 (10 × 2) to figure out the amount.

$$3{,}240 \div 10 = 324$$

$$324 \div 2 = 162$$

so, $3{,}240 \div 20 = 162$

Kylie splits the amount into parts that are easier to divide by 20.

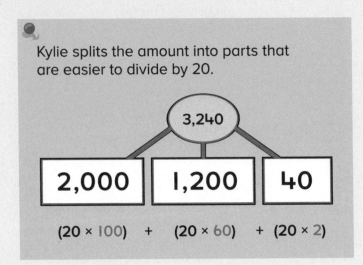

2,000	1,200	40

$$(20 \times 100) \quad + \quad (20 \times 60) \quad + \quad (20 \times 2)$$

What steps do Blake and Kylie follow?

How could you use Blake's strategy to calculate $1{,}280 \div 40$?

How could you use Kylie's strategy to calculate $3{,}850 \div 35$?

Step Up   1.   Complete each equation.

a. $1{,}390 \div 10 = \boxed{139}$

b. $260 \div 10 = \boxed{}$

c. $3{,}400 \div 10 = \boxed{}$

d. $1{,}810 \div 10 = \boxed{}$

e. $690 \div 10 = \boxed{}$

f. $5{,}070 \div 10 = \boxed{}$

g. $6{,}120 \div 10 = \boxed{}$

h. $7{,}090 \div 10 = \boxed{}$

i. $1{,}780 \div 10 = \boxed{}$

2. Complete each equation. Show your thinking.

a.

$850 \div 50 =$ ☐

b.

$940 \div 20 =$ ☐

c.

$2,860 \div 20 =$ ☐

d.

$3,750 \div 50 =$ ☐

e.

$480 \div 15 =$ ☐

f.

$1,250 \div 25 =$ ☐

Step Ahead

A baseball team wins a prize of $7,280. There are 40 players on the roster, but only 20 players played in the tournament. How much will each player receive if the prize is shared equally among everyone on the roster?

$ _____

Step In

Helen buys this car.
She makes equal monthly payments over three years.

$7,380

Do you think her monthly payment is more or less than $200?
How did you decide?

What amount should she pay each month?

This is much harder to figure out. I know it is more than $200 because $36 \times 200 = 7,200$. That gets me close to the amount.

Helen calculates the answer like this.

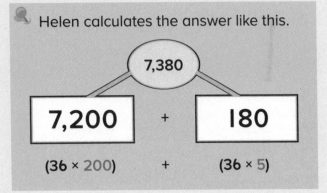

7,380

| 7,200 | + | 180 |

(36 × 200) + (36 × 5)

$36 \times ? = 180$

$36 \times 10 = 360$

so, $36 \times 5 = 180$

How does she partition the amount to make it easier to divide by 36?

What amount does she pay each month?

How could you split 36 into factors to make it easier to divide?

36 can be split into factors $9 \times 2 \times 2$. This could make it easier to divide.

Step Up

1. Complete the equation. Show your thinking.

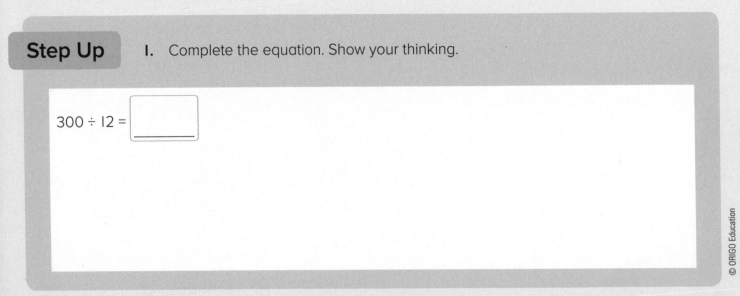

$300 \div 12 = $ ____

2. Complete each equation. Show your thinking.

a.

$315 \div 15 = \underline{}$

b.

$672 \div 16 = \underline{}$

c.

$1{,}092 \div 26 = \underline{}$

d.

$1{,}222 \div 47 = \underline{}$

Step Ahead Solve this problem. Show your thinking.

Manuel wants to buy a car that costs $8,640. He can make equal monthly payments over 36 months or 48 months. How much more will he pay each month if the payments are calculated over 36 months instead of 48 months?

$ \underline{}

Think and Solve

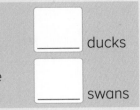

There are ducks, swans, and geese swimming in a pond.

- For every 3 ducks, there are 4 swans.
- For every 2 ducks and swans, there are 3 geese.
- There are 21 geese in the pond.

a. How many ducks are in the pond?

_____ ducks

b. How many swans are in the pond?

_____ swans

Words at Work

You can use the partial-quotients strategy to calculate 3,650 ÷ 50. Write about another method you could use to find the solution.

Ongoing Practice

1. Convert each amount to fluid ounces. Write equations to show your thinking.

a.

6 qt = ☐ fl oz

b.

3.25 qt = ☐ fl oz

2. Complete each equation. Show your thinking.

a.

8,680 ÷ 70 = ☐

b.

7,560 ÷ 30 = ☐

Preparing for Module 7

Write each number in expanded form.

a.

4,987 _____

b.

15,306 _____

c.

22,451 _____

Algorithm

Algorithms are rules used for completing tasks or for solving problems. There are standard algorithms for calculating answers for addition, subtraction, multiplication and division problems. This example shows the division algorithm.

$$
\begin{array}{r}
2\ 0\ 8 \\
4\overline{)8\ 3\ 2} \\
-8 \\
\hline
0\ \ 3\ 2 \\
-3 \\
\hline
2\ 2 \\
0 \\
\end{array}
$$

Area

Area is the amount of surface that a shape covers. This amount is usually described in square units such as square centimeters (cm^2) or square inches (in^2).

Capacity

Customary Units of Capacity		Metric Units of Capacity	
8 fluid ounces (fl oz)	I cup (c)	1,000 milliliters (mL)	I liter (L)
2 cups	I pint (pt)		
2 pints	I quart (qt)		
4 quarts	I gallon (gal)		

Common Fraction

Fractions describe equal parts of a whole. In this common fraction, 2 is the numerator and 3 is the denominator.

$\frac{2}{3}$ is shaded

The denominator shows the total number of equal parts (3). The numerator shows the number of those parts (2).

A **common denominator** is one that two or more fractions have in common.

Equivalent fractions are fractions that cover the same amount of area on a shape or are located on the same point on a number line.

For example: $\frac{1}{2}$ is equivalent to $\frac{2}{4}$.

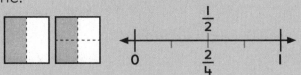

Proper fractions are common fractions that have a numerator that is less than the denominator. For example, $\frac{2}{5}$ is a proper fraction.

Improper fractions are common fractions that have a numerator that is greater than or equal to the denominator. For example, $\frac{7}{5}$ and $\frac{4}{4}$ are improper fractions.

A **mixed number** is an improper fraction that has been changed to show the whole part/s and the fractional part. For example, $\frac{13}{6}$ is equivalent to $2\frac{1}{6}$.

Coordinate plane

A **coordinate plane** is a rectangular grid which has a horizontal axis called the *x*-axis and a vertical axis called the *y*-axis. The **origin** is where the axes meet.

An **ordered pair** is two numbers that describe a specific point on a coordinate plane. These numbers are called coordinates. Marking ordered pairs on a coordinate plane is called graphing or plotting.

Decimal fraction

Decimal fractions are fractions in which the denominator is 10, 100, or 1,000, etc. but are always written using decimal points. For example: $\frac{3}{10}$ can be written as 0.3 and $\frac{28}{100}$ can be written as 0.28.

A **decimal point** indicates which digit is in the ones place. It is positioned immediately to the right of the ones digit. For example, in the numeral 23.85, 3 is in the ones place.

A digit's **decimal place** is its position on the right-hand side of the decimal point. The first decimal place to the right of the decimal point is the tenths place. The next place is called hundredths. For example, in the numeral 23.85, 8 is in the first decimal place so it has a value of 8 tenths.

Expanded form

Expanded form is a method of writing numbers as the sum of the values of each digit. For example: $1.842 = (1 \times 1) + (8 \times \frac{1}{10}) + (4 \times \frac{1}{100}) + (2 \times \frac{1}{1000})$

Exponents

Exponents are often used to represent multi-digit numbers. Using exponents involves repeatedly multiplying a base number. The diagram shows that 10^3 is equivalent to $10 \times 10 \times 10$, so $10^3 = 1,000$.

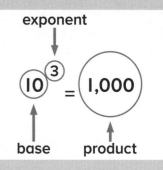

Factor

Factors are whole numbers that evenly divide another whole number. For example, 4 and 5 are both factors of 20 and 20 is a multiple of both 4 and 5.

STUDENT GLOSSARY

Length

Customary Units of Length		Metric Units of Length	
12 inches (in)	1 foot (ft)	10 millimeters (mm)	1 centimeter (cm)
3 feet	1 yard (yd)	100 centimeters	1 meter (m)
1,760 yards	1 mile (mi)	1,000 meters	1 kilometer (km)

Line plot

A **line plot** is used to show data.
On this line plot, each dot represents one student.

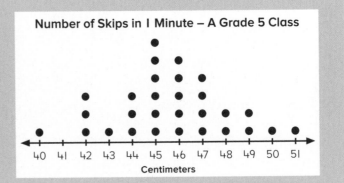

Mass (weight)

Customary Units of Mass		Metric Units of Mass	
16 ounces (oz)	1 pound (lb)	1,000 grams (g)	1 kilogram (kg)

Order of operations

If there is **one** type of operation in a sentence, work left to right.
If there is **more than one** type of operation, work left to right in this **order**:

1. Perform any operation inside parentheses.

2. Multiply or divide pairs of numbers.

3. Add or subtract pairs of numbers.

Parallelogram

A **parallelogram** is a quadrilateral with exactly two pairs of parallel sides.

Perimeter

A **perimeter** is the boundary of a shape and the total length of that boundary. For example, the perimeter of this rectangle is 20 inches.

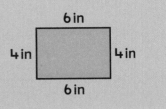

Triangle

A **scalene triangle** has no sides that are equal in length and no angles equal in size.

An **isosceles triangle** has at least two sides of equal length and at least two angles equal in size.

An **equilateral triangle** has three sides of equal length and three angles equal in size.

Volume

Volume is the amount of space that an object occupies. This amount is usually described in cubic units such as cubic centimeters (cm^3) or cubic inches (in^3).

TEACHER INDEX

Academic vocabulary 16, 28, 40, 54, 66, 78, 92, 104, 116, 130, 142, 154, 168, 180, 192, 206, 218, 230, 254, 266, 278, 292, 304, 316, 330, 342, 354, 368, 380, 392, 406, 418, 430, 444, 456, 468

Addition
Common fractions 11, 86, 163, 196–9, 202–7, 261, 287, 324
Decimal fractions 158–61, 163–164, 165–9, 175, 212, 224, 260, 286, 287, 305, 354, 386, 430, 445, 462
Estimating 87, 131, 158, 164–7, 196, 197, 206
Five-digit numbers 93
Four-digit numbers 93
Mixed numbers 17, 175, 208–11, 213–15, 219, 324
Standard algorithm 93, 164–7, 175
Three-digit numbers 22, 87, 98, 131, 136, 381
Two-digit numbers 381
Word problems 99, 149, 197, 205, 215

Algebraic thinking
Equivalence 304, 380, 468
Order of operations 26, 27, 30–3, 35–9, 41, 54, 174, 201, 207, 289, 335, 389, 391, 400, 425
Patterns
  Addition 363
  Coordinate plane 402–6, 408–11, 413, 469
  Division 384, 385, 396, 401
  Multiplication 225, 274, 275, 359, 363, 369, 396–9, 401
  Ordered pairs 402–11, 413, 469
  Relationships between patterns 398, 399, 418
  Shape 396, 399
Problem solving
  Think Tank problems 16, 28, 40, 54, 66, 78, 92, 104, 116, 130, 142, 154, 168, 180, 192, 206, 218, 230, 254, 266, 278, 292, 304, 316, 330, 342, 354, 368, 380, 392, 406, 418, 430, 444, 456, 468
Word problems
  Addition 99, 149, 197, 205, 215, 254
  Area 380, 393, 426, 427
  Capacity 111, 150, 151, 381
  Common fractions 105, 134, 135, 197, 205, 215, 251, 254, 279, 289, 291, 293, 296, 297, 299, 304, 309, 314, 315, 321, 327–9, 332, 333, 335, 338, 339, 342, 419, 431
  Decimal fractions 104, 116, 179, 180, 367, 377, 379, 383, 390, 391, 469

Algebraic thinking (continued)
  Division 217, 221–3, 226, 227, 22 321, 328, 329, 332, 333, 335, 338, 339, 342, 349, 355, 377, 379, 383, 390, 391, 419, 431, 447, 454, 455, 469
  Length 139–41, 355
  Mass 117, 150, 151, 345, 393
  Mixed numbers 134, 135, 215, 254, 264, 265, 309, 314–6
  Money 78, 342
  Multiplication 23, 58, 59, 61, 149, 155, 279, 289, 291, 293, 295–7, 299, 304, 309, 314–6, 328, 329, 335, 338, 339, 342, 367, 369, 390, 391, 469
  Perimeter 393, 422, 423, 425
  Subtraction 179, 251, 254, 264, 265
  Two-step 23, 32, 33, 36–41, 61, 76, 77, 99, 150, 151, 180, 205, 215, 217, 221, 229, 251, 254, 296, 297, 299, 304, 316, 355, 418, 423, 425, 427, 429, 430, 455
  Volume 76, 77, 428–31
  Using symbol for unknown 296, 330, 332, 391, 469

Comparing
Common fractions 79, 105, 127, 134, 135, 312, 313, 317
Decimal fractions 102, 103, 106, 107, 111,
Seven-digit numbers 14–6

Data
Bar graph 363
Interpreting 114, 115, 152, 153, 155, 292, 352, 353, 369, 392, 456
Line plot 114, 115, 152, 153, 155, 352, 353, 369

Division
Basic facts
  All facts 48, 255, 348
Estimating 458, 459
Four-digit numbers 187, 193, 217, 221–3, 225–31, 349, 355, 419, 425, 434, 435, 437, 443, 447–9, 451–3, 455, 457
Fractions 87, 120, 121, 122, 125
  Common fractions 322, 323, 325–35, 337–9, 342, 355, 419, 425, 431
  Decimal fractions 372, 373, 376–9, 382–5, 387–93, 438, 454–7, 460, 461, 463–7, 469
Mental strategies
  Partial quotients 29, 35, 41, 193, 216, 217, 220–2, 226, 228, 401, 406, 419, 425, 454, 456, 460, 461, 464, 465

ORIGO Stepping Stones • Grade 5

Division (continued)

Think multiplication 326, 327, 330, 331, 333–5, 337, 342, 349, 355, 372, 373, 376–9, 382, 383, 463
Use factors 226, 228, 230, 419, 425
Patterns 384, 385, 401
Related to common fractions 320, 321
Related to multiplication 284, 285, 287, 292
Remainders 181, 222, 223, 413, 446, 447, 451
Standard algorithm 436, 437, 439–55
Three-digit numbers 35, 41, 110, 186, 187, 216, 217, 220–3, 226–9, 272, 362, 407, 413, 419, 425, 431, 434–7, 439, 442–7, 455
Two-digit numbers 29, 181, 401, 436, 437, 439, 440, 441
Word problems 217, 221–3, 226, 227, 229, 328, 329, 335, 338, 339, 349, 355, 377, 379, 383, 390, 391, 419, 431, 447, 454–6, 469

Estimating

Addition   87, 131, 158, 164–7, 182, 183
Division 458, 459
Multiplication 44–7, 49–54, 56, 57, 181, 187, 193
Subtraction 172, 173, 176–9, 182, 183

Fractions

Common fractions
Addition 11, 17, 163, 198, 199, 201–11, 213–5, 219, 254, 287, 324
Comparing 79, 105, 127, 134, 135, 196, 197, 312, 313, 317
Division 322, 323, 325–35, 337–9, 355, 419, 431
Equivalent 67, 73, 87, 93, 99, 120–3, 125, 128–33, 137, 142, 169, 205, 207
Estimating 196, 197
Finding common denominators 73, 120–3, 131, 169, 202–5, 207–11, 213–5, 219, 246, 247, 249–53, 255–9, 261–3
Improper fractions 128–30, 132, 133, 137, 142, 244, 245, 247, 258, 259, 273, 306–9, 312, 313, 316, 317, 413, 439
Language 128
Mixed numbers 17, 23, 55, 82–5, 90–2, 95, 99, 111, 117, 126–30, 132, 133, 137, 142, 208–11, 213–5, 219, 244, 245, 252–4, 256–9, 261, 263–7, 273, 306–9, 311, 314–6, 324, 407, 413
Models
Area 99, 120, 132, 142, 246, 282, 300–2, 305, 306, 320, 325, 401

Fractions (continued)

Length 123, 282, 288, 296, 320–3, 332, 333
Number line 11, 126, 127, 201, 244, 261, 273, 283
Set 284, 285, 287, 290
Multiplication 249, 267, 279, 282, 283, 288–97, 299, 300–3, 305–9, 311–17, 323, 326–31, 333–5, 337–9, 355, 360, 361, 401, 407, 413, 439
Related to division 284, 285, 287, 320, 321
Subtraction 23, 105, 111, 117, 201, 219, 244–7, 249, 250–59, 261–67, 324
Unit fractions 284, 285, 287–9, 322, 323, 325–29, 331–35, 337–9, 355
Word problems 105, 134, 135, 197, 205, 215, 251, 254, 264, 265, 279, 289, 293, 295–7, 299, 309, 314–6, 321, 327–9, 332, 333, 335, 338, 339, 419, 431
Decimal fractions
Addition 86, 125, 158–61, 163–5, 168, 169, 181, 206, 212, 224, 260, 286, 287, 293, 299, 305, 348, 386, 445, 462
Comparing 102, 103, 106, 107, 111
Data 114, 115
Division 372, 373, 376–9, 382–5, 387–93, 438, 456, 457, 460, 461, 463–69
Estimating 158, 164–7, 172, 173, 176–9, 182, 183
Hundredths 55, 61, 73, 79, 82–7, 125, 159–61, 163–73, 175, 178, 179, 181–3, 212, 224, 255, 261, 267, 293, 299, 325, 331, 337, 343, 358–61, 363, 366–73, 375–9, 382–93, 414–7, 419–21, 424, 438, 439, 445, 450, 456, 457, 460, 461, 463–9
Models
Area 55, 82–4, 87–90, 92–4, 331, 358, 360, 364–6, 372, 373, 387
Number line 49, 73, 84, 85, 158, 159, 163, 170, 171, 249, 267, 359, 363
Multiplication 358–61, 363–71, 375, 381, 390, 391, 412, 414–7, 419–21, 424, 438, 439, 445, 450, 451, 457, 469
Ordering 102, 103, 106, 107, 345
Rounding 108, 109, 112, 113, 117, 278, 363, 439, 278, 363, 439
Standard algorithm
Addition 164–7, 299
Subtraction 172, 173, 182
Subtraction 170–3, 176–9, 182, 183, 206, 213, 249, 255, 261, 267, 310, 325, 331, 337, 343, 348, 386, 451, 462

Fractions (continued)

Tenths 79, 158–61, 163–7, 170, 172, 173, 175–7, 181–3, 206, 224, 249, 255, 261, 286, 293, 299, 305, 310, 331, 337, 348, 358–61, 363–5, 369–73, 375–9, 381–93, 412, 439, 451, 457, 462, 463
Thousandsths 88–7, 99–101, 104–9, 111–3,
Word problems 104, 179, 367, 377, 379, 383, 390, 391, 469

Measurement

Area
  Composite shapes 41
  Regular shapes 35, 41, 104, 299, 349, 380, 381, 393, 426, 427
  Rule for calculating 35, 426
  Word problems 380, 393, 426, 427
Capacity
  Conversion
    Gallons, quarts, pints, cups, fluid ounces 144, 145, 154, 225, 231
    Liters, millileters 317, 346, 347, 350, 351, 354, 375, 381
  Customary 111, 144, 145, 150, 151, 154, 225, 231
  Metric 317, 346, 347, 350, 351, 354, 375, 381
  Word problems 111, 150, 151, 350, 351, 381
Length
  Conversion
    Feet, inches 61, 138, 139, 213
    Kilometers, meters 341, 343, 350, 351, 355
  Meters, centimeters 55
  Miles, yards, feet 140, 141, 142,
  Millimeters, centimeters, meters 305, 340, 341, 349, 350, 351, 354, 355
  Yards, feet, inches 140–2, 219,
  Customary 117, 138–42, 213,
  Metric 49
  Word problems 117, 139, 350, 351, 355
Mass
  Conversion
    Kilograms, grams 311, 344, 345, 350, 351, 354, 387, 393
    Pounds ounces 146, 147, 149, 154
  Customary 146, 147, 149, 150–5, 222, 223, 369
  Data 152, 153, 155, 352, 353, 363, 369
  Metric 16, 304, 345, 350–4, 363, 380, 387, 393, 468
  Word problems 150, 151, 345, 350, 351, 393
Perimeter
  Irregular polygons 305, 423

Measurement (continued)

Regular polygons 181, 393, 422, 423, 425
Rule for calculating 422
Word problems 393, 422, 423, 425
Time
  Conversion
    Hours, minutes 127, 131
  Duration 131
  Elapsed 137
  Hours and minutes 125
  Word problems 28
Volume
  Composite prisms 74, 75, 175
  Language 62, 78,
  Rectangular-based prisms 62, 63, 67–71, 73, 79, 169, 428–31
  Rule for calculating 65, 68, 69, 428
  Unit cubes 64, 65, 163
  Word problems 76, 77, 428–31

Money

Dollars 78
Transactions 414–7, 419–21, 458–61
Unit costs 466, 467

Multiplication

Estimating 44–7, 49–54, 56, 57, 181, 187, 193
Extending
  Four-digit numbers 44–7, 49, 56, 57, 193, 225
Fractions
  Common fractions 249, 267, 279, 282, 283, 288–95, 299–303, 305, 308, 309, 312–15, 326–9, 333–5, 338, 339, 360, 361, 401
  Decimal fractions 358–61, 363–7, 370, 371, 375, 381, 390, 391, 414–7, 419–21, 424, 445, 450, 451, 457, 469
  Mixed numbers 306–9, 311, 314,–6, 407, 413
Factors 70, 71, 79, 116, 192, 254
Mental strategies
  Double and halve 148, 200, 336, 375, 414, 415
  Doubling (and repeated doubling) 420
  Partial products 17, 50, 52, 56, 162, 267, 306, 307, 337, 343, 366, 367, 370, 371, 387, 420, 421, 445, 463
  Round and adjust 416, 417, 419
  Use a known fact 124, 360
  Use factors 10, 29, 60, 148
Models
  Comparison (tape diagram) 143, 149, 155
Patterns 225, 274, 275, 279, 359, 401